the fun habit

the fun habit

HOW THE PURSUIT OF JOY AND WONDER CAN CHANGE YOUR LIFE

MIKE RUCKER, PH.D.

ATRIA BOOKS
New York London Toronto Sydney New Delhi

An Imprint of Simon & Schuster, Inc.
1230 Avenue of the Americas
New York, NY 10020
Copyright © 2022 by Michael Rucker

All rights reserved, including the right to reproduce this book or portions thereof in any form whatsoever. For information, address Atria Books Subsidiary Rights Department, 1230 Avenue of the Americas, New York, NY 10020.

First Atria Books hardcover edition January 2023

ATRIA BOOKS and colophon are trademarks of Simon & Schuster, Inc.

For information about special discounts for bulk purchases, please contact Simon & Schuster Special Sales at 1-866-506-1949 or business@simonandschuster.com.

The Simon & Schuster Speakers Bureau can bring authors to your live event. For more information or to book an event, contact the Simon & Schuster Speakers Bureau at 1-866-248-3049 or visit our website at www.simonspeakers.com.

Interior design by Jill Putorti

Manufactured in the United States of America

1 3 5 7 9 10 8 6 4 2

Library of Congress Cataloging-in-Publication Data

Names: Rucker, Michael, author.
Title: The fun habit : how the disciplined pursuit of joy and wonder can change your life / Michael Rucker, Ph.D.
Description: First Atria Books hardcover edition. | New York, NY : Atria Books, 2022. | Includes bibliographical references and index.
Identifiers: LCCN 2021057127 (print) | LCCN 2021057128 (ebook) | ISBN 9781982159054 (hardcover) | ISBN 9781982159061 (trade paperback) | ISBN 9781982159078 (ebook)
Subjects: LCSH: Joy. | Happiness. | Discipline.
Classification: LCC BF575.H27 R835 2022 (print) | LCC BF575.H27 (ebook) | DDC 158—dc23/eng/20220112
LC record available at https://lccn.loc.gov/2021057127
LC ebook record available at https://lccn.loc.gov/2021057128

ISBN 978-1-9821-5905-4
ISBN 978-1-9821-5907-8 (ebook)

In memory of Brian Rucker. When we meet again, I hope I find you with Bourdain and Cornell, drinking scotch and eating well, accompanied by Farley and Hedberg, who have us all in stitches. Your memory serves as a reminder to make the most of every day, which includes seeing this book through to the end. As a result, there is going to be a lot more fun in the world, and I know that would make you happy. I love you, bud.

Contents

Author's Note		ix
Introduction		xi
1.	Fun Is the Antidote	1
2.	Time to PLAY	22
3.	SAVOR Every Moment	51
4.	Enjoyment *After* the Moment	73
5.	The Great Escape	86
6.	The Mystery	103
7.	Friendship Is Weird	119
8.	Fun and Parenting: From Bassinet to Empty Nest	132
9.	Bring Your Fun Habit to Work	154
10.	The Pleasure of Hard Fun, or How to Accomplish Almost Anything	180
11.	Fun Is a Force for Change	200
Conclusion: Finding Ultima		217
Acknowledgments		227
Endnotes		235
Index		255

Author's Note

I started writing the final draft of this book at the beginning of 2020. Then, as I am sure you are aware, something quite extraordinary happened—a global pandemic. I handed off the finished manuscript just as the United States was about half-vaccinated and returning to some kind of precarious new normal. Otherwise put, I wrote this book during what will (hopefully) be the least fun years any of us ever *collectively* experience in our lifetime.

The ideas in this book had been battle-tested under "normal" circumstances, but the COVID-19 pandemic resulted in a completely foreign landscape. During the pandemic's most challenging periods, fun was not at the top of anyone's agenda, including my own. In May 2020, I got extremely sick, an aftereffect of an initially mild COVID-19 infection and the coalescing of the period's various stressors. I lost the ability to sleep for months, which made daily functioning, let alone fun, almost impossible. While there were times that the lessons in this book served me to my great satisfaction, there were also times that I struggled with impostor syndrome, writing chapter after chapter on fun while not experiencing much of it personally. Despite my setbacks, I still consider myself lucky. Millions of people lost their livelihood, lost their loved ones; the most unfortunate lost their lives. In addition to an uncontrollable virus during the pandemic, people worldwide were reckoning with systemic racism and injustice, wrestling with political turmoil, battling the challenges of climate change, and the list goes on. With so many physiological and psychological safety needs unmet, it's no wonder that there weren't many of us concerned about the pursuit of higher needs.

If the grim landscape had a thin silver lining, it was that it provided many with a once-in-a-lifetime opportunity to observe their former life—its schedules, rhythms, distractions, and obsessions—from enough distance to ask important questions: Am I living the life I want? What is accidental, and what is by design? Can I live more deliberately? And even, yes: *Can life be more fun?*

For those working through such questions, this book could not have come at a better time. Whether we completely comprehend it or not, the pandemic made us intimately familiar with what you will see are key concepts important to this book. We experienced how painful it is to waste our precious time, locked out of many of the activities we love. We suffered from a lack of live interaction with friends and family and felt the damage that can occur when we are not personally connected to something other than ourselves. We realized the truth in the assertion, "security is mostly a superstition," and all longed to return to the "daring adventure."[1]

It's time for all of us to jump back into the *daring adventure* and reclaim our fun—not just for ourselves, but as a restorative path for our loved ones, and as you'll discover, for society as well.

Introduction

I have spent most of my life searching for happiness. It was like a puzzle that I could never quite figure out. As an adolescent, I was a hopeless wannabe with an agonizing desire to find my rank in the social structure of my small hometown of Davis, California. Unhappy at home, I emancipated as a teenager to see if happiness was somewhere out there in the world, waiting for me. It's been quite a journey since then.

People have always wanted to be happy, but the idea of happiness as a learned skill has never been so popular. Today, there's a happiness-industrial complex of gurus, psychologists, institutions, and organizations attempting to "solve" the happiness problem for good. Book after book is written on how to experience more happiness from neurological, psychological, religious, and spiritual perspectives. The promise of happiness, separate from wealth, achievement, or any other external factor, strikes a major chord. Many of us feel helpless nowadays as we try to journey toward the good life against what sometimes feel like impossible headwinds.

For everyone, from baby boomers unable to reconnect with the joys of the past to younger generations experiencing record levels of loneliness, anxiety, and burnout, the pursuit of happiness holds out hope as the answer to our problems. The thinking goes that if we can only activate our "happiness switch," other challenges in life will lose their edge.

INTRODUCTION

Inner satisfaction can be found no matter how grim our circumstances. Did I mention that the office now has a Zen room?[1]

As you will soon discover, pursuing happiness in and of itself can be a trap. In fact, for almost all of us, chasing happiness makes us anything but. I know because I fell for that happiness trap myself. Back in early 2016, I felt I had checked all the boxes in the pursuit of happiness: A good marriage and two healthy children. Successful endeavors as both an entrepreneur and an intrapreneur. A two-time Ironman. Well-traveled, having stepped foot on every continent. A Ph.D. with published, peer-reviewed research. Various accolades for being influential in my field. Most would say I had it all. Objectively, life was good. Furthermore, as a charter member of the International Positive Psychology Association, I had positioned myself at the cutting edge of research into happiness. Naturally, I put all the latest findings to use in my own life. As a member of the Quantified Self community, I optimized my life not only qualitatively, but quantitatively as well—logging my good days and bad days, constantly looking for correlations and ways to improve. I had reached a pinnacle. There was little else I could do to make myself happier, no technique I had yet to employ.

I'm an avid blogger, and in support of this hobby, I send a quarterly newsletter on or around the twenty-third every three months (December, March, June, and September). June 23, 2016, was business as usual. I hit send on my newsletter, which was essentially a victory lap that life at that moment was amazing. Toward the end of the newsletter, I celebrated recently checking off a bucket list item with my beloved brother, Brian—riding the tallest roller coaster in the world, the Kingda Ka.

At some point within twenty-four hours of hitting send on that newsletter, my brother passed away unexpectedly from a pulmonary embolism. It felt surreal: Just as my friends, family, and followers were reading how much I enjoyed the experience that he and I had shared, Brian's tragic passing ensured there would never be another such opportunity. As the shock wore off, I found myself deeply sad and unsettled. This period opened an uninvited path to questioning everything.

A short time later, I found myself in the hospital needing major hip

INTRODUCTION

surgery. When I woke up after the procedure, I couldn't feel my legs. Lying in the hospital bed, I struggled to stay positive. I'd built my life around staying physically active and benefiting from a positive mindset. Now I was adjusting to the reality I would never competitively run again, and emotionally, I was a wreck. The traditional tools of positive psychology were failing me. No matter how much I meditated or wrote in my gratitude journal, happiness remained elusive. I finally had to admit to myself these tools had lost their utility. A believer in happiness, yet not able to feel happy, I experienced significant cognitive dissonance. I'd thought I had life figured out, and now I was lost again.

The feeling in my legs returned, thankfully. And, as I recuperated in the months that followed, something significant began to dawn on me. I began to wonder whether trying so fervently to be happy had been part of the problem. Because when I stopped criticizing myself for being unhappy, something amazing happened. The energy I was burning up relentlessly focusing on my happiness ultimately became available for use elsewhere. Instead of perseverating on the gap of what was missing, I began to make better choices in the present moment, using my time to take action and have fun. As you'll soon read, this ranged from simple stuff like finding creative ways to ensure my wife and I had scheduled time to connect, to an unorthodox approach to physical therapy that afforded me the opportunity to be a better dancer while connecting with my daughter.

Over time, this realization blossomed into a full-blown epiphany. I finally saw how futile, even counterproductive, my efforts to grasp and then hold on to happiness had been—not just in that time of crisis, but for years. The work of being happy had been eating into the limited time and attention I had for experiencing life.

Scientifically, my epiphany made perfect sense. Happiness evolved for a reason: to lure us toward those things and activities that improve our chances of survival. If we always felt satiated, we would have little motivation to move forward. Sometimes *dissatisfaction*, not happiness itself, is what drives us. Yet, even though many of us understand this conceptually, the quest for happiness remains universal. Just as Sisyphus mindlessly rolled his boulder uphill only to watch it tumble back down, we struggle endlessly with the effort of becoming and then staying happy without ever questioning the value of the effort itself.

Personally, I'd now arrived at the belief that my deliberate concerns of being happy only drew my attention to what was missing, making me more unhappy. (I have since come to learn that emerging research on the science of happiness, which I'll be sharing in the pages of this book, supports this insight.) I began to accept that being sad about my brother's death, and then fearful for my physical recovery, were appropriate and inevitable responses to real tragedy. Grief and pain are part of the human experience. But in the thralls of pursuing happiness, instead of accepting this fact, I had deepened my misery by trying to subdue grief and avoid pain. I'd been so overprescribed on the need to be happy, I hadn't honored the need to process, to feel, to mourn.

But if deliberately chasing happiness left me miserable, what was the alternative? Is there anything we humans *can* rely on to pull us through periods of darkness? I began to ask less introspective questions. Instead, I focused on compassionately exercising my autonomy and agency in alignment with my values. As I set aside the self-recrimination and began to get more active, despite my state of grief, a second, crucial insight clicked into place: I couldn't always make myself happy, but I could almost always have fun. I could create moments of enjoyment and pleasure by being deliberate about it—yes, even while owning that I was sad. As you'll soon read, fun can coincide with a variety of emotional states, or even transcend them altogether.

Unlike happiness, fun isn't a reaction to your circumstances. It's an action orientation, one you control and can enact almost anywhere, anytime. It's also enormously beneficial, physically and psychologically. Instead of concern about what might be missing, a bias toward fun affords immediate gains.

Fun is a direct neurological route to improving our well-being—and yet, as I would find, it is also a skill that requires some training, at least for anyone deeply engaged in the serious business of adulting. Kids embrace fun naturally, but as adults we face three obstacles:

INTRODUCTION

1. We're conditioned as we age to believe that trying to have fun is childish, even inappropriate.
2. We undervalue the mental and physical benefits of fun.
3. We're put off by the counterintuitive fact that fun for busy adults requires discipline, which sounds . . . well, not fun.

By the time you finish *The Fun Habit*, you will be armed with clear and compelling scientific evidence for the life-sustaining value and importance of fun. You will learn tactics and techniques for making fun a regular part of your life in a way that feels comfortable and authentic, not forced or phony. These techniques have dramatically improved my well-being, and I've used them to help others with wonderful success.

I'm no guru descending from the mountaintop. When I say it's time to stop chasing happiness and start having fun, these principles are fully grounded in peer-reviewed research. My team and I have spent years authenticating the ideas and strategies you are about to discover. We all have the agency to live more joyful lives; we just do not have the right tools. This book solves that problem.

chapter 1

Fun Is the Antidote

*There was a time in my life when I thought
I had everything—millions of dollars, mansions, cars,
nice clothes, beautiful women, and every other
materialistic thing you can imagine.
Now I struggle for peace.*
—RICHARD PRYOR

One winter's day in arid Phoenix, Arizona, a man named Will Novak received an email inviting him to a bachelor party. It sounded like a lot of fun: a wild skiing weekend in Vermont. There would be an '80s theme, BBQ and Italian food, beer, and beautiful fresh snow. There was just one wrinkle. Will had never heard of the groom, Angelo, or any of the groomsmen; one of them had sent him the invitation by mistake. (Remarkably, there was a groomsman named Bill Novak.) Still, reading the email put Will in a good mood. He was the father of a ten-month-old baby, and the levity was welcome.

So, laughing to himself, he wrote back: "F*cking count me in! From the contents of this email, Angelo sounds tremendous and I want to help send him off in style. I hope his bride (or groom) to be, is awesome." He included his T-shirt size.

He never expected to hear back. But he had sent a ripple into the universe, and it landed. The groomsmen thought Will was hilarious—so hilarious he'd make a great addition to their party. Soon he received their answer: "If you're serious, we're serious, get here."

Will was stunned. *Was* he serious? The trip would cost him almost a thousand dollars. Meanwhile, he had a wife and a baby and felt the financial pain of having renovated a fixer-upper. And . . . these were total strangers. On the other hand, he hadn't been skiing since he was fourteen. His life was full, but like most first-year parents, diaper blowouts and sleep deprivation were, for the moment, what passed for adventures.

So instead of declining, he doubled down. He started a GoFundMe campaign, "Help me go to the bachelor party of a stranger." It's one thing for a sleep-deprived new dad and a bunch of dudes in party-planning mode to commit to something so completely random. But now dozens, and ultimately hundreds, of people hopped on, stopping whatever more serious thing they were doing that day to log in to GoFundMe and throw in a few dollars. Before the day's end, Will's trip was fully funded. Ultimately, 224 people contributed $4,615, and the campaign was shared 6,300 times. (The extra money went to a "college/food/toys/whatever the baby needs fund" for the groom and his then-fiancée, who were expecting.)

If you find all this ridiculous, put yourself in Will's shoes for a moment. Consider what the experience felt like:

The giddy silliness of a good joke
The adrenaline of taking a risk
The pure joy of leaping from the mundane into the extraordinary
The thrill of spontaneous travel and an opportunity to play
The reward of making new friends
The chance for a healthy escape

Will's story, distilled to its elements, is pure, unadulterated fun. With his partner's blessing, he boarded a plane and had a good time. He made memories he'll remember his entire life. To others, he became a legend. Someday his kids will see the pictures and laugh in disbelief that their dad did something so spontaneous.

My point in telling you this story isn't that you should want to emulate Will Novak or throw out your day planner in favor of something completely new. That's not at all what this book is about. At the end of the day, the point of the story isn't Will at all, but all those people who cheered his adventure from the sidelines. Their viral fervor is revealing. There's a reason people funded Will's campaign, and many other fun (but arguably "pointless") funding campaigns on the Internet:

We live in a world in which people are critically fun-starved. Instead of having fun ourselves, we click a few buttons and farm it out to guys like Will.

Fun is—or should be—one of the fundamental goods available to all of us. We don't get through life without enduring periods of disappointment, pain, and loss. Fun is the magical balm that makes the slings and arrows bearable.

From birth, fun is essential to the development of the human brain; in a game as simple as "peekaboo," humans lay the seeds of making sense of the world. As children, fun helps us develop basic social and motor skills, establish and test boundaries, and define ourselves in relation to the rest of the world. In our adolescence and early adulthood, we use fun to explore life, discovering who and what gives us pleasure, and to role-play different identities ultimately leading to a mature sense of self. (In the wise words of Chef from the TV show *South Park*, "There's a time and a place for everything, and it's called college.")

As we travel through adulthood, when life becomes more deliberate, fun becomes both a tool for enrichment and an escape valve from life's pressures. It also keeps us healthy: The laughter and good humor that often accompany fun reduce anxiety, decrease stress, enhance self-esteem, and increase self-motivation. Fun improves respiration and circulation, lowers your pulse and blood pressure, and helps release endorphins into the bloodstream. Fun relieves loneliness and boredom. Fun is one of the keys to vitality as we age.

That's the truth and the potential of fun, or at least it should be. The sad reality is that most of us all but abandon fun after early adulthood because, "We've got to grow up sometime, *right*?" In a piece for the *Wall Street Journal*, "An Overlooked Skill in Aging: How to Have Fun," Clare Ansberry exposes that throughout adulthood many of us forget how to have fun. We let these important skills weaken due to the false belief they provide little value, when the truth is, "laughter, levity, enjoyment, diversion—can act as antidotes to stress, depression, and anxiety."[1]

You bought this book, so you probably already had the suspicion that our lives are perversely short on fun. Well, reader, you're special. Many dismiss fun as childish, extraneous, distracting, or even dangerous. I know this because I've seen many people's dubious reactions when I tell them I'm writing a book re-centering people on fun. Some glance over their shoulder nervously. Others chuckle and redirect the conversation. Still, others nod enthusiastically, only waiting for the opportunity to build their case for why, given their situation, fun cannot be prioritized.

In a society that prizes productivity above all, we have bought into the notion that fun is a "nice to have." Instead of dedicating daily quality time to fun, we relegate it to once-a-year vacations, and maybe one-off weekend adventures if we're lucky. The United States has the least paid-vacation time among developed countries, according to the human resources firm Zenefits,[2] and yet many U.S. employees have to be prodded by their companies to use it. Day by day, we give a majority of our waking hours to work, growing resentful of our to-do lists. And in this impaired state, we begin to live vicariously through goofy outliers like Will who meander through our social feeds, instead of choosing our own adventure, each and every day.

When I say, "choose your own adventure," I don't mean cross-country travel to party with strangers, or anything so radical. **I mean living life intentionally, starting with a conscious decision to adopt a bias toward fun each and every day—in the life you have now, not some fantasy of tomorrow. Call it a *Fun Habit*.**

Building your habit starts with a re-understanding of what fun is, and why it's far more essential to our health, happiness, and success than we've been led to believe.

All Work and No Play

How did we get here? In the United States and Europe, most of us have been marinated in that old Protestant work ethic, the spiritual underbelly of the American Dream: Hard work is a virtue. To the Puritans, success defined not just our self-worth, but our spiritual worthiness. Your literal soul was in the balance. In this context, hard work and its output become very serious business!

And if work is holy, that makes distractions from work—aka fun—not just worthless, but *evil*.

Following from this same gospel, hard work is all that's needed to create wealth and live the American Dream—despite the fact that modern sociology suggests that the relationship between poverty and the individual is much more complex. This was vividly demonstrated by the journalist and social critic Barbara Ehrenreich in her book *Nickel and Dimed*,[3] in which she recounts what happened when she tried to live off a series of minimum-wage jobs. In short, working hard wasn't enough to overcome the massive inefficiency of living hand to mouth, without personal savings or a meaningful social safety net.

And still, the notion that through work we rise (in every sense) remains deeply entrenched. Our sense of self-worth rises and falls with our productivity. Author Rahaf Harfoush notes in *Hustle & Float*[4] that the emphasis on work as a virtue—however divorced it may be from pleasure, meaning, or the fruits of labor—was extremely helpful as the Industrial Revolution subdivided work into ever more menial tasks, whose output could be measured and optimized. This so-called *algorithmic work*—work done in a repeatable sequential pattern—is how many people used to make a living.[5] For instance, my grandfather owned a foundry in Oklahoma. He and his fellow employees got to work at the same time every morning. Each day, each person knew what was expected of them. The work was physically taxing, so late nights weren't an option. You knew what was expected, you did your work, and you got paid. The rest of your time outside of work was yours to keep.

In the 1970s, we welcomed the Information Age. Many workers

stopped building widgets, and instead found their livelihood in the emerging field of "knowledge work." With intellectual property and innovation now the work product, we are no longer workers operating machines with sprockets and cogs. We *are* the sprockets and cogs, and our ability to perform is exploited and over-optimized just like the equipment on an assembly line. We have become the machines that now output the goods that create profit for others.

Complicating the picture, productivity has become increasingly hard to measure in recent years. Unlike assembly lines, creative work is driven by nonlinear thinking and processes, and no longer follows a consistent pattern. As a result, our work now has an ill-defined finish line. Without the well-defined goals afforded by algorithmic work, we are left with blurry indications of whether we've put in an honest day at the office. Anxious to earn our keep, we find ourselves always "on." Meanwhile, new forms of communication that make us accessible almost anywhere, at almost any time, are compounding the problem. Nowadays, with so many of us working from home, our work seemingly has no end. We work, eat, and sleep within the same physical space, so there is no tangible transition that tells our mind we're "off" from work. Instead, we're answering emails until our head hits the pillow.

In recent years, the flailing tentacles of the "gig economy" have further upended the balance. For those who earn their living on platforms such as Uber, Lyft, Fiverr, Instacart, and DoorDash, work is crammed into every possible nook and cranny of life. Attracted to gigging by the false promise of autonomy, gig workers are often unaware that there are powerful forces in place to make sure a significant portion of the value created by their effort goes to someone else. Worse, the game mechanics of these platforms are set up to trick gig workers into working more and more for less and less pay. If you're a gig worker, a quick Internet search will introduce you to numerous confessions of software developers stricken with guilt because their skills were used to rig the game against you.

The illusion of control and conscious manipulation of workers in the app-enabled gig economy is extreme—but not entirely unique. Unless you work for yourself, few employers are perfectly transparent about their top priority: to squeeze as much out of every resource—including people—as they can. Such corporate sleight of hand was called out in the *Slate* article "My Disturbing Stint on a Corporate Wellness App." Author Ann Larson theorizes that her company's workplace wellness app's furtive purpose was to shift the blame for the ill effects of low-pay, backbreaking work from employer to the employee, while also making it possible for her to do more debilitating labor, longer.[6] Companies that make a mission of sharing the wealth with employees are out there, but they're not the norm.

Without boundaries between work and life, "Give it 110 percent!" takes on a new and nefarious meaning. For all kinds of workers, burnout is at an all-time high in the United States. Corporations hire popular speakers like Gary Vaynerchuk (who insists you need to "hustle"[7])* and Grant Cardone (who proclaims the glory goes to those who work "10X"[8]). These messages sound great from the stage, but an increasing number of empirical findings make it clear that those who are inspired by these messages will likely pay a considerable toll. In his book *Dying for a Paycheck*, Jeffrey Pfeffer, a professor of organizational behavior at the Stanford Graduate School of Business, outlines the extent to which the "always on" demands of the modern workplace are harming us.[9] In an interview with Insights by Stanford Business, Pfeffer credits Nuria Chinchilla of IESE Business School with coining these maladaptive behaviors as "social pollution."[10] The harm from this pollution—invasive work priorities—goes beyond simply destroying friendships and family ties; it is literally killing some of us. Findings from the World Health Organization and the International Labour Organization indicate that long working hours led to 745,000 deaths in 2016, up 29 percent from similar data reviewed in 2000.[11]

Getting workers to produce more for the organizations they serve is not a new concept. Frederick Winslow Taylor's 1911 opus, *The Principles of Scientific Management*—in which Taylor famously tells the story of how he got pig-iron handlers to increase their daily production from twelve tons to

---

* I have met with Gary, and I believe his intentions are well-intended (and I assume the same for Grant). Gary has really softened his stance on "hustling" over the past few years and I feel it is important to acknowledge that here.

forty-seven tons by upping their wages and closely managing the cadence of work—still informs management theory and practice today, despite all the dramatic shifts in our economy described earlier. (And despite Taylor's undisguised contempt for at least one of the laborers and phlegmatic that he more nearly resembles in his mental-make-up the ox than any other type.")[12] I recall as a doctoral candidate learning about goal-setting theory.[13] Edwin Locke and Gary Latham (thought leaders in the study of organizational behavior since the mid-1960s) made a name for themselves for their methods using ambitious business goals to increase worker production. All this to say that the evolution of optimizing us to be working machines has a long history, but more recently corporations are trying to sell us the message that "the grind" is a badge of honor. In reality, it's poisonous.

Let's face it, if you aren't hustling . . . if you are not answering your emails on the toilet . . . if you are not walking your ten thousand steps . . . then you must be a slacker, *right*? Honestly, it is mind boggling how hard we have been duped. These practices of sacrifice come at a terrible cost. A component of our well-being relies on fun, play, and leisure, and modern life has eroded our opportunities to enjoy these essential components of vitality.

Springing the Happiness Trap

As I related in the introduction, I am one of many whose response to this pressure cooker was to make "being happy" a relentless goal. In doing so, like many, I stepped into a trap of quantifying this aspiration across all aspects of experience that bring us joy. Let me give you an example. I like to meditate. Hoping to "optimize" my experience of meditation, I bought a device to provide neurofeedback so that I could learn how "well" I was meditating. The experience soured quickly, however, as the device's software kept prodding me to meditate more instead of simply allowing me to relish the experience. As it is with so many activities these days—we are encouraged to use apps and gadgets to track almost every aspect of our lives, from sleep to exercise, to something as intimate as the number of days we have been with the person we love.[14]

Instead of enjoying activities on our terms, we turn them into statistics to be parsed. We compare today's version of ourselves to yesterday's version, while also comparing ourselves to the Joneses next door. We fixate on the gap between our current state and our accidental desires that are more a matter of happenstance, when we could be moving toward meaningful experiences that really feed us and help us grow. Happiness becomes a mirage that we can only see clearly from a distance; once we arrive, we discover there's not much there—and start to scan the horizon again in what ultimately becomes an infinite loop.

It's not our fault: Science suggests the deck is stacked against us. Our brains are actually *programmed* to fixate on the gap between where we are and where we think we'll be happy. A bit of jargon academics use to signify that something pertains to pleasure is the word *hedonic*. When we talk about having a hedonic experience, it typically has two components—anticipatory and consummatory pleasure. Science once believed that we were primarily driven by the pursuit of consummatory pleasures—a fancy way of saying we do things to feel good. Science has now come to understand that, for a lot of us, what really drives us in the pursuit of pleasure is often not the experience of feeling good itself, but the allure of pleasure from a potential reward or positive outcome and the accompanying good feelings when we have predicted correctly. There are three reasons for this:

1. We are good at anticipating. If you've done any prior reading on happiness, you likely have heard of dopamine before. Dopamine got its common nickname, the "happy" hormone, because it was originally understood to be the neurotransmitter that helps us experience pleasure. But as the neuroscientist Dr. Blake Porter put it when I interviewed him, "The dopamine pleasure story is pretty dead at this point, in neuroscience." As scientists began to study dopamine, they noticed something surprising: It often spikes *before* we do something fun. Where we once thought dopamine was integral in experiencing something fun and pleasurable, we now know that the heightened sensation it's connected to is primarily in the *anticipation*.[15] And, in fact, the anticipation isn't necessarily connected to pleasure at all. Scientists now believe dopamine's evolutionary purpose was to ready you for something unexpected, by heightening your arousal. The quality of the "something" itself? Dopamine doesn't care. Dopamine is now also believed to be connected to goal pursuit, providing a jolt of motivation to get us to the finish line.

Urged on by dopamine, then, we haphazardly *pursue* happiness, instead of genuinely enjoying the gift of happiness itself.[16] The desire to alleviate this craving is, by design, insatiable. And so, we find ourselves on a hamster wheel that science aptly calls the "hedonic treadmill." You might also see it referred to as hedonic adaptation, hedonic relativism, or the happiness set point—but all of these concepts in general refer to our tendency to overestimate the impact that life changes and events will have on our happiness. That, more often than not, once a change becomes familiar, our happiness returns to our unique "set point"—the same level of happiness that existed for us prior to the change. We are no happier than before, so we head back out on our pursuit for something more.

From the hedonic treadmill follows two more "silly human tricks" that make happiness elusive.

2. We are good at adapting. Any outcome in life—whether good or bad—generally only has a limited, temporary impact on our subjective happiness. Happiness begins to slip away as soon as we grab it. For decades science has been applying adaptation-level theory to try and understand why good things don't seem to last, but it was a 1978 paper by Philip Brickman, Dan Coates, and Ronnie Janoff-Bulman about lottery winners that really got people's attention.[17] What these researchers found is that we can have amazing, unexpected experiences—winning the lottery, for example—and life is temporarily thrilling, but that we have a tendency to adapt. We eventually acclimate to our new reality and return to whatever default level of happiness we were originally accustomed to. In fact, when we are not deliberate in our approach to our changing circumstances, we risk being less happy because of new complications (e.g., for lottery winners, the arrival of pressure from friends and family who want to share in the good fortune) and new responsibilities (as The Notorious B.I.G. would say, "Mo money, mo problems"). The good news is that more recent research shows that all hope is not lost, even for lottery winners. We can indeed improve our life satisfaction, if we are able to assimilate good fortune effectively.[18] We can "outsmart" adaptation, if given the right tools.

3. We are good at comparing. Feeling happy can often have less to do with our actual experience, and more to do with how we think it compares to someone else's.

Much of how we perceive happiness is predicated on shared experience. In this way, our happiness is almost like a mass hallucination. We compare ourselves against others in whatever consensus reality we are living in within that moment.

For example, a French sociodemographic study noted that, when given a choice, people usually don't want to have "more" in any abstract sense. They just want to have more than those around them. When participants in the study were asked if they would prefer to have an IQ of 110 while others had an average IQ of 90, or an IQ of 130 while others had an IQ of 150, many participants chose the first option, even though that would mean having a lower IQ overall. Similarly, many preferred four weeks of vacation if others had two instead of six weeks of vacation if others had eight.[19]

Inherent in all of us are deep-seated evolutionary mechanisms predisposing us to the hedonic treadmill. You finally take that vacation, and it doesn't make you as happy as you thought because it didn't live up to the hype. You finally get that promotion, but your elation wears off as you adapt into the new role. Worse, you find it's not what you expected. Your child relishes the excitement of holiday gifts, only to have their world fall apart when they compare their good fortune to that of their cousin's who happened to get something a little bit cooler. The positive aspects of these experiences prove ephemeral, and we return to our original state (that pesky happiness set point) or sometimes feel even worse.

Enter the Nothing

Have you ever seen the movie *The Neverending Story*? In it, an all-powerful, malevolent force called *The Nothing* is devouring the magical world of Fantasia, leaving behind only a bleak emptiness meant to signify an utter lack of imagination in the "real" world. That's how I've come to think of mindless media consumption and other soul-sucking activities—a seemingly unstoppable *Nothing* capable of sucking pleasure and meaning from life . . . if we let it.

Let's take social media consumption, for instance. Social media platforms can be effective for having a bit of fun, connecting with others, and relishing and reminiscing over our memories. I certainly enjoy engaging with people and sharing online, so I'm not trying to demonize these tools. It's important to remember, though, that these applications are specifically engineered to invade and commandeer our leisure. They compel our attention through contrived engagement levers. As the software reminds us that certain events have been socially rewarded, we slowly learn to rank our memories through comments and likes, instead of the intrinsic merits of our experiences.

These types of game mechanics—meant to keep us using the platform—can lead to unintended behavior change, as little by little we do things to make the "Gram" happy, instead of making ourselves happy. We forgo situational intimacy and dilute it through the act of vicarious displacement. As our audience grows, validation increasingly comes from outside sources, from a *Nothing* army—strangers who have little or no real interest in us or our well-being.

Our experiences, instead of being ends in themselves, now are a means toward status through strange virtual currencies that have almost no value, and for most of us, are pretty much good for *Nothing*. Seeing another uptick in the like counter leaves you temporarily satiated by that release of dopamine. The fleeting gratification is easy to access and enjoyable, so you return for more, again and again. Sounds a bit like a budding addiction, doesn't it? That's because it is. Emerging science suggests these practices are changing the structure of our brain and making us more prone to depression and anxiety.[20] In fact, some researchers argue that rising statistics in suicide and depression coincide with the expansion of smartphones and social media usage.[21] The work of Dr. Jean Marie Twenge, a professor of psychology at San Diego State University, has been particularly prominent around the idea of smartphones destroying mental health. Although some have criticized her for being overly negative in her interpretations, her research shows that social media likely has a significant negative effect on our well-being.[22]

In *The Compass of Pleasure*,[23] an entire book dedicated to the science of what makes us feel good, author David J. Linden points out that pain was once thought to be the opposite of pleasure—until we started studying that trickster dopamine and discovered that pain, too, can activate our reward circuits. We now understand the opposite of pleasure to be *ennui*—dissatisfaction resulting from a lack of stimulation and enrichment. If ennui is an enemy of fun, the *Nothing* is fun's ultimate villain.

Fun's Secret Weapon, Oxytocin

The way we believe we are staying happy these days is doing little to enrich our lives; it is simply effort that gets lost in the void of the *Nothing*. We work hard at being happy for little lasting reward, and when happiness is elusive, we are left wondering why.

To all this, fun is the antidote—maybe even literally, neurochemically. You see, fun shared with others is connected to a second, equally important feel-good hormone that we don't talk about enough: oxytocin. We earn some of our oxytocin through prosocial interactions and engaging in experiences that connect us to others. Oxytocin gives us that real sweetness of something larger than ourselves, while dopamine is metaphorically feel-good saccharin.

Without conscious control, we let others commandeer our time. It leaves us feeling trapped and powerless because we know it shouldn't be that way. We ignore our primal urges for agency and autonomy and placate those feelings by donating to Will's adventure, or by posting a #tbt photo and watching the likes trickle in. The problem is that's not real connection. We push those buttons while ignoring the people we're sharing a meal with and call this virtual exchange social engagement, while deep inside a feeling nags that life is passing us by. All we've done is thrown another moment into the *Nothing*.

When we have a bias toward fun, we start to take back control. When we prioritize sharing in deliberate experiences, when we actively seek out meaningful social interaction with others through fun, we escape the need for dopamine's IV drip. As such, fun is an antidote to the hedonic treadmill, enriching our lives instead of simply repressing our true need to feel alive and connected.

Oxytocin release appears to be more than merely pleasurable; research suggests it protects us from our own negative impulses. When Dr. Volker Ott at the University of Lübeck in Germany and his colleagues gave a group of twenty healthy men oxytocin, their self-restraint increased and their snack consumption decreased, leading the researchers to conclude that oxytocin can have a significant effect on controlling reward-related behavior.[24] When we prioritize activities that enrich us with oxytocin, satisfying our need for fun, we're better equipped to move beyond instant gratification and make better choices about how to invest our time and attention. Encouraging the release of oxytocin also appears to support the bonds of connectedness through helping us experience empathy more deeply. As such, we go from feeding the *Nothing* to feeding ourselves and those we genuinely care about. When oxytocin is present, we tend to act more prosocial and better actualize that it's not about ourselves and how we rank against others, but rather that we are better when we are supporting each other.[25]

Note: Oxytocin and dopamine have real and studied links with behavior. Science is beginning to gather pieces of the puzzle but concedes that the full picture of how they work in the body is far more complex than our current understanding. Neurotransmitters aren't an either/or; they're interrelated and symbiotic, and they are put to a variety of different uses by the body. So, while it's not really *oxytocin* vs. *dopamine* in the brain—in fact, they're more like playmates who need each other to have fun—they're useful here as metaphors for what we should value and why.

A Simple Theory of Fun

Fun has been so villainized, marginalized, obfuscated, and ignored that it needs a do-over. Our adventure together begins by understanding the true nature of fun. Happiness is a state of mind, but fun is something you can do.

It doesn't require education, money, or power. All it requires is intentionality. If happiness is a mirage, fun is your backyard oasis. By the end of this chapter, we are going to start to take immediate action. That's how fun does.

From the point of view of science, fun is comparatively undiscovered territory. In that way, it's like lightning, which humans have watched with fear and awe since the dawn of mankind. Lightning is spectacular, it is real, and in some cases, it can be destructive—and yet even today, exactly how it manifests is a mystery.[26] Scientists disagree about how thunderclouds charge, and how they initiate a spark. Lightning breaks basic rules of physics.

Similarly, much about fun remains mysterious. Scientific knowledge about its origins is largely speculative. One theory is that early in our evolution we figured out having fun supports our brain's development.[27] Having fun with others taught humans how to cooperate and develop mutual agreements that set the stage for future social norms and consensus. As our ancestors engaged in fun and play, they developed rewarding relationships and beneficial, prosocial agreements that are the underpinning of modern group dynamics. Because of this aspect of fun's power, fun likely facilitated the growth of our societies, or so the theory goes.

These are guesses. The truth is no one knows fun's evolutionary origins for sure or why having fun is so useful in helping us thrive. But unlike *happiness*, a subjective construct defined by human perception, fun is demonstrable, observable, real, and immediately in our grasp. It is primal and universal, operating at a level deeper than culture—a fact that's readily evident when you remember that many animals seek fun, not just humans. Fun is as simple as two dogs playing and as complex as the pathway accredited to some of Albert Einstein's most significant discoveries.

For those who desire a simple definition of fun, here you go: **fun is engagement in pleasurable experiences.** But let's go a level deeper because fun is also so much more. Fun is:

1. Biased Toward Action

Fun is immediate. You're either having fun or you're not. In science, we define the affective quality of experience through the label of *he-*

donic tone, more commonly referred to as *valence*. In the spirit of keeping things simple, the words *hedonic* and *valence* are the only two pieces of pop psych jargon I'd like you to remember as we progress. Experiences that are positively valent are pleasurable, the ones that are negatively valent are not. When we bias ourselves toward fun, meaning we restack the deck in our favor for more positive experiences, we start racking up gains.[28] In contrast, when we concern ourselves with "becoming" more happy, by proxy we are subconsciously identifying ourselves as unhappy (or at best not happy enough). This gap within ourselves—this lagging indicator of well-being—becomes our focus, part of our identity, crowding out the empowering belief that we have agency regarding how we spend our time.

2. Prosocial

Fun is inclusive. It's not reliant on the "you can't pour from an empty cup" and "put your mask on first" attitude that many who focus on happiness convey. Instead, fun often transports you outside yourself. I loved how the neuroscientist Dr. Lisa Feldman Barrett put it when we spoke: "You dislodge yourself from the center of your own universe for a few minutes." You move from a *me* space to a *we* space.

Fun is predisposed to benefit not just you, but all who share in it. Take laughing with friends, for instance. As the comedic actor John Cleese nicely put it, "It's almost impossible to maintain any kind of distance or any sense of social hierarchy when you're just howling with laughter. Laughter is a force for democracy."[29]

This isn't to say that fun requires the company of others. Solitary fun is just as important and may be particularly important to introverts. That said, the people we care about can be our most potent sources of fun. As well, when I say fun is prosocial, I also mean that fun is not something you have at someone else's expense. Interestingly, when the word *fun* first appeared in the English language, probably in the late 1600s, it initially meant a cheat or a hoax. That connotation remains today when we say, "I had a little fun at someone's expense," and maybe has contributed to our dim attitude toward fun in general. Let's do away with that baggage. Going forward, let's agree that it isn't fun if you have to hurt someone else to have it.

3. Autonomous

Fun's prosocial slant makes some feel like advocating for fun is just another form of the office bully telling you to smile more. Unlike happiness (that's been quantifiably defined by science), fun is uniquely yours to define. Your fun is autonomous, it's uniquely yours, and you own it. The only commonality fun shares with us all is positive valence—the energy that fills us up. When others push their idea of fun upon you it can be harmful. This practice is another reason fun has gotten a bad rap, and we'll address this issue in the chapter about fun at work.

4. Extraordinary

Fun has so many levels—evident from the emerging smirk you get from reading a funny comic to the immersive wave of physiological and psychological pleasure you feel from peak experiences. Fun can be cuddling with a partner watching Netflix for one and gloriously beating a drum set for another. The best part, as we'll discover, is that no matter what fun means to you, it can lead you to transcend the ordinary. There is a miraculous area of fun that sits beyond science, beyond measurement.

I like to think of valence as two colors of a roulette wheel. I'll let you decide which color represents positive experience and which represents negative. Yours to pick. When we develop a Fun Habit, we rig that winning color in our favor. We cannot ensure the ball will never fall in negative valence, but we can usually influence our time in such a way that we index more good experiences than bad. We can also learn to enjoy our experience even when things don't break our way. Why I love the roulette analogy though, is the wheel's green pockets. Fun at its best transcends the dichotomy of unhappy and happy. There is a special pocket of fun you cannot find on a linear scale. It lies beyond valence. We leapfrog simple aspirations of greater subjective well-being and acknowledge them for what they are, trivial concerns of the self. These peak moments are momentarily absent of happiness and sadness, and those lucky enough to find them describe the experiences as wonder beyond the grasp of words. These liberating leaps have the potential to connect us to something greater—something that, as you'll see, I have come to call *The Mystery*.

Hall of Fun: Albert Einstein

Albert Einstein's 72nd birthday party at Princeton University, Princeton, New Jersey, 3/14/1951

Despite his complex mind, Einstein was known to be a lot of fun. You inevitably know the cropped version of this iconic portrait, but you might not know the backstory. The photo was taken by Arthur Sasse, on March 14, 1951, Einstein's seventy-second birthday. In the uncropped photo, we can see Einstein sitting in a car, between his wife, Elsa, and Dr. Frank Aydelotte, the head of the Institute for Advanced Study. The story goes that as they were leaving his birthday celebration for their home in Princeton, New Jersey, Einstein was repeatedly asked to smile at the cameras. When Sasse asked for one last photo, he defiantly made a funny face. Einstein liked the resulting image so much, he immediately ordered multiple copies so he could sign and send them to friends as a joke. Later on, he used this photo to make greeting cards.

Einstein rarely let others get in the way of his fun. He was quick to joke, rarely wore socks (he thought that the shoes should do the job), let his mustache and hair grow, and gave interviews on his porch in fluffy pink slippers. His commitment to fun ran deep—and yet when Sasse sent his photo to editors for publication, they debated whether it was even appropriate to make it public, given Einstein's eminence. It only ever saw the light of day because Sasse related how much the great scientist himself loved the image.

According to Walter Isaacson's biography, *Einstein: His Life and Universe*,[30] the personality traits that contributed most to Einstein's greatness were curiosity and nonconformism. Scientific studies suggest that humor and intelligence are associated. People who show an aptitude for fun also seem to have superior cognitive abilities.[31] Einstein was excellent proof of that. Legend has it that Einstein said his other great idea (after relativity) was adding an egg while cooking a bowl of soup, so that you can boil an egg without making an extra pot dirty.

Fun Is Not a Gateway Drug

My guess is that some of you only need a nudge. A gentle reminder to realign. I get excited when I hear from someone who at first blush wrote off fun as nothing more than whimsy, only to use some of the tactics you are about to learn and discover that more enjoyment was waiting right in front of them the entire time.

For those of you who are still resistant, let me assure you I am not trying to sell you a gateway drug. Having a Fun Habit isn't about making sure you're at Burning Man next year (unless that's what you consider fun). Nor am I asking you to ignore or deny all in life that is difficult, wrong, and upsetting. That would be toxic positivity—the damaging belief that we shouldn't have negative emotions. As we'll learn later, limiting our range of emotions has a serious downside, and the reality of life is that it's just not possible to be happy all the time. It's harmful to pretend otherwise. So, let's scroll past that "positive vibes only" meme right now and accept there will be hours each week we need to spend on unpleasant tasks to be contributing members of the human race. In addition to our daily routines, we will inevitably be faced with surprises, some of which will suck.

What I am suggesting is that society has now devalued fun and leisure so much it's significantly harming us. Just as it was once popular to villainize rest and recovery while championing sleep deprivation—a practice fading away only after it's been exposed as asinine and unhealthy—it is time that we stop villainizing fun in the same way, because an enjoyable life is just as important as a well-rested one.

If you find yourself pushing back against the idea of having more fun, fearful that dialing up enjoyment runs the risk of rampant self-indulgence or escapism—then I ask you to evaluate how this reaction might speak to your own current worldview on renewal. Taking back our control, our autonomy, and finding enjoyment has never been more important. The sooner we are able to realize that the better. Let's get started.

Take Action: Create A Fun Booster

Building your Fun Habit starts here: Explore your photos and find an image that exemplifies fun for you. Ideally, you will be in the photo, a visual artifact of a moment or time when you experienced the pure joy of living. (If you can't find one of you, any photo that documents a fun experience will do.)

Print the photo and keep it near your desk; dress it up with a nice frame or a hand-drawn border, if that speaks to you. When you're feeling down or doubtful, look at the picture. That's step one. Step two is to use the image to vividly re-create in your mind the experience that surrounded that photo.

Like most of the recommendations in this book, this activity is informed by research. In a study published in the *Journal of Happiness*, researchers looked at how different kinds of reminiscing boosted mood. Students were randomly assigned to spend ten minutes a day either reminiscing by replaying a happy memory in their thoughts (called cognitive imagery), or reminiscing using memorabilia, such as photos or scrapbooks. A third control group was asked to spend the ten minutes thinking about current conditions. They found that both of the reminiscing groups reported increases in the percent of time they felt happy in the following week—but that happiness increased more in the cognitive imagery group.[32]

With this in mind, glancing at the photo is good. Using it as the launching point to mentally relive a fun day is even better. That is why we dedicate an entire coming chapter to reminiscing. For now, though, simply let your chosen image be a reminder that you're not only capable of fun, you're on a path toward genuine and lasting well-being, no matter what challenges life brings your way. *Fun lights the way forward.*

chapter 2

Time to PLAY

*I'm here today because I refused
to be unhappy. I took a chance.*
—WANDA SYKES

Hopefully after reading chapter 1, you now share my passionate perspective on the innate and wondrous value of fun and are eager to learn and use the strategies in this book to harness fun's power. You also recognize the obstacles and headwinds and are ready to join the fight against the status quo. Here's how you strike the first blow: by adding novel, pleasurable activities into your daily life, starting today. In addition, identify and begin to remove any resistance that stands in the way of moving from theory to practice. Let's start immediately on building momentum.

"I don't have time" is the reaction I most often get when I encourage people to schedule more fun into their daily lives. The objective of this chapter, therefore, is to provide everything you need to fix that. Building a Fun Habit means seizing each day as an opportunity for enjoyment. In this chapter, you'll learn how to restack your deck with positive experiences that enrich you and compound over time, leading to better and better choices.

The PLAY Model is a simple but powerful tool to support that journey. What you're going to do with the PLAY Model is radical, even countercultural. It's also liberating. In the past you may have been encouraged to audit your calendar for productivity. You may have even taken a course or paid someone to help you squeeze more usefulness out of every minute. Summon, now, your most rebellious self, and **instead of auditing your calendar for *productivity*, audit it for *fun*.** In fact, since *audit* is listed in *Webster's Unabridged Dictionary of the Utterly Unfun*, let's *revolutionize* your calendar instead. Be brave. Give yourself permission to see through clear eyes, independent of the beliefs and priorities that may have driven your decisions in the past. I promise that in doing so, you'll uncover hidden opportunities to increase your fun, even *without* sacrificing productivity.

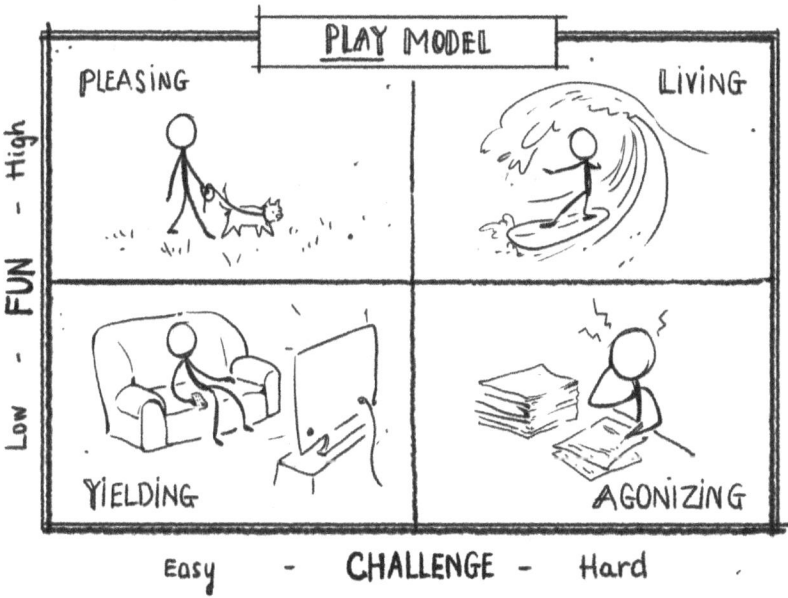

The PLAY Model asks you to sort each of your activities using two axes—their level of challenge and their degree of fun—which creates four quadrants:

* * *

Pleasing activities are those that are easy to execute and enjoyable. They are the moments of joy and delight punctuating our day-to-day life. Only you will know what these activities are, but examples include time catching up with a friend, unstructured play with children and/or pets, personal hobbies, and so on. Activities in this category are often viewed as frivolous, but science tells us they are anything but. Matthew Killingsworth, while completing his doctorate at Harvard University, found activities associated with momentary happiness are also associated with greater life satisfaction.[1] Though short-lived in duration and requiring little investment, these activities when compounded contribute to that elusive feeling most of us are looking for—that our life is worthwhile and fulfilling. Momentary fun, therefore, is an important fixture of our menu of activities.

Fun but challenging activities sit in the *Living* quadrant. Meaningful fun is sometimes experienced outside our comfort zone (although we can relish the moment further once we're back in comfort). This includes experiences like mastering a new skill, tackling an invited challenge, or doing something exhilarating like a challenging hike that leads to majestic views. These are generally not activities you can engage in all the time. However, when we engage in peak experiential activity, often triggered by challenge, risk, physical exertion, natural wonder, rich insight, or deep personal interactions, the payoff is significant. What type of fun truly makes you feel alive?

Agonizing activities are challenging to execute and bring us little to no joy. It is fair to say life is not meant to be all fun. Most of us have joyless work and unpleasant tasks that nevertheless need to get done. The Agonizing list looks different for everyone, but examples might include work and personal responsibilities, domestic responsibilities (e.g., cleaning and yard work), or other obligations (e.g., taxes). These activities might be a little bit harder to identify, because our true preferences are obscured by emotional or cultural baggage. For example, when my wife and I audited our own lives, we were surprised to find we both put our kids' evening bath time in the Agonizing category. (**Side note:** Loving your children to pieces doesn't mean that some aspects of parenting aren't drudgery. A 2004 survey of 909 working mothers in Texas found that childcare was about on par with housework regarding their level of enjoyment engaging the respective activities.)[2]

The last activity type is *Yielding*. These activities are easy to execute but don't add much value to our lives. Often they simply pacify us. Mindless social media use or TV channel surfing fall into this category. So might friendships of convenience, or social gatherings that you join because you feel obligated. For some people, most or all of their leisure time is spent Yielding. Time spent in this quadrant simply feeds the *Nothing*.

Where Are You Today?

Time to get curious: How are you *really* spending your time?

Your task is straightforward. For one week, log your activities by hour (168 hours in a week) and evaluate where they fall within the PLAY Model. There are two ways to go about this. If you're someone who keeps a thorough daily calendar or journal, and you want a quick-and-dirty readout, you can work from the past week of your calendar.

For a more thorough evaluation, track your time each day for the next week.*

Track everything: sleeping, making meals, eating meals, commuting, working, leisure time, family time, fights, sex, sports—all the joy and tedium of seven days of life.

As you go through the exercise, it will become clear quickly which activities maximize and which squander opportunities to build your Fun Habit. Once you identify distractions and obstacles, it becomes easier to diagnose the changes that need to be made to improve your outlook.

---

* (Don't wait, start today. You can download the PLAY time tracker here: https://share.michaelrucker.com/time-audit.)

* * *

This is the moment where most books would offer an assessment. You'd total up your numbers and we'd spit out a score and your "Fun Type." I created a tool to do that online, but only for lighthearted novelty (https://share.michaelrucker.com/fun-type). We are not going to do that here, because we've already defined fun as necessarily autonomous. The last thing I want to do is box you into an identity or rank you against a perceived right way of being. The point of this self-evaluation isn't to *rank* at all. It's about *fit*—looking carefully at the choices you're making about how to spend your time and considering whether they are in alignment with what supports your well-being, now and in the future.

Ultimately, we want to ensure a healthy balance of time spent in the Pleasing and Living quadrants and to decrease our time in the Yielding and Agonizing space (where it makes sense). It is important to note that you also should have dedicated time for rest and renewal. Although the goal here is definitely to have more fun, too much of anything can burn us out.

For those of you who are inevitably asking themselves, *Okay, but how much time should I be seeking to spend on fun?* Here's a starting place: *two hours a day*. This recommendation is grounded from two empirical sources: first, research from Dr. Marissa Sharif, Dr. Cassie Mogilner Holmes, and Dr. Hal Hershfield that suggests the "Goldilocks" sweet spot for leisure time is between two to five hours a day (more than five hours and the weight of being overly nonproductive might have a negative psychological impact),[3] and second, data around Americans and leisure time that indicate what's average in the United States, suggesting that two hours is at least an attainable baseline for most of us.

According to the results of the American Time Use Survey by the Bureau of Labor Statistics, on average, people in full-time employment have 4.09 hours per day of leisure time.[4] This includes 3.34 hours on weekdays and 5.87 hours per day on weekends. Not surprisingly, people with no kids at home have more, 5.93 hours per day. But even people with kids report 4.12 to 5.00 hours per day. And although Pew research indicates that modern fathers in heterosexual relationships[5] are trying to close the gap of parental parity, it is important to note the gap still exists between parental gender roles.[6] Modern moms in heterosexual relationships remain at a disadvantage when it comes to leisure. The Pew Research Center reports that moms, on average, have 2.7 less hours of leisure a week when compared to fathers.[7]

It's hard to guess how participants would have rated their free time using the PLAY Model, but the researchers counted the following activities as leisure: watching TV, socializing, reading, exercising, playing sports, relaxing, playing computer games, and other similar activities.

If you think that four to five hours of daily free time is a lot (or more than you thought), a survey by the insurance company Direct Line that included two thousand people suggests that the optimal amount of free time for us is actually *six hours and fifty-nine minutes*![8] In other words, in this particular study, the amount of free time *desired* was quite a bit more than what most people actually enjoy.

Trying to find almost seven hours of free time per day might not be realistic for many of us. However, almost all of us should have agency over at least two hours of our day, so that is a good place to start.

A New Take on Affluence

Most people spend a lot of time thinking about affluence in the financial sense. We fixate on the perceived scarcity of money in our lives. Some of us fixate on generating more than we need. Meanwhile, we spend very little time building *time affluence*. If fun, experience-rich lives are our goal, this is a mistake. A 2010 study by Cassie Mogilner Holmes reveals that merely shifting our *thinking* toward time rather than money can help usher more fun into life. When Mogilner Holmes gave study participants an exercise that led them to think about money, they focused on productivity as a value. Meanwhile, when she led participants to think about time, something exciting happened: In at least their short-term thinking, they immediately prioritized social connections over work.[9] It's easy to extrapolate from there that focusing on time affluence might make it easier to appreciate the upside of fun. Other studies have shown that people who prioritize time over money are generally happier. In one, professors at UCLA and the University of Pennsylvania found that while Americans tended to choose money over time, choosing more time was associated with greater happiness long-term.[10]

Despite a lot of worry to the contrary, "productive life" and "fun life" are not necessarily in opposition to each other. Happily, shifting time away from work need not dampen your professional performance. In fact, I've seen the opposite happen to me and to people I work with. Taking time to relax and restore makes us more productive, with better work and better results (this works if you're fortunate enough to have the freedom and financial security needed to pull these levers, which sadly not everyone does). Increasingly, businesses have recognized that there are diminishing returns to extending work hours beyond a certain point, particularly for people engaged in the creative, heuristic work we discussed in the last chapter.

There's one final way that time affluence can help restack your deck toward fun. Wealth is generated by investing in opportunities for future returns. Not enough of us think about time in the same way, especially our leisure time. As you consider an activity, ask yourself if it's an investment or merely a cost. Fun is enrichment, not expense. For example, thirty minutes Yielded to looking at other people's vacation photos in your social feed? *Cost*, a contribution to the *Nothing*. Thirty Pleasing minutes spent working on the details of your next vacation? *Investment*! Time spent in Pleasing and Living activities don't just satisfy us in the moment but enrich us in the future as well. Yielding activities are occasionally investments, but more often are costs. Agonizing activities? Even more so, but unlike Yielding activities, Agonizing activities can be a means to an end. They are costs, but sometimes necessary ones—the housekeeping of life. Yielding activities, meanwhile, are generally at our own discretion.

Ultimately, what they say about money—"Here today, gone tomorrow"—is even more true about time, so it's vital that we get more intentional about it. Time is a finite resource, of course, so building time affluence means finding ways to increase the amount of time you have control over. For that reason, our work with the PLAY Model starts by taking things *off* your plate, not adding them.

TIME TO PLAY

Make Life Less Agonizing

If you've completed your time audit, you probably have already had some eye-opening revelations about how you've been using your time. Now comes the first step toward time affluence: subtracting what you can from what agonizes you. Let's make you some space.

Of course, we can't avoid everything that belongs in the Agonizing quadrant. But when people use the PLAY Model, they are always amazed at how many activities they can simply . . . stop doing . . . only because they had never evaluated their habits with a critical eye before. Ironing is one very basic but universal example. Unless you're in a handful of fields that demand starch, you could probably throw out your iron and no one would notice. So, stop buying clothes that require ironing. There are quite a few household and personal maintenance chores that you might do less frequently—or stop entirely—once you realize the true aggregate cost of "maintaining appearances."

I am fortunate to have Nir Eyal as a friend. Nir wrote the bestselling book *Indistractable* and is an expert on building habits. From his wisdom, I learned how to reduce dramatically the time I spend on one of my top Agonizing quadrant activities: email, and especially the email *chain*—the long, distracting back-and-forth that one innocent message inevitably sparks. "But I've got to answer people," I'd complain. "It would be rude not to." Nir's solution was brilliant. "Mike," he said, "If you don't want to receive so many emails, *stop sending them*." I was so focused on what other people were doing *to me*, it never occurred to me what I was doing to *them*, and further, that I had more control than anyone in the volume of email I was chained to. So, I started to check in with myself before writing an email: Is the communication truly necessary? Most of the time, the answer is *no* and I move on. I have also come up with my own strategy. I almost never respond to an email forward that only has this word in the body copy, "Thoughts?" If the content in the forward lacks enough substance that it doesn't inspire the forwarder to provide any context, it's almost always a clear indication it's not worth my time, either. These two tactics of reducing an Agonizing activity have put at least three hours back in my week that I now repurpose for more fun endeavors.

Sometimes what you can't subtract entirely, you can outsource. Earlier I mentioned the Agonizing experience of trying to get both of my kids bathed every night. Let me start by saying that my wife, Anna, does not consider a daily bath "maintaining appearances." It's a fact of life. Skipping more than two nights a week is not an option in our household. (I can only imagine how unkempt and malnourished my children would be without my better half.) We love spending time with our kids, and yet something about bath time brought out the worst in all of us. They never wanted to get in, so we had to fight them every step of the way. They sensed our stress, and intentionally wound us up. When we tried to cut the time in half by putting them in the same tub, they fought with each other, making it worse. Things got so dysfunctional that neither Anna nor I wanted to be the one in charge, so we'd each try to wait out the other, with one grim martyr finally stepping up to the plate. It was *Agonizing*.

When we first thought about the problem, we got stuck on the idea that we needed to hire a nanny, which we couldn't afford and didn't really need or want. As things got worse, one of us finally said, "What about hiring a babysitter three times a week, just for dinner and bath time?" At first, we thought it was kind of weird to bring someone in just for baths—then we decided we didn't care. It just might work for us. And guess what? We found a babysitter, Caitlin, that our kids love. She brought all kinds of fun energy to the activity (like literally pretending my youngest was a burrito while drying him and wrapping him up in a towel), and my kids stopped fighting (sometimes) and now have fun with the various antics. As a result, Anna and I started having three dinner dates a week and watched our resentments evaporate while having the opportunity to reconnect as a couple. Then something unexpected happened: Once baths with the sitter became something they looked forward to, my kids stopped fighting with us so much when it was our turn. Of course, we borrowed some techniques from Caitlin ("the fun one"). All in all, bath time became less Agonizing. We subtracted three bath times from our week, gained three date nights with each other, and ended up with *more* quality time with our kids overall. Talk about a win.

Here are a few typical Agonizing quadrant activities I hear about again and again, and ideas to eliminate or reduce their footprint in your life:

- *"Round the Clock" News, aka "Doomsurfing":* Too much bad news, particularly when the events are out of our control, can be Agonizing, affecting us negatively even beyond the time we spend viewing and reading it. That said, we all want to be informed. Consider getting your news once a week, in a thoughtful, concentrated hour, from a handful of trusted sources, rather than through a social media feed. Turn off any mobile news notifications. I've seen people go as far as scheduling specific, explicit time to "worry" to avoid being anxious about world affairs the rest of the week (an old psychology trick). Give yourself a finite amount of time and then move on.
- *Ghost on Meetings:* Is there anything more Agonizing than a meandering, impactless meeting that interrupts productive work? My friend Brad Wills, when he was an executive at a tech firm, encouraged his direct reports to abandon any meeting where their presence was a waste of time. That's right: He told them to walk out silently, and then protected them when people complained. Not everyone is lucky enough to have such an enlightened boss—but politely declining to attend some of the meetings on your schedule may be easier than you think.
- *Reconsider the Gym:* I'm someone who helps design health clubs and loves them, and even I will tell you: If you hate the gym, *don't go!* It's not for everybody. Instead, pick a physical activity with no commute, like body weight exercises in your own home or a nature hike in a nearby park. (**Health clubs:** The takeaway here is to create more fun and inclusive offerings so you *are* the fun choice.)
- *Outsource Routine Tasks Like Your Laundry:* This is pretty obvi-

ous, but I know many, many people who thought they couldn't afford an expense like this—until they finally did it and wished they had done it years earlier. Consider the time you'd save spending the extra dollars, and then look at what you might cut in your budget to accommodate the new expense. And laundry is just the start. From bookkeeping to having someone wait in line for you, there are a lot of creative ways to exchange money for time back on your calendar.

- *Eliminate Agonizing Steps at Work:* Analyze your work processes to make sure that annoying administrative or process steps justify their effort. That sounds simple, but most of us have many learned-but-untested assumptions about how to do our work. My friend Rosemary is a UX/UI designer. She was taught that wireframes—very basic line drawings showing the elements and layout of a new digital offering—were an absolutely essential, do-or-die step of the design process. But after many years in her niche, they began to feel both Agonizing to produce and unnecessary. She began experimenting with skipping them completely and found that there was no difference in the end result for her clients. Bye-bye, wireframing. What onerous tasks might you eliminate?

- *Housework:* Share the burden with your children! My friend Christine was doing all the housework herself, thinking that her kids were too young to make a meaningful contribution to the household chores. She finally decided to give them a chance anyway—and found that her kids were completely capable of washing the dishes and their clothes, two of her most hated tasks. Based on the frequent resharing of an eye-popping infographic called "Age Appropriate Chores for Kids"[11] in my social feeds over the past years, presumably many parents underestimate the potential contributions their kids can make toward household chores. The graphic, created by home economics expert Toni Anderson based on her own experience as a "happy housewife," recommends starting your kids on basic chores between the ages of two and three, as bananas as that may sound.

Stop Yielding to the *Nothing*

If you discovered during your audit that you're spending a lot of time in Yielding activities, don't beat yourself up—that's great news. Yielding is time you already control, where small changes in your behavior can produce immediate and dramatic wins. One of my favorite examples comes from the author of Creative Trespassing,[12] Tania Katan. Some years back, she was working for a super-extroverted CEO who encouraged employees to do everything together—his approach was, "Let's have work lunch together. Let's do everything. Let's go pee-pee together," she joked when she told me the story. The style was not a good fit for Tania. She needed some time away from her colleagues and the office each day to do her job well. So instead of Yielding to the established social culture, she started taking a solo walk every lunch break. She'd stroll aimlessly or walk to a coffee shop to meet a friend. The plan was solitude and free space to think, but then other employees started approaching her to ask if they could escape with her. "I inadvertently started a walking revolution," she said. (Later, when she met her wife, a visual artist and professor who runs the Museum of Walking, their shared love of wandering on foot became a point of connection.)

As Tania experienced, we sometimes yield our social life to cultural pressure. We'll talk more about applying intention to our social lives in chapter 7.

For now, let's turn our attention to the most pervasive, common, and wasteful Yielding activity: mindless consumption of social media, news, and entertainment content.

Do me a favor: Take out your phone and find the feature that tells you your average daily screen time. *What's that giant sucking sound I hear?* It's all those precious hours of your day being vacuumed into the *Nothing*.

Based on recent findings from Nielsen,[13] we are now spending almost half of our day engaged with media and content. Don't get me wrong.

Watching a favorite TV show or movie can fit happily into the Pleasing quadrant (especially when you're sharing the experience with friends or loved ones). However, we know from years of research about media consumption that mindlessly watching television correlates with being unhappy,[14] and that those that don't spend all their time sitting in front of a screen generally tend to be happier.[15]

Social media, handily delivered via a useful device that travels with us everywhere, has taken the consumption problem to new levels. At this point, we're all familiar with the studies revealing the ill effects of too much scrolling—for example, the college students who reduced their social media time to thirty minutes per day and enjoyed rapid and significant improvement in their depression and loneliness.[16] We know that social media companies, like junk food companies, have made turning us into addicts a near perfect science. We know these things, and yet we still reach for our phones the moment we have downtime—whether it's two minutes or two hours. On top of that, we may identify or defend our social media use as "fun" or "relaxing," despite the fact that the science overwhelmingly shows us that after a certain point, it is anything but.

So why do we perceive it as such? The short answer is that when we find ourselves in neutral or negative valence—in other words, not having fun—social media is often the easiest way to escape our discomfort. Also, we crave novelty and social interaction, and the anticipatory reward of dopamine tricks us into the cognitive error of thinking social media provides both.

And so, we fall into the *Nothing*. Like any habitual Yielding practice, its impact on our memories of experience is quite literally that—nothing. We lose that time forever. That is because our brains are efficient. We often encode noneventful routine activities as a single memory. If you had two hundred copies of the same thing, would it be efficient to hold on to the other 199? Common events are encoded in our memory as a single experience. Think of an old commute pattern. Do you remember the fifty times you went somewhere, or do you remember the "one" way you used to get somewhere and recognize you used to do it the same way all the time?

So how do we save ourselves from Yielding, whether to social media or any other false friend? Unlike alcoholics, we can't pour the liquor down the toilet. Few of us are going to give up our mobile phones. I know one woman who bought a combination safe and had her husband lock her phone away a certain number of hours of the day. (It helped, until she started refusing to turn it over.) I myself use apps such as BlockSite that block my access to sites that I've identified as soul-sucking.

The answer brings us to the next phase of your work with the PLAY Model.

Expanding Your Fun File

As we've discovered, reducing Yielding activities that have become habitual isn't easy and sometimes requires help. One form of help comes from behavioral science, which tells us that when we try to quit an unhealthy habit, we're much more likely to be successful if we replace the existing habit with something else. For example, smokers who are instructed to chew gum when they would have otherwise smoked cigarettes have higher success rates than those who aren't nudged toward a replacement activity.[17]

Enter the Fun File. The Fun File serves up a broad menu of activities you've already brainstormed and vetted as being in the top two quadrants of the PLAY Model. Instead of having to think deliberately in those moments that you need an alternative, you can scan your list and pick something fun. It's like grabbing for that stick of gum. With a list in hand, we are better positioned to take action rather than wander into old habits.

Creating Your Fun File Has Three Main Steps

Step One: The Brainstorm
Start by determining the most reliable way for you to document and store your list (e.g., pen and paper, Word file, Google Docs, Evernote, etc.). Then, start brainstorming all the things from your past and present that bring (or have brought) you pleasure and enjoyment. Everything from small pleasures (playing with your dog) to elaborate ones (taking your dog on a road trip).

Repeat the exercise with your eye toward the future. What things might bring your future-self pleasure and enjoyment? What have you never done but might like to try? An example from my future-self is traveling to space. I've already scraped together my down payment to be a part of a Virgin Galactic flight.

Some people find that they benefit from setting a time limit for this exercise, while others like to brainstorm over several days or weeks. Do whatever works best for you.

Step Two: Adding Structure
Some will argue that being so methodical about fun that we build a premeditated list creates a contradiction, making thinking about fun more a burden than a reward. I disagree, and here's why: Developing an organized list of options both gives us freedom of choice, as well as provides a mechanism to guide our choice. Science suggests that we increase the likelihood of a fun outcome when we are able to reduce the mental workload of having to always think of new options. And in the world of human desire, the need for autonomy and the need for structure are a dynamic duo.[18] Most of us crave both.

Adding structure to our list has the added benefit of generating even more interesting ideas for fun. Research by Dr. Eric Rietzschel and colleagues suggests that some of us become more creative when we're given structure because order relieves some of the cognitive load of having to pull ideas out of thin air. Once we see patterns of where we find fun, similar ideas will likely come easier (e.g., "I clearly like concerts, what are some bands I'm not thinking of that would be really fun to see?"). Furthermore, we can use this spared brain power for decision making and taking action. When we're systematic and intentional, we are better focused on what's important—*actually having fun!*

The question we need to ask is: What's the right amount of structure for our Fun File? The good news is not much! There are only two elements I believe are essential . . .

1. A sorting order of categories that is meaningful to you (e.g., activity type, difficulty to achieve, time of year, etc.).
2. Your "short list." (To see my current short list, visit https://share.michaelrucker.com/fun-list.)

Step Three: The Short List
The final step to complete your Fun File is possibly the most difficult: From the long list you generated, pick your favorite **eight to fifteen achievable choices** as your go-tos in the upcoming months. All the items that make the short list should be achievable (e.g., it would be fun for me to compete in another Ironman, but that is no longer possible since I now have a hip replacement).

Brainstorming and being expansive regarding your options was an important starting place, but having hundreds of activity ideas at the ready is not a recipe for fun. It's too much of a good thing, or what science calls *overchoice*.

To illustrate the problem of overchoice, imagine it's a Friday night at home, and you plan to watch a movie. Would you rather start your evening by picking from a list of a thousand movies or a list of ten? If you said ten, you've intuitively predicted what a study exploring that very question determined: Computer users trying to choose a movie to watch made better decisions and enjoyed their choice more when working from a short list of films.[19] With a list of one thousand movies, you could easily fall asleep hours later, movie yet unwatched, still in the act of watching trailers and deliberating.

Overchoice makes it hard to prioritize, and in some cases, this leads us not to choose at all. *Why is that?* Remember how we are really good at comparing? When presented with ideas for fun, our brain assesses every option against the next one, trying to predict which one will be the most enjoyable. We don't want that happening with our Fun File.

If you're wondering how I landed on a list of eight to fifteen items, that, too, was informed by science. In a study of people choosing from sets of six, twelve, or twenty-four items, brain activity measured by MRI scans showed that twelve items led to the highest level of contentment. The scientists concluded that the brain probably performs best when given between eight and fifteen choices.[20]

If fun requires that you be a rebel and settle on a list of seventeen items, go for it. What's more important than the exact number is that your list includes at least some options that have the potential to take you to the Living quadrant. If you're finding it difficult to identify what a future peak experience might look like for you, look no further than the next section.

Five Gateways to Peak Experience

The American Psychological Association Dictionary of Psychology defines peak experiences as, "a moment of awe, ecstasy, or sudden insight into life as a powerful unity transcending space, time, and the self."—a terrific way to describe the height of the Living quadrant.[21] When I went looking for what you might call "gateways" to such experiences, I unexpectedly found some of my answers in a familiar childhood place: video games. Games, by design, guarantee a unique blend of pleasure and challenge, risk and reward that define the Living quadrant—although, unlike IRL fun, the thrills only last as long as the power button is on. But what if you applied the underlying design assumptions to make real life more fun?

According to his résumé, Alexandre Mandryka develops video games—twenty-four games, to be exact, that have sold more than fifty million copies. I instead like to think of him as one of the world's foremost experts in creating the conditions for peak experience. Remarkably, Mandryka's insights on how to create a thrilling game operate like a template for how to create a remarkable peak experience. Use some or all of these insights to broaden your horizon as you develop your Fun File over time. You'll see very quickly that you don't need to climb Mount Everest to have a more exhilarating life.

TIME TO PLAY

1. Leveling Up

Mandryka says that in gaming, peak fun is achieved by alternating between periods when you increase your challenge and periods when you enjoy your mastery. Put another way, you get more thrill from moving between an anxiety zone and a comfort zone than being constantly in either state. For a real-world example, recall what it was like to first ride a bike. Riding with training wheels is an incredible thrill—until it's not. Then off come the training wheels, and we're briefly terrified until—*Yesss!*—we gain our balance and enjoy a new high. When that gets old, we start experimenting with speed, acceleration, distance, and maybe even stunts. We vary the challenge of the route to develop mastery or find unfamiliar scenery for variability.

Interestingly, balancing challenge with skill is an integral part of Mihaly Csikszentmihalyi's acclaimed theory of flow, which describes the immersive, almost hypnotic state artists, musicians, and other highly skilled individuals find themselves in when they've achieved mastery after thousands of hours of practice of their craft. Flow state is indeed a type of peak experience—but it can require considerable investment. Fun Living quadrant experiences, meanwhile, are happily available to almost everyone, simply by balancing challenge against mastery. The joy from "leveling up" can happen at any level.

Mandryka also believes that challenging players to level up protects them from "a pleasurable but mind-numbing grind that leaves you feeling empty." In other words, pleasure connected to a learning experience insulates us from the *Nothing*. "That type of game that provides pleasure and can be played without effort and thus without limit, I call addictive. It is the type of entertainment that tricks our body and brain to focus on meaningless glitter and look for the next release of dopamine," Mandryka wrote on his blog.[22]

2. Learning + Self-Determination

Learning is fun—when it's a path we've chosen ourselves. Maybe you read about the boss in France whose team, thinking it would be fun, surprised him with a *Top Gun*–style experience in a French fighter jet. Surprise birthday parties instill terror in some people—how well do you think surprise aerial acrobatics went over? Before the flight, a watch measured the boss's heart rate as being in full tachycardia. Once in the air, at 870 miles per hour and 2,500 feet, he panicked and hit the eject button. Whatever his level of general interest in aerial dogfighting, I think we can all agree that's the kind of activity you want to *choose*, not have thrust upon you. There are peak experiences, and there are traumatic ones. (The man did safely parachute back to Earth, but the plane was destroyed.)[23]

What feels intuitively true appears to be backed by science: Both learning and fun benefit when they are aligned with self-determination. You're less likely to have a breakthrough (not the kind through the roof of a jet) if you're experiencing someone *else's* idea of a good thrill. One small-scale research project into the characteristics of an after-school design lab—where children and their teacher built, designed, and played with different tools—found that children had the most fun when allowed to take responsibility and make choices on their projects. When analyzing the interactions that happened at the creative lab, the authors came up with a simple formula for fun: self-determination + learning.[24]

3. Uncertainty

Mandryka aptly linked self-determination to yet another fun gateway: "Fun is the desired exploration of uncertainty," he wrote. Humans are attracted to uncertainty; we enjoy the shivery anticipation of not knowing what's next. When we read a book, don't we enjoy it more if it includes twists and unexpected turns?

Alan Dix, the director of the Computational Foundry at Swansea University, found that adding an element of surprise can transform even a boring activity into a fun one. For example, waiting for a kettle to boil can be quite mundane. However, if a bird pops out and sings when the kettle boils, this suddenly adds a bit of whimsy to the activity. In his position paper, Dix notes that this experiment might sound silly, but he was after fun, not cool.[25] No one ever confused a trick kettle with a peak experience, but when you apply uncertainty to more meaningful activities, it can boost them into the Living quadrant. (More on this when we discuss variable hedonics in chapter 3.)

4. Intensity of Emotion

Crafty game designers are aware that immersive games don't require elaborate graphics to provide players with fun. Usually, they build on basic human emotions and instincts and provide us with some mystery and magic—something we have been hardwired to respond to through thousands of years of making sense of the world through storytelling.

I don't think I need to provide studies to connect emotion to peak experiences. Falling in love, marriage, childbirth, and other milestones linked to personal relationships are typically high on people's lists. Spending time nurturing and developing close relationships—likely sources of intense positive emotions—is an important gateway, and accessible to most of us.

That said, emotional intensity isn't only found in relationships. Try thinking about your life in creative terms. If your days are feeling flat, ask yourself: How can I add more action and suspense to my story? What major climax might I start to work toward this month (or year)? If your life lacks a dramatic arc, it's fully in your power to invent one.

5. Risk-Taking and Edgework

Physical thrills aren't for everybody, but they're definitely a gateway activity for some. Stephen Lyng is a pioneer in the sociology of voluntary risk-taking, which he calls *edgework*. Lyng suggests that many are willing to engage in activities that bring a risk of physical harm and require special skills because they provide a unique and therefore fulfilling experience.[26] Peak experiences often take us outside of the limited, commodified set of activities we pursue in day-to-day life. This sets them beyond professional status, efficiency, and income, as observed by George Ritzer in his book *Enchanting a Disenchanted World*.[27] Maslow, too, counted being unmotivated by the "needs and drives of the ordinary sort" as a facet of peak experiences.[28] For example, a study of BMX riders (people who use their bikes to perform dangerous stunts) by Shane Scott and Mark Austin of the University of Louisville found that the fun had was connected to more than just the physical thrill.[29] Participants described their risk-taking as a way to escape society's constraints. The fun they have while riding is, in a way, a rejection of the rationalization and commodification of an ordinary world.

Of course, risk-taking has its downside. I was struck by the video Sky Brown, a skateboarder as famous for her young age as for her competition stunts, shared after a devastating fall in 2020.[30] She failed to land on the half-pipe after flying up one side and went hurtling through the air before being knocked unconscious. A helicopter rushed her to the hospital. In the video, speaking weakly from her hospital bed with a black eye, she says she normally doesn't share her accidents, because she prefers people see the fun side. But after her worst fall, she wanted fans to know "It's okay to fall sometimes . . . I want everyone to know that whatever we do, we're just going to do it with love and happiness." For anyone exploring edgework, the key is evaluating both the risk and reward. Understand what's at stake and consider activities where the real risk is lower than the perceived risk—for example, exploring rock climbing, but maybe not free climbing, if you're not an experienced enough climber.

Still looking for more? In *Toward a Psychology of Being*,[31] Maslow identified *sixteen* aspects of peak experiences. Based on this work, here are a few more suggestions where you might direct your Living quadrant energy. Seek out activities that:

- Help you leave behind inhibitions
- Leave you feeling at one with the environment
- Give you a sense of completion
- Allow for artistic expression and free-range creativity
- Make you feel powerful and/or unique

Avoid the Enemies of Fun

Now that we've talked about gateways into the Living quadrant, how about some guardrails: What are the potential pitfalls and limits of fun?

Addiction, Dependence, and Obsession

In my day job, I am surrounded by fitness fanatics. Knowing that I'm a two-time Ironman, you might suspect I qualified at one point as well. In the health club business, we have a saying about chronic exercisers, "They're either running toward something or away from something." Imagine a person who spends fifteen hours a week at a gym who's not going there to pay the rent. Some might say that's someone who's truly committed, but, in fact, that's the threshold that sports behavioralist Mark Anshel says defines *exercise addiction*.[32] Many experts agree that *dependence* on exercise—itself a healthy way to have fun—can present a considerable behavioral problem for some people (e.g., "The rest of my life needs to fit around running").

Excessive fun, in which self-control and autonomy are lost, gives fun a bad rap. David J. Linden, the professor of neuroscience and the author of the book *The Compass of Pleasure* we discussed in chapter 1,[33] contends the brain doesn't know the difference between vice and virtue. We activate the same circuits in the brain when we take heroin or have casual sex as we do when we engage in virtuous acts such as meditating or giving a gift. This could also help explain why fun, which is fundamentally good, can turn bad under circumstances of excess. Repeated experiences cause long-term changes in our neural structures, a process known as neural plasticity. Memories get stored in the brain, and as such, Linden argues that addictions might actually be a form of learning. Certain activities produce natural feel-good neurochemicals like endorphins (e.g., runners get a "runner's high"). The feeling of euphoria a pleasurable activity produces is compelling, so we gravitate toward it again and again, possibly ignoring all common sense about what's good for us.

To determine whether one of your passions is drifting toward unhealthy obsession, try applying Canadian psychologist Robert J. Vallerand's "dualistic model of passion."[34] Vallerand distinguishes between harmonious passions (healthy) and obsessive passions (harmful). Experiments that build on Vallerand's model show that harmonious passion, defined as a strong inclination to engage in an activity willingly and with a sense of volition, creates positive emotions and improves life satisfaction.

Obsessive passions, meanwhile, are not enriching. When we stop, we feel empty. For instance, you played golf all weekend even though you had shared duties with your partner that you had agreed upon beforehand (that didn't get done). Afterward, instead of satisfied, you feel ashamed or guilty. You might also experience:

- Withdrawal, similar to an addiction: "If I cannot exercise, I feel irritable."
- An inflexible attitude: "I need to do it, even if it hurts me or others."
- Blindness to risk: "I'm all in." In Vallerand's study, obsessively passionate cyclists continued with their activity even when there was snow and temperatures dropped below zero. Vallerand's experiments show that obsessive passion is also involved in addictive behaviors, such as pathological gambling that can lead people to lose everything.[35]

When self-control and self-regulation are gone and the activity takes over, the dark side of fun is revealed, as the pursuit of pleasure indeed turns painful.

Clinical Depression

If you're struggling with depression or another form of mental illness, please don't take on the additional burden of trying to "fun" your way out of it. It's a very unfortunate reality that not enough of us get the assistance we need because of the stigma attached to asking for help. Whether due to neurochemistry or trauma, some mental health conditions are best treated with the help of a professional, medication, or both.

For instance, you cannot will yourself out of treatment-resistant depression. Trying to do so could be potentially fatal. Early in my twenties I was hospitalized with a virus that resulted in neurological and psychological complications that I wouldn't have been able to navigate myself. Accepting help pulled me out of a dark hole and allowed me to thrive my last three years as an undergrad. I've also used SAM-e

(S-adenosylmethionine) to improve my mood during various periods of high stress. If you need it, there is no shame in seeking help. Once you get the help you need, fun will be there waiting for you.

Overwork and Lack of Sleep

It's very simple: Life is no fun when you don't get enough sleep. Sleep deprivation is an increasingly prevalent public health hazard. According to the research on the physiology of sleep and cognitive performance conducted by the National Sleep Foundation, adults should get between seven and nine hours of sleep a night.[36] In contrast, if we get less than that for several days, we start developing a sleep deficit, making it more difficult for our brains to function.[37]

Furthermore, we're working too hard. Dr. Charles A. Czeisler, a professor of Sleep Medicine at Harvard Medical School, indicates we should have eleven consecutive hours of non-work-related activity for any given twenty-four-hour cycle of time. Also, we should have at least one day completely off a week from any work activity—ideally, two in a row—which will help us avoid some of the poor sleep hygiene habits that often lead to sleep deficits. Dr. Czeisler also believes that we should not work more than sixty hours a week.[38]

If you're one of the more than a third of U.S. adults who report they're getting fewer than six hours of sleep a night,[39] piling on new activities, no matter how fun they are, is not going to help you. No activity is restorative at that point. Fun will become just another thing you need to grind out. Time poverty and overwork, which we discussed earlier, are closely related.

Mistaking Fun for High Arousal

Let your own needs and desires, not someone else's definition of fun, shape your habit. Dr. Iris Mauss, the director of the Emotion & Emotion Regulation Lab at Berkeley, has made major contributions to the science of happiness. When we spoke, she pointed out that in American and Western culture, we tend to associate "fun" with high-arousal (e.g., energized, excited) positive experiences. "I think, we as a culture have under-emphasized what [Stanford associate psychology professor] Jeanne

Tsai calls *low-activation* or *low-arousal positive emotions*, like calm, peace, serenity." Quietly reading a book, meditating, and gardening are all low-arousal activities that some people might not classify as *fun*, and yet can be exactly that. They also provide balance and renewal, which so many of us are sorely lacking.

Over-Optimizing

When I meet people who are enthusiastic about my work, especially young, tech-oriented people, many of them tell me how good they are at finding spare minutes for fun amidst the crazy pace of their working life. "I work like an animal, so I've been tricking out every minute," one young entrepreneur told me. "When I go to the bathroom, I jump on Tinder and line up dates." The people who say this tend to be part of a subculture that's relentlessly focused on self-optimization and life hacking. Many of them also tell me that I'm wrong to discourage their eighty-hour-a-week work schedule, because they're actually having fun on the job. That may be true—and yet, at some point, living within that bubble, they are prioritizing a very small window of experiences over the grand breadth of what life has to offer. Their ability to plan dates on the toilet and fit fun into ever smaller units of time may give them a sense of accomplishment, but at some point, almost all of us need to find things to subtract from our schedule. Intentionality is the ultimate goal, not hyper-optimization of time usage.

Becoming More Intentional

My hope is that you're leaving this chapter with a heightened understanding of both the finite nature of time and the many opportunities your time represents. Contrary to the cliché, every moment *doesn't* count; a fun, happy life can sustain a certain amount of tedium or even adversity. And yet if we don't seriously reconcile with the fact that time is ultimately a finite and scarce resource—though we rarely know exactly how scarce, both a blessing and a curse—we will squander time and fail to invest in activities that produce compounding fun.

The people I know who spend the most time in the Living quadrant are relentlessly intentional about it. They are busy people, so they schedule their fun. We often mistakenly think that "magical moments" shouldn't require planning. While it's true that magical moments are near impossible to contrive, you do have to commit to making space for them in your life. To do so effectively takes a bit of planning and some discipline.

I became intimately aware of how important such a commitment can be when I lost my brother a lot sooner than I ever expected to. He was only forty-one. The death of a loved one is never easy, and I was emotionally unprepared for it. One thing that has helped me as I've worked through my grief in the years since is savoring the fact that we created so many happy memories in our adult years, despite not living in the same state much of the time.

My brother and I had a long tradition of sharing bucket list experiences with each other. We went to Oktoberfest in Munich and Second City in Chicago. When he lived in Indiana, we went to Dark Lord Day—a festival for craft beer lovers packed with music from heavy metal artists—an event Brian discovered while looking for an adventure for us. (He loved craft beer; I love heavy metal—it was a great pairing.)

Just a month before he passed away, we shared our last trip together. At the time, I was working two jobs and immersed in a very stressful company reboot. When business brought me to New York, I knew immediately that I'd carve out some time to meet my brother, who then lived in Princeton, New Jersey, even though it meant saying no to some professional demands. We made a plan to travel to Six Flags Great Adventure in Jackson, New Jersey. If you're a roller-coaster person, you might know that this particular park is the home of the Kingda Ka, the tallest roller coaster in the world and the second fastest. It was an obvious choice because it was relatively convenient. Still, for me it would be an eight-hour round trip, and I'd be lying if I said there weren't moments I grumbled to myself about the inconvenience.

When we got to the park that day, I left behind all those worries. We were both happy to be reunited, and full of excitement—with a tiny bit of apprehension, too. Ten years before, we had tried to ride some roller coasters at a Six Flags in California and left disappointed. My brother, a big guy, was a hair too big to fit in most of the rides' safety harnesses. Now in New Jersey, as we walked to the coaster, we both became increasingly nervous. *Would we be denied the Kingda Ka?*

When it was our turn in line, we rushed to our seats. We both knew what we needed to hear, the click of the harness's buckle. No click, no ride. I looked over nervously as my brother squeezed himself in, but my heart told me we were going to be okay. With all the effort he could muster and a deep exhale, my brother sucked in his chest, and with a little help from the park's staff, we heard the click!

Within moments of that sound, we were off. The ride was magnificent. It was all we had hoped for. *It was so much fun!* We couldn't stop talking about it the rest of the day. Although we would be turned away from other rides that day, it didn't matter. We had conquered the beast! My brother took me to the airport the next day, and before he dropped me off, we enjoyed a victory feast. During that meal together, we jabbered like children, going over every minute of the experience. It's one of many fond and fun memories I have of being with my brother.

Kingda Ka, Jackson Township, New Jersey, 5/14/2016

TIME TO PLAY

If you're cagey about scheduling fun, I promise you this: There's plenty of room for spontaneity and surprise within that seemingly rigid box on your calendar. Sometimes you have to be a "stickler for fun," as counterintuitive as that sounds, in order to make the space to allow for the unplanned, the elated, the extraordinary. (And sometimes you schedule something promising that turns out to be about as fun as a bag of rocks. It happens—so then you try again.)

There's no way to take total control of the future. We can always count on life to surprise us—and that's not a bad thing, even though it's sometimes painful. All we can do is the best we can with the time we have.

Hall of Fun: Mark Sutherland
Creator of *Abby's List: A Dogumentary*

Have you ever heard of a dog with a bucket list? For Mark Sutherland and his whippet, Abby, such a list changed both their lives. When Abby turned thirteen, Mark could see his sweet girl was slowing down. She was weak and arthritic, sometimes walking with a limp, and veterinarians warned him about cancer. Mark began to feel like they were on borrowed time; he had lost two previous whippets at the same age.

At the same time, Mark was jobless for the first time in many years. "I thought, we should take a road trip," he says.

Mark started brainstorming a funny bucket list on Abby's behalf: peeing on Redwoods (the world's tallest trees), getting room service in Vegas; riding the It's a Small World ride in Disneyland. Over time, the list became populated with more meaningful "firsts": meeting new friends (dolphins), running in the snow, camping.

Mark put his life in storage, and they took to the road. The plan was to start at the beach in Southern California, travel cross-country for a couple of weeks, then end by putting Abby's paws in the Atlantic. When Mark and Abby were camping on Little Haystack Island in Canada, something completely unexpected happened:

Abby's health improved. She lost her limp and started scampering up rocks again. "She was starting to run and starting to smile. I truly watched her aging in reverse," says Mark.

At that point, he threw out his original plan; he'd keep traveling as long as he could. Three weeks became almost three years. Abby's quality of life held until she got cancer. But in the weeks before she died, she improved once more. At last, they were able to make it to the Atlantic—the original ending to their trip Mark had imagined but had set aside as the trip took on a life of its own.

Over the course of those three years, he filmed more than one hundred hours of footage, which is now a full-length feature documentary. Mark says, "One of the real themes of the film ends up being *get off the couch and live life*. It doesn't mean we can't do meaningful things. But we can also make conscious decisions to enjoy what we're doing along the way."

chapter 3

SAVOR Every Moment

You know, a lot of people think that just 'cause you work out, lift weights, eat right, and do what people tell you to do that you'll live a long life, maybe you will. But, why do people measure life by the years instead about how good the years were?
—GABRIEL IGLESIAS

With the help of the PLAY Model, you've now removed some of the waste as well as added pleasurable new activities into your daily life. In this chapter, we'll take a more alchemical approach, using a set of tools I've assembled that can help *transform* your daily life for more joy and satisfaction.

The SAVOR system, grounded in science and empirical evidence, consists of five elements:

- Story editing
- Activity bundling
- Variable hedonics
- Options
- Reminiscing

There's no better way to introduce you to SAVOR than to show the transformative power of putting even some of the tools into practice. A couple of years before fun saved my life, my doctoral practicum assignment was assisting a major California hospital network after one of its doctors completed suicide. His death was a wake-up call that many physicians in the network were suffering under the all-encompassing pressures of their work. Although burnout can affect any of us, it's commonly studied among health care workers because these roles offer researchers convenient opportunities for examining interpersonal stressors. In these studies, one job consistently ranks among the most affected: physician. While the suicide was a terrible shock for the organization, survey data collected from doctors throughout the network suggested that a larger crisis was brewing.[1]

When I arrived, the chief medical officer (CMO) of the hospital network was open to new ideas and highly motivated to take action. He was inspired in particular by the growing body of academic literature on building resilience through positive psychology techniques. Could these strategies be used to improve physician well-being? If we could somehow teach doctors to be more resilient, the CMO hoped, we could protect them from burnout.

After some initial meetings with the CMO, we decided I would work with the hospital group's Well-Being Committee—a committee that, beyond the CMO and myself, included over a dozen physicians, all representing different groups within the hospital system. Helping any group of people build resilience isn't simple, and this environment would prove even more difficult than most. Reviewing the hospital group's suggestions, I could see that many would be hard to implement in the face of entrenched social norms. They all included some component that would take the physicians away from their work and involved some component of outside learning. With time as scarce a resource as it was in this environment, the risk of this kind of experimentation going nowhere—or worse, creating more burnout—outweighed any potential benefit.

If the committee couldn't point us in the right direction, perhaps the at-risk physicians could. I started meeting individually with doctors, and right from the start, a theme emerged: putting the job before yourself.

Finishing medical school requires an enormous amount of effort. Med students are required to effectively abandon self-interest, adopting a relentlessly selfless mindset centered on seeing the commitment through to the end above all other factors—including personal well-being. For many doctors-in-training, this means forgoing everything that does not align with this commitment—even things as simple as taking a night off to see a movie. To survive medical school, future physicians radically eliminate the elements of their lives that don't contribute directly and visibly to their success, including life experience and self-care.

You may not have gone to med school, but this likely still feels familiar to you. Med students represent only one of the more extreme manifestations of what is now a nearly universal mindset among aspiring professionals. Convinced that success and meaning in life are derived primarily from salaried work, we prioritize our professional path and force the rest of our life to fit in the leftover space.

In talking to the at-risk doctors, most of whom were well beyond their med school days, I could see that this reprogramming of priorities—away from their own needs in favor of the needs of the job—did not resolve itself on its own. As a physician matures into the role, their single-minded passion for being a doctor naturally fades over time as life's other needs reemerge. As these doctors settled into their careers, the appeal of being "only" a doctor diminished. The preexisting conviction that perseverance and passion would be enough to sustain their spirits was gradually exposed as a lie. Inevitably, there was a painful reckoning with what had been sacrificed in the name of the job, and this reality ate away at their psyches. Medicine is among the most admirable, useful, and important professions, but even those most dedicated to the vocation need a life outside of duty. Without it, opportunities to learn and gain worldly experience, the kind that enriches us with insight and wisdom, prove elusive.

As my work progressed, I developed personal relationships with a handful of physicians from the committee. One physician in particular displayed an inspiring willingness to explore cutting-edge ideas. I'll call her Antonia.* Antonia joined the Well-Being Committee because she had faced burnout herself. Shaken by the recent suicide in the hospital network, she wanted to do all that she could to help other physicians improve their own well-being. She also found it disconcerting that, little by little, her personal life had all but vanished over her years as a hospitalist.

We decided to work together to see what small changes she might make to begin to feel more personally fulfilled and present. While Antonia was excited to make changes, she was unsure where to start. I suggested she think back to her life before med school, or when she was a child. "How did you spend your time? What made you smile?" I asked. Almost immediately, she said, "Drawing"—and then just as quickly dismissed it as a silly hobby. She had never been a "real artist." Together, we practiced **story editing**—refining the lens through which we assign values and priorities—to recognize drawing as something truly important to her well-being. The fact was, drawing had once been a significant source of pleasure for Antonia. It had just been deprioritized over time to the point of nonexistence in the crucible of med school. Far from being a superfluous hobby as she'd once seen it, the lack of self-expression and play in Antonia's life had been a significant contributor to her burnout.

At first, it was hard for her to reconnect with her long-lost passion, but we didn't give up trying. We went through her schedule, looking for periods in her day that lent themselves to a few minutes of creative release. She found she was able to **bundle** drawing into the time she spent responding to patients in the evening. She began sketching cartoons that satirized the difficult situations she encountered. Doing so, she found, helped her relieve stress and also put her in touch with her artistic and emotional side. From this early win, we explored additional **options**, like participating in activities her children enjoyed. Once we got the momentum going, her "Fun File" started to get pretty large. Rather than

---

* I have a tremendous amount of respect for the physicians I worked with during my fieldwork on the Well-Being Committee. An immutable component of the practicum contract with the hospital group was confidentiality. Antonia represents a real person, but I have changed her name and blended our experiences with other elements of that engagement to create an amalgamation that preserves her anonymity.

let it become an overwhelming and unactionable dumping ground, we whittled her options down to a few favorites and turned our attention to making those a reality. For example, while Antonia already kept a gratitude journal, we fine-tuned that practice so that the emphasis was on recording and **reminiscing** about her most delightful memories.

Make no mistake, I had a humble batting average working with these physicians. Many scoffed at fun as a trivial distraction from their important work. Antonia and the few others who were open to it, however, began to see it as a restorative tonic, and eventually as a safe and legal performance-enhancing drug. The truth is doctors who enjoy life make better doctors.

After I left the Well-Being Committee, I occasionally grabbed coffee with Antonia to check in on her progress. It gave me pleasure to see the new smiles that accompanied the renewed agency she found. She had expanded on her hobby outside of her working hours and was building a website that explored the link between art and wellness. In fun, she and I had discovered a new kind of medicine for burnout. I felt like a scientist whose experimental drug had just passed a successful clinical trial.

As you read the next section, ask yourself: What invisible stories about myself and my life have a negative effect on my ability to have fun? Are these narratives still useful, or, like Antonia's old mindset, are they relics that need challenging? How can I keep these stories from inhibiting my progress?

Story Editing

I first learned about story editing in the book *Redirect* by Dr. Timothy Wilson. Wilson's book explores the power our beliefs have in shaping our subjective reality. As Wilson explains, people possess the ability to "edit their personal stories in ways that lead to sustained changes in their behavior and well-being."[2] Story editing helps us correct the faulty mindset that fun is foolish and a poor use of time.

With our "always-on" lifestyles, powerful social norms inhibit us from valuing fun, let alone having any ourselves. Story editing is the first step in breaking through those inhibitions. In fact, simply becoming aware that these inhibitions exist and committing to living more joyfully is half the battle. With practice, story editing can also help turn the most mundane circumstance into an opportunity for joy, simply by giving ourselves the mandate to enjoy fun as an act of radical self-care.

To begin the process, start by examining any lingering prejudice you may have about fun. In particular, remind yourself that having fun and being a high-functioning adult are not mutually exclusive. (If you're still in doubt, keep reading: I'll be unpacking this further throughout the book.) Fun isn't "extra," it's a vital component of your personal well-being. This redirection of your personal narrative is the first step to gaining your power back and letting go of your old script. Fun needs to be woven into your identity.

Producing pleasurable thoughts on command takes deliberate practice, so be patient with yourself. In fact, for many of us, the simple act of trying not to focus on our worries can be draining. In one experiment conducted by Wilson and his colleagues from the University of Virginia, when given a choice between fifteen minutes spent sitting and thinking or enduring an electric shock, two-thirds of men and a quarter of women took the shock.[3] Further research out of the University of Virginia by Sarah Alahmadi and her colleagues revealed that when we aren't mindful, we don't prioritize pleasurable thoughts, likely because we tend to underestimate how enjoyable and beneficial such thoughts can be. The research group concluded that, without such awareness, we might never prioritize pleasure at all.[4] Most of us work hard all our lives to reach some end goal—achievement, accolades, money—not realizing that when we reach these milestones, we will lack any significant capacity to enjoy them.

That said, when we have the right kinds of triggers—reminders that it's okay to relax into our thoughts and enjoy the moment—we get it. In one study, researchers gave two groups of people a "thinking aid" to promote thinking about topics that they enjoy. After participants generated a list of enjoyable topics, researchers asked them to think about those topics for a few minutes. In the days that followed this induction, the experimental group received reminders of their topics, whereas the control group did not. Participants who received the reminders found it easier to concentrate on enjoyable topics, their minds wandered less, and they enjoyed the activity more than the control group.[5] We'll learn how to harness the power of this in the next chapter.

Since we appear to be predisposed to avoid thinking about fun, incorporating simple reminders into our life can help bring what we enjoy thinking about back to the front of our conscious. A bit of guidance ("redirection") can even help you reframe life's most mundane moments—stuck in a long line, waiting for water to boil—as opportunities to think about what is most enjoyable. During life's little lulls, you want to avoid the FOMO (fear of missing out) our social media feeds drive and instead find ways to bask in your own delightful memories. You can do this right now in a variety of ways, from reviewing the Fun File you created in the last chapter to setting intermittent calendar reminders for yourself of fond memories from the past (think of Facebook's On This Day feature, except with this method you are in complete control of what you'd like to reminisce about).

Successful story editing can also help you develop a growth mindset, a concept introduced by researcher Dr. Carol Dweck in her book *Mindset*.[6] Dweck found that people with a growth mindset have an enhanced sense of agency. They see themselves in the driver's seat of their lives. They believe that they can have a positive impact when it comes to improving themselves and their situations. Without a growth mindset, people see their abilities as fixed attributes and their lives as essentially outside their control.

To adopt a growth mindset, reinterpret negative occurrences in a way that promotes improvement. For example, when you face rejection or make a mistake, choose to think, "I love a good challenge. Next time, I'll practice harder and have even more fun along the way."

In contrast, with a fixed mindset, you might interpret any setback as the final word: "That wasn't fun. I must not be any good at this. At least I'll never have to do it again."

If this type of reframing proves difficult, start small: Tell yourself that your upcoming weekend is a vacation. That simple, just set the intention. This small mindset shift has been shown to have a positive effect,[7] delivering some of the psychological benefits of an actual vacation. Once you experience the palpable benefit of a small mindset shift, you'll feel empowered to try larger ones.

As you practice story editing, you will start to see opportunities for fun where you never have before. For instance, you can treat your lunch hour like a true "break" and take the opportunity to do something fun, like reconnecting with an old friend over a meal. Get lucky enough and you might just find your soul mate like (as we discussed in the previous chapter) Tania Katan did. At the least, you will begin to rediscover your once-strong appetite for it as soon as you see the impact fun has on how you feel.[8]

Hall of Fun: Bill Murray

Bill Murray is, of course, the star of many beloved blockbuster Hollywood films—*Caddyshack* and *Ghostbusters*, to name just two—as well as many indie films in his career's second act. But in recent decades, he has become more than a celebrity. You might call him a modern-day folk hero. There are dozens of stories in which everyday strangers invite Murray to join them in fun—and are then shocked when he says yes. There was that time in New York City when he accepted an invitation to join a group of strangers for karaoke, and then stayed all night, buying drinks and singing. Or that time that he crashed a wedding photo shoot, to the bride and groom's mutual delight. Or that time that he went to an anthropology students' party in Scotland and stayed to do the dishes. These now-legendary stories—many of which have been verified by Tommy Avallone in a documentary called *The Bill Murray Stories: Life Lessons Learned from a Mythical Man*—all speak to an admirable refusal to elevate himself above the rest of the world, taking instead whatever adventure comes his way.[9]

Murray, who got his start at Chicago's Second City before graduating to *Saturday Night Live*, has always written his own script when it comes to his career. He famously doesn't have an agent or manager, and filters offers through a personal voicemail box that he checks when he feels like it. The blockbuster success of *Ghostbusters* vaulted him to a new level of stardom, and yet he experienced it as a career low due to the simultaneous flop of a passion project—so he took four years off to study history and philosophy at the Sorbonne in Paris. When Charlie Rose asked him in 2014 what he wanted that he didn't have, Murray didn't ask for an Oscar. He spoke of his desire to be more fully present. "I'd like to really see how long I could last as being really here, really in it, really alive in the moment," he said. When Jimmy Kimmel called him on his seventieth birthday in 2020, he said, "I still think I would be tried as a juvenile if I got into any real trouble." He took that call on a Snoopy phone.

Activity Bundling

Having audited your use of time in the last chapter, you're now acutely aware that, in any given week, you simply cannot have it all. I do not possess the wizardry to add hours to your day, but I can help you achieve something similar with activity bundling.

In a way, activity bundling *is* a kind of magic—it adds more hours of fun to your week without the need to add hours. It's a process of examining the way you spend your time and judiciously incorporating other, positive elements into moments that might otherwise be underutilized. Of course, there are foundational activities—sleep, meditation, time dedicated to unstructured thought—that could be harmed by this practice. But, done carefully, activity bundling can transform many of life's most mundane or difficult moments into more enjoyable experiences. Think of Antonia incorporating a drawing practice into her nightly duty of having to respond to patients, for instance.

The simple practice of bundling activities increases the number of opportunities for more fun in any given week. Activity bundling can be done effectively in any quadrant of the PLAY Model. For instance, you can double your fun by combining two Pleasing quadrant activities (say, enjoying a comedy show and catching up with a friend), or combine an Agonizing activity (like cleaning your house) with a Pleasing activity (like catching up on your favorite podcast or audiobook).

Another approach is to bundle activities in succession to reward yourself for an activity you want to get done but don't find pleasurable. Behavioral scientists have long understood that pleasurable activities are a strong motivator to perform unpleasant ones. In the 1920s, Curt Paul Richter of Johns Hopkins Hospital found that rats increase their physical activity when they are hungry and anticipate food.[10] David Premack studied this phenomenon further and established the Relativity Theory of Reinforcement, more commonly known as Premack's Principle: "Any response A will reinforce any other response B, if and only if the independent rate of A is greater than that of B."[11] Put more simply, when we make something fun *dependent* on doing something not so fun, we become more likely to do the not-fun thing.

If you are a parent, you already know this type of bundling works because you have likely coerced your child into doing something important with the allure of a rewarding activity afterward. "Clean your room and then we can all go get ice cream!" The science supports that you can just as easily apply this strategy to accomplishing your own essential, yet Agonizing, tasks. Fun is a great motivational tool. *Why not use it?*

One caveat here: This method can backfire, big time, with one experience degrading rather than complementing the other. Be thoughtful and realistic about what activities bundle well together. For example, listening to an audiobook by your favorite author while walking your dog might sound good—until one day you become so engrossed in what you're hearing that you notice too late that your dog is snacking on garbage. (This actually happened to a friend of mine. Even when her dog wasn't exploring the neighborhood buffet, he was too big a distraction. She also came to realize that she didn't enjoy listening to novels as much as she enjoyed reading them.) Another risky example is bundling intellectually rigorous work (e.g., tax preparation) with trying to watch your favorite show with your favorite person. In this scenario, the work will likely become Agonizing, and the joy of time spent with your friend or partner goes out the window. It's important to know this tactic has limits and using it with abandon can be harmful.

With practice, activity bundling has made a tremendous impact in my own life. As you might imagine, going from Ironman athlete to never being able to significantly run again at the age of forty-five was not an easy transition. Running had always been a form of therapy for me, so when my doctor told me that my femoral head was sitting on my pelvis and running was no longer an option, I was crushed. Unable to maintain my previous activity level, I gained significant weight and became hyperglycemic—not a good look for someone whose livelihood is supported, in part, as a health advocate.

Moonlight Race, Davis, California, 7/12/2014

Told that my only option for staying active was to get a hip replacement, I went through with the procedure. The first few weeks after surgery it was quite difficult to keep up with my two rambunctious children. The recovery took a particular toll on the relationship with my daughter. Our bond up until that point had always involved being active together. The initial physical therapy was both unavoidable and Agonizing, and I wanted to get back to having fun with my daughter quickly. The solution, for me, was activity bundling.

My daughter had a budding interest in dance, so instead of spending monotonous hours feeling alone in physical therapy sessions, I found a dance instructor capable of cocreating medically appropriate moves for me that would be fun enough to keep my daughter and me engaged. The activity evolved into a weekly dance ritual in the Living quadrant that allowed me to reconnect with my daughter, get healthy, put us on a path toward mastery, and best of all, have a ton of fun together.

Variable Hedonics

> It just felt real good. You know why? Because you waited five months for it. If you starving and somebody throw you a cracker, you gonna be like this: "Goddamn, that's the best cracker I ever ate in my life! That ain't no regular cracker, was it? What was that, a saltine? Goddamn, that was delicious. That wasn't no saltine, though. That was... that was a Ritz. That wasn't a Ritz? God, that's the best cracker I've ate in my life."
>
> —EDDIE MURPHY, *RAW*

Research shows that when we are deprived of something pleasurable, we enjoy it more intensely when it's reintroduced. It can be as simple as taking a break from an enjoyable activity or otherwise changing up our routine. This is because variability disrupts hedonic adaptation, the brain's tendency to "set" our enjoyment level. As discussed in chapter 1, we each have a happiness set point. Hedonic adaptation is what brings us back to that set point regardless of external circumstances. Remember, your brain doesn't want you to feel good all the time because the whole point of happiness is to incentivize positive behaviors. You get what you want, you feel good, and then that good feeling fades. This is part of the hedonic treadmill.

Leif D. Nelson of the University of California, San Diego, and Tom Meyvis of New York University found that inserting an unexpected break into a positive experience—for example, a massage—makes that experience more pleasurable. The converse is also true. When you take breaks from things that are not fun, you make them even *less* fun. In starting the adaptation process again after a break, you become freshly aware of the stimuli you'd previously become accustomed to. For example, if you're trying to get some work done despite the noise at a construction site, you will eventually tune that noise out and warm to your task—until you take a break, at which point you will be freshly reminded of the distraction, making for an even more unpleasurable experience.[12]

Nelson and Meyvis found that the valence associated with the experience didn't make a difference—both positive and negative experiences gained in intensity after a break. As such, you should make a habit of eliminating downtime during Agonizing activities and introducing breaks and other variation into pleasurable ones.

For example, in a study of chocolate consumption, people who abstained from eating chocolate for a week enjoyed it more when they returned to eating it compared both to a group instructed to eat as much as possible and one that ate their usual amount.[13] Temporarily giving up something you find fun can sometimes be an effective route to more enjoyment later on.

Of course, depriving oneself of good things to enjoy them more down the road might not work for everyone, indicated by a considerable drop-out rate in the chocolate-restricted group.

Introducing uncertainty is another way to get more fun out of an activity. In another experiment, conducted by Timothy Wilson, Wilson and his colleagues gave gifts to the study's participants. One group was told who gave them the gift and why, while the other group was left wondering. The people left uncertain stayed in a positive mood for longer.[14] Variable hedonics is woven into wonder, curiosity, and mystery. Artists, magicians, and entertainers rely on these tools because they are so effective at elevating an experience. In fact, a little variation can make the experience of fun feel like it lasts longer. When life becomes routine, time passes more quickly in our perception. Variety—a break from routine—slows time's perceived passage. In fact, simply by attending closely to what you are doing, being mindful of something you usually do automatically, you can stretch your perception of time.

The reason doing anything novel forces our brain to slow down is that it hasn't developed mental shortcuts (sometimes referred to as *heuristics*) for processing the new incoming information. Think of driving: When you had your learner's permit, driving was an overwhelming sensory experience. You struggled to watch the cars ahead of you and all three mirrors, remember the rules of the road, and actually operate the vehicle with your hands and feet. Your brain was working overtime and you were exhausted by the end of each lesson. With practice, however, your brain figured out which pieces of input it needed to focus on—the brake light on the car just ahead, for example—and which pieces of information could be ignored. Over time, most of the action of driving became automatic and unconscious for you. Now your daily commute barely registers and most of your conscious attention is on the day ahead. If you added variety to your drive—wearing a thick pair of mittens and dark sunglasses, for example—you can bet you'd experience your next commute with a sense of mindfulness and present awareness you haven't experienced since you earned your license. (Don't try that, of course.)

Routine experiences typically escape our memories—for instance, can you remember in detail what exactly happened on your commute two weeks ago? As such, you perceive them as happening much more quickly. Dr. Dinah Avni-Babad and Dr. Ilana Ritov from the Hebrew University of Jerusalem conducted six experiments into the influence of routine on people's estimation of time. In all six studies, people estimated the length of a routine activity as shorter than a nonroutine activity of the same duration.[15]

When you fill your life with fun and novel experiences and feed your brain lots of new information—learning, traveling, meeting new people, trying new activities—you look back on life in general with greater satisfaction. Neuroscientist David Eagleman describes time as a rubbery thing that can stretch when our brains are fully switched on. An experiment Eagleman did together with Chess Stetson and Matthew P. Fiesta showed that time-slowing occurs when we code a memory as an intense, rich experience (which usually happens when you do something new or exciting). In the study, participants experienced free fall for thirty-one meters before landing safely in a net. When asked how long the fall felt like it lasted, the participants' estimates were 36 percent longer than the ones they made about others making the same leap. The authors concluded that "a richer encoding of memory may cause a salient event to appear, retrospectively, as though it lasted longer."[16]

Variable hedonics have a downside, too. It isn't just about stretching time; it's also about your satisfaction rising or falling as you compare yourself to others. Remember that euphoric feeling the last time you got a promotion? As I teased in chapter 1, your elation likely wore off as you grew into the new role. You initially enjoyed the pleasure of being rewarded for your hard work, the higher income, and the upward shift in social status. Then your situation lost its luster. The familiar yearning for something more returned. You adapted to the professional and financial concerns of your new social status. Despite your improved circumstance, concerns you had before the promotion boomeranged back into your awareness. *What happened?* As evolution intended, your expectations reset to match your new peer group—their achievements, their artifacts, their status. That initial high of satisfaction faded, and you were back on the hedonic treadmill.

In *The End of History and the Last Man*, political scientist Francis Fukuyama argued that humans desire some things "not for themselves but because they are desired by other human beings."[17] Most of us try to keep up with the Joneses, one way or the other, but the actual Joneses we compare ourselves to tend to change as our status evolves. Unless you take deliberate action to circumvent this cycle, your rat race will never end.

Study after study confirms that our subjective happiness is influenced not only by how much we have (absolute levels of income and position) but how we compare ourselves to others (relative levels of income and position). This phenomenon is known as "positionality." In defense of humanity, most of us are happier with feeling we have slightly more than others (those we compare ourselves to). Having a lot more does not seem to have the same effect.[18]

Unfortunately, in this case, variability is part of the trap. The reward of *just a little more* is always within reach if only we work a little harder. And so, our proverbial treadmill never ends—*unless* we intentionally keep our set point constant based on our own personal, intrinsic desires. When we own our definition of success, the pressure of external influences is mitigated, and the Joneses have less power over us. We can then refocus our energy toward things that actually bring us meaningful delight.

Some people find another solution to positionality: They position themselves at the top of the heap. They do this by leaving their home for a country where their native currency is worth more, local politics give them more freedom, and like-minded bohemians give them a sense of belonging.[19]

For instance, it is not uncommon for Westerners to take advantage of positional economics in places like Goa, Bali, and Thailand. Some see this as ethically dubious, while others argue that this maneuvering allows developing economies to flourish. Either way, there is no denying that when your expectations are level-set, taking advantage of positional economics improves the utility of your resources and increases your opportunities for fun.

Benefiting from positional economics does not require you to move to another country. With a little research, you can usually find these advantages fairly close to home. Relocating to an area with a lower cost of living has an almost immediate positive impact because it frees up resources for things that are a lot more fun than rent or mortgage payments—increasing your quality of life and improving your options. This is known as "lifestyle migration," and it is exactly what my wife and I did when we fled the expensive Bay Area for the lower cost of living in the Carolinas.

Dr. Michaela Benson and her colleague Dr. Karen O'Reilly define lifestyle migration as "spatial mobility of relatively affluent individuals of all ages, moving either part-time or full-time to places that are meaningful because, for various reasons, they offer the potential for a better quality of life."[20] When discussed in academic literature, the phenomenon isn't solely defined as lifestyle migration. This strategy goes by all sorts of names: international retirement migration (IRM), amenity-seeking migration, residential tourism, and (international) counter-urbanization. Regardless of what science calls it, the commonality among the people that use these types of strategies is that they vary their position to improve their access to pleasure. And while affluence certainly widens your options, there's some version of this available to people with more modest means—for example, moving farther from an urban center, or to an area where labor is in short supply so wages are higher.

A word of caution: Moving, by itself, does not guarantee you will have more fun. If you decide to take advantage of positional economics, make sure you plan ahead. Things go off the rails when we let our proverbial "bar"—our set point—succumb to adaptability. The secret sauce for more fun is manipulating the variables of experience while holding our expectations static. It's also important not to let our imaginations run wild, to romanticize what a particular destination might offer us.[21] For instance, you might move to rural France because of the image you hold of the place: peaceful landscape, vineyards, colorful villages. Once you get there, it might not live up to your expectations, inevitably leading to considerable regret. Do your research and be realistic in your expectations and more fun is almost guaranteed.

Options

When you have access to better options, you make better choices. Since your goal is more fun, let's explore how you can increase your options for fun. There are plenty of opportunities for serious fun available to anyone willing to put in a bit of work. As seen from my work with Antonia, increasing your awareness of viable options for fun is an important step in the process. Opportunities are bound only by the limits of your imagination. Sometimes you just need to brainstorm and get inventive. This builds further on the work you've already done on your Fun File.

A great way to brainstorm more fun options is by using a coaching practice called the *five options technique*. As the name suggests, you simply push yourself to come up with five new options for fun—activities you're not currently engaged in—that are realistically doable in the coming weeks and months. These ideas might include going to a movie with an old friend, taking a course on something interesting, picking up a neglected hobby, and so on. If you get stuck coming up with five, ask yourself these questions:

- What are some activities that connect me to fun and joy from my past?
- What are some fun things my friends are doing that I might like to try?
- What are some fun things I can bundle with the things I am already doing now?

When you have at least five, identify one option you can immediately attempt. If you have a hard time choosing just one option, visualize how each option would make you feel once it is successfully completed. Use your feelings regarding each activity as a gauge for which option makes sense to go after first. Once you have chosen your option, work backward to identify and execute the steps needed to turn your new opportunity for fun into a reality.

Ingenuity is another great way to unlock options for fun. Private events and VIP experiences are fun for many reasons. One of the most obvious is the fact that they are exclusive. However, it is often easier to beat the gatekeepers than you think. All you need to do is find a key to the back door. One of my favorite ways of getting access to an otherwise inaccessible activity is to find a way to contribute. I generally do this by finding a way to volunteer. I have used this strategy effectively not only to attend conferences I can't afford but to hobnob with celebrities at A-list events.

SAVOR EVERY MOMENT

As a graduate student in the late '90s, I was fortunate to backpack around Europe one summer. During my trip, I learned of a "Cinema Against AIDS" event taking place at the Cannes Film Festival in France. It was an invitation-only party for the international filmmaking elite. There was no way I was getting in through the front door. So . . . I went through the back door. How? *I asked.* I asked, "How can I help?" The cost of admission for a nobody like me ended up being a day of putting celebrity gift bags together with a bunch of fun, awesome people. Then, the gatekeepers let me in.

Sixth Annual Cinema Against AIDS Gala,
Cannes, France, 5/20/1999

As part of the event, there was a charitable auction. Elizabeth Taylor wanted to bring attention to a particular auction item and had requested a young man help her up on stage. Since I fit the bill, the event organizers asked me, the volunteer guy from earlier, if I wouldn't mind doing the job. I accepted, of course, not knowing that it would lead to my fifteen minutes of fame. The next day, basking in the afterglow of an amazing night, I walked out of the accommodations I was sharing with several other starving students and, to my surprise, saw myself and Liz on the cover of the

Nice-Matin—one of France's more popular newspapers. All of this became an option for me because I invented a way to obtain access to a fun evening.

You can also make a habit of expanding your options through travel hacking and fun hacking. Travel hacking is the strategic art of using credit card points to accelerate the rate at which you accumulate travel rewards, like free flights. When my wife and I first started travel hacking, we were both a bit intimidated. After a few months, however, that was quickly replaced by remorse that we hadn't started sooner. Done properly, the rewards stacked up faster than we ever could have imagined. And while good information on travel hacking used to be obscure, the latest strategies are now as close as a Google search.

What is not as well-known is that many credit card reward programs can also be applied to increasing options for fun experiences—opportunities like member-only entertainment events, private tours, and exclusive dining invitations with celebrity chefs. Reward opportunities are so broad nowadays, I refer to the practice of accumulating reward points as fun hacking (since it's no longer about just travel). With a little effort, your options become almost limitless. Fun hacking isn't as prevalent an idea as travel hacking because many reward cards are associated with travel companies. Furthermore, information regarding the card's experiential benefits is often buried amongst all the other features of the card. To unearth your possibilities, simply call your credit card company and ask where you can find your available options for life experience. Personally, my favorite fun hack is VIP concert experiences. I traveled using points to see My Morning Jacket during their One Big Holiday tour. If concerts aren't your thing, you will undoubtedly find a spectrum of new options that suit your preferences and taste. Now that you know where to look, you're on your way to more fun. (For a list of credit cards that offer experience rewards, visit https://share.michaelrucker.com/rewards.)

Reminiscing

Reminiscing is a great way to step off the hedonic treadmill. As the psychologist Nico Frijda aptly put it, "Adaptation to satisfaction can be counteracted by constantly being aware of how fortunate one's condition is."[22]

The positive benefits of gratitude are well-established. Gratefully *reminiscing* about fond memories is gratitude on steroids, employing a form of appreciation known as dispositional gratitude. Dispositional gratitude is characterized by (1) an appreciation for others, (2) an appreciation for simple pleasures, and (3) a sense of abundance.

When you establish a reminiscing routine through acknowledging gratitude for past experiences, it keeps you mindful that fun is abundant. Put into practice, reminiscing in this manner mitigates feelings of regret and deprivation by giving you a concrete prompt to fully appreciate life's pleasurable experiences. A habit of acknowledging the pleasure in your life naturally increases your overall sense of gratitude, amplifying fun's positive effects.

Science has been critical of some forms of acknowledging gratitude. For instance, Sonja Lyubomirsky, from the Department of Psychology at the University of California, Riverside, and her colleagues found that those who logged their gratitude in a journal once a week saw a benefit, but once it got to three times a week, those benefits all but vanished.[23] One of the dangers of gratitude journaling is that some people can struggle to find things to be grateful for—and for them, the exercise can actually end up causing harm by serving as a reminder that their lives aren't currently fulfilling. This can lead to ruminating on the gap between yourself and happiness. Even so, most experts agree that the general act of being grateful—experiencing and expressing gratitude—has a significant positive impact on our well-being.[24] What makes reminiscing through gratitude different from run-of-the-mill gratitude—the standard practice of searching for things to be grateful for—is that it is action-oriented in that we are actively participating in the things for which we are grateful. We celebrate our gains and bask in the agency we have to create things to be grateful for.

Put into practice, the SAVOR system can transform an ordinary life into a remarkable one. Challenge your assumptions (and mine!). If something is not working, subtract it. Bolt things on as you find new things that work. Make this your own. If you have already put some of these ideas into practice, relish in the relief that the pull to conform to social norms is being lifted. You are now benefiting from new ways to bring delight, wonder, and play into your life and the lives of those closest to you.

We are far from done yet! It's time to level up even further by creating a feedback loop—one that supports a perpetual positive upward spiral of continual growth.

chapter 4

Enjoyment *After* the Moment

*Whenever I think of the past,
it brings back so many memories.*
—STEVEN WRIGHT

Lately society's primary response to the pressure of a noisy, overscheduled life has been to stress enjoyment in the moment. *Be here, now.* Indeed, being mindful can help us better relish the present. Recognizing the power of the precious now, à la Eckhart Tolle, Spencer Johnson, and all those that came before them, is an important corrective and a great complement to having more fun. Being present also helps with memory formation; put simply, it ensures we don't miss the exciting details. But it's important not to forget that we have another, less discussed resource to relish our fun further: enjoyment *after* the moment. The *be here now* folks may not approve, but if you're not being thoughtful about how to relish fun memories through reminiscing, you're leaving some of life's joys on the table—the fun you had yesterday, last year, or last decade.

The purpose of this chapter is to help you get the most out of the "R" in SAVOR—reminiscing—by extending fun's power beyond the moment it occurs. There are plenty of books and Internet essays that fine-slice the art of mindfulness, to get the most out of every moment, in the moment. Reminiscing, as I define it, is (almost) the opposite: a tool for *after the moment*. I want you to be able to make the most of your memories, both positive and negative, so that they contribute as much as possible to your well-being even years after the fun.

I present four strategies, each with tactics, to help you:

1. **Time Travel.** Peak moments in life happen fast and are few and far between. Reminiscing allows us to expand these moments beyond their short time frame.
2. **Curation.** This means emphasizing the good memories, while mining the bad for your benefit. Yes, even bad memories can contribute to well-being.
3. **Prompts.** Just as you learned to schedule fun, you can schedule time for reminiscing, aided by technology.
4. **Feedback.** As you develop your Fun Habit and try new things, you're learning a lot about what really lights you up and what you might pass on next time—if you pay enough attention. Taking time to evaluate your experiences *after the fact* closes the SAVOR loop so that over time you get better at picking activities that have a much higher likelihood of bringing joy.

Strategy One: Time Travel—Take the Past with You

The biggest, most fun moments in your life are often just a matter of hours. Honoring this reality can ensure you make the effort to effectively hold on to important memories. While it isn't the focus of this chapter, temporal awareness in the moment can help—reminding yourself how quickly things pass, to ensure you enjoy things while they last. For example, so many can barely recall their wedding day. The best piece of advice I ever got in this regard was to constantly check in with myself that day, to notice my own feelings and elation amidst the joyful pandemonium. To take the time to take mental pictures. Because I was given this sage advice, even with a few too many cocktails in me, I can recall that amazing evening because I took time to relish the event shortly after it was over, committing to memory some of my favorite moments. Be careful with this one though, because reminding yourself

ENJOYMENT AFTER THE MOMENT

how quickly moments pass can easily turn into negative rumination that dampens the fun.

Again, the focus is on enjoying our peak experiences in the moment, and then relishing the memory *afterward*. While any of the tactics offered in this chapter can help relive these moments, my favorite when it comes to events like weddings, vacations, and other once-in-a-lifetime experiences is what I call the "treasure chest." I've got one, and I'll be honest: It's heavy. Your treasure chest can be for tangible things or—for the space-deprived—digital assets (or a combination of both). Either way, it should be filled with memorabilia that takes you back in time. That might include old train tickets, leaflets of places you visited, refrigerator magnets, photographs, small objects, quotes. But just like fun itself, it's up to you to decide the best way to reminisce on your fun memories. Instead of me prescribing something for you, here's a grab bag that I've collected of cool ideas for storing memories. Have some fun picking the ones that work for you.

- Creating a holiday jar. When you go somewhere fun, collect a few items during the journey (e.g., stones, seashells, pieces of fabric, postcards, drawings). Arrange them all in a glass jar and keep them as a decoration on a shelf.
- Instead of keeping a formal journal, write down short stories or vignettes describing your favorite moments and keep them in a folder, adding new ones as you go along. Like Antonia, my daughter likes to draw, so she's adapted this tactic through cartooning.
- Any type of themed photo album. Wedding albums are great, but any meaningful event can be worthy of an album. There are so many affordable options now for printing that you don't need to worry if the book takes on some wear and tear from frequent use. You can always reprint. You could also make an expensive archival copy of a really important event that stays on the shelf, alongside a cheaper version appropriate for sticky-fingered children.
- There is a whole art to scrapbooking. This isn't something I have ever tried personally, but there are clearly a lot of crafty people that find this type of remembrance fun. A quick Google

search should give you more than enough good ideas to get you started.
- If there is something that really lights you up, surround yourself with the activity's artifacts by creating a personal museum. For my dad, that's great jazz albums and various tubas that remind him of the hobby he loves to engage in. For entrepreneur and serial collector Jeremy Fissell, who you'll meet later, that's a warehouse full of boom boxes that he loves restoring.

> **Hall of Fun: David Spade And Chris Farley**
>
> Change and loss are part of life, but relics can play an important role in helping us feel connected to important people and events in our past. On the twentieth anniversary of *Tommy Boy* in 2015, David Spade shared on Facebook that a promotional poster for the film hangs in his office, signed by his costar and best friend, Chris Farley, who died in 1997 at the age of thirty-three. The two comedians signed posters for each other as jokes, but decades later, the poster serves as an unexpectedly poignant reminder of their incredible friendship. Spade said that if he thinks about it too long, he'd bawl, "Like now. As Chris would say. What a p*ssy."[1]

Strategy Two: Curating the Past to Improve the Future

At our house, we love the movie *Inside Out*. If you don't know it, this is an animated feature that primarily takes place in the mind of a young girl named Riley. It's intended for kids, but because it's Pixar, the writers consulted with two top research psychologists to craft a story that's not just fun for all ages, but also a canny exploration of the psychology of memory formation and our emotions. As the story line progresses, we meet the embodiment of five of Riley's emotions: Joy, Sadness, Disgust, Fear, and Anger. Joy (played by actress Amy Poehler) narrates the story.

ENJOYMENT AFTER THE MOMENT

Joy does her best to ensure Riley's memories are fun-filled. She does this for good reason: The experiences we focus on are at the core of who we are, what we become, and how we perceive the world around us.

Relishing the memories we make with our new Fun Habit comes with a host of psychological benefits. Dr. Barbara Fredrickson (and others after her)[2] have made a compelling case that expanding and documenting our positive emotions have long-term adaptive benefits.[3] Researchers from MIT found that activating positive memories can help suppress depression.[4] Fun memories, it seems, are more than pleasant anecdotes at cocktail parties. They help us build enduring intellectual, social, and psychological resources. When life is not so fun, they offer emotional resilience. As such, when we cultivate fun and extend the habit's benefit through the practice of deliberate reminiscing, we increase our probability of a better future.

Journaling is an extremely efficient and effective way for us to store memories and process our experiences, synthesizing events and activities into a coherent narrative. It gives us the power to own our personal story. In the pages of a journal, we can curate, prune, celebrate, and lament as we see fit.

If you think journaling is a good tool for your SAVOR system, here are some suggestions for entries with the goal of helping your SAVOR practice:

The Basics
- Whether you write your entries in bulleted lists or descriptive narratives, try to include memorable details about the experience you are describing. *Why* was it fun? *How* did you feel? *Who* were you with? *Where* was the setting and *when* did things take place? If you're not into writing, being prescribed a set word count or length of time you need to write can discourage you from the practice. Nonetheless, it is important to at least quickly get down enough details that when you return to the entry, you'll be able to recall the event. I have found that if I use too much brevity I'll look back at an entry and not have it jog any recall of what happened. Don't let this happen to you. If

you are someone who enjoys writing, *have at it*—another great way to have fun.
- In your journal entry, if you can, include an anchoring artifact. Something that reminds you of the event (a photo, song lyrics, a video clip if you're using an online or electronic journal). By including an artifact in this way, the memory exists in both your subjective mind and in a tangible form in objective reality. Having this type of anchor improves our recall and helps ensure we will remember the event in the future.

These basics are good enough, but to level up, you can play with adding elements from the science of savoring. I have been influenced in particular by Fred Bryant and Joseph Veroff's book *Savoring: A New Model of Positive Experience*,[5] which explores how we process positive experiences. Their book, while academic in presentation, is full of useful tips to better savor your experiences, which includes reminiscing. I have adapted some of my favorites that apply to journaling and listed them for you below, but for anyone looking to do a deep intellectual dive, I highly recommend picking up their book.

Juice Up Your Journaling
- Include elements of the experience that are specific to how it made you feel. It's one of the few times in the book that I'll encourage you to be a bit ego-driven. Was the memory from the Living quadrant? If so, *why*? What about the memory lights you up? What about it gave you a sense of belonging? What about it gave you a sense of pride? How did it make you grow?
- Gratitude is a powerful tool when used effectively. If it feels right, document the components of the memory that make you feel grateful. Are you grateful for something leading up to the memory? Are there components of the memory itself you are grateful for? Is there gratitude to be had for the friendships on display? Are you grateful for the memory connecting you

to something bigger? For example, the sense of awe or wonder that was brought forth by what took place?
- Lock in the memory by using a tool taken from mindfulness called *sensory-perceptual sharpening*. When describing your memory try to include elements that were noteworthy from your senses. How did the food taste? How amazing were the acoustics in the theater during the concert? How did the autumn air smell on the hike? How did the kite you two were flying look while you held his hand in the park? How did her touch feel after not seeing her for a semester?
- If it feels natural, engage in some visceral behavioral expression as you write your entry. Physical expressions of joy give your brain additional pieces of evidence of the memory's positivity. This can provide a significant boost to the practice of reminiscing. Try literally laughing out loud as you document your fun memory and see if it works for you.
- Before you end your entry, anticipate a similar event happening in the future. We can extend our ability to relish a memory by anticipating a similar event again (even better if you actually plan for it to happen again during the process). The anticipation of something good happening in the future is an effective savoring technique.
- After you are done documenting your memory, try sharing the retelling with others in some form. Either by quite literally sharing the entry with the people involved or with others you think would enjoy it; or recounting the entry some other way, like sharing it verbally in some fashion or posting a version of it on social media and tagging those involved.
- Acknowledge any elements that were not fun. Do this by including any challenging moments you experienced (thoughts, emotions) and how you dealt with them—possibly transforming something not fun into something positive if that transformation happens organically and authentically through the process of retelling. By including things that were not fun

(maybe even as separate entries) you provide the backdrop to further appreciate the good times, as well as valuable feedback about perhaps what not to do in the future.

It's Not All Fun

While I'm recommending that you dial up both your fun experiences and their place in your memory, the point is *not* to ignore or repress memories that weren't so fun, or to try to be positive all the time. In this regard, *Inside Out* proves wonderfully instructive again: When Joy tries to prevent Sadness from recording any memories, Riley's psyche (and the movie) goes into crisis, and everything falls apart. Only when Riley finally actualizes her sadness can she move forward to build more fun memories. This tracks well with the findings of psychologists Brett Ford, Phoebe Lam, Oliver John, and Iris Mauss, which have shown that acceptance of our emotions and thoughts (both negative and positive) is a predictor of good mental health.[6]

I mentioned my admiration for Barbara Fredrickson's work on the value of emphasizing the positive. Initially, Fredrickson's work in this area only focused on positive emotions; however, it soon became clear during her research that negative emotions are just as important, as long as they don't prevail. Some even go as far as to say that if we only pay attention to the positive, we can become aloof or unfocused. Dr. Kevin Rathunde suggests that in a creative endeavor, there should be a dialogue between the positive and the negative, trying to integrate the two for the best result.[7] Some psychologists (e.g., Dr. Dan Siegel) advise the technique "Name It to Tame It"; studies show that if we name our negative feelings (e.g., *I feel angry, I am afraid*), their potency reduces as we are able to integrate the left and right sides of the brain and lower the response of the amygdala and other limbic areas.[8] This technique can be particularly useful to help children calm down when they feel agitated or insecure.

I recommend that whatever method you choose for remembrance, you pay homage to some negative emotions and thoughts to help you appreciate the good. Let me give you a few personal examples:

- I have a scheduling tool I use to make sending holiday cards more efficient. I have not removed loved ones that have passed away from the master mailing list. Instead, each year I manually uncheck the box for these friends and family, one by one. This gives me the prompt to remember the good times I had with each of these people and also keeps them in my thoughts during the holidays.
- I used to look at the six-inch surgical scar on my thigh as a constant reminder that I will never be able to enjoy a long-distance running event again. That was until I used the story-editing strategy to change the scar's purpose. Now, when I let this artifact grab my attention, I use its symbolism to remind me about all I was able to accomplish athletically. Also, how grateful I am that the surgery has given me back the mobility to make new fond memories with my kids. Sometimes, it even serves as a great reminder to get something fun and active on the calendar with them (since I might need a revision at some point, which could reduce my mobility further).
- I do journal, and mostly about fun stuff. Yet, when something is exceptionally not fun, I write that down, too. I generally don't go back to those entries, but within the process of writing them down I do find it cathartic to get the moments of pain out of my head and onto paper. Also, if my kids ever discover my journals, I want to make sure they know that my life wasn't all fun; that we all go through periods requiring resilience and fortitude—but that even during periods of pain, we should be assured that we will find fun once again.

One last thing to consider: Experts warn that journaling can lose its potential benefits if it's done for the wrong reasons; for example, if we don't explore our experiences to gain insight, or if we become too self-absorbed.[9] Despite the many people and products that push daily entries, I have been unable to find any credible proof that such frequency is needed for journaling to be effective—and lots of anecdotal evidence that a daily requirement can burden you with a sense of duty, which isn't very fun. Along with this duty comes more think and less do. Dr. Tasha Eurich, organizational psychologist and bestselling author of the book *Insight*, put it to me this way, "By writing in a journal every day, you reap a kind of navel-gazing or cycle of self-pity. A better approach may be, instead, stand back at a pivotal moment—for instance, you are making a decision, or you've got something big that you want to figure out—and use journaling as more of an event-based methodology rather than a habitual one." As such, find a schedule that works for you and play around with different methods of journaling. If building the habit feels difficult, maybe start with Strategy Three.

Strategy Three: Prompts—There's an App for That

Many people use productivity software to easily create reminders to stay on top of the work obligations they have in their daily lives. In fact, sometimes these systems can feel like you're a servant to a cruel master. Whether that's days where it seems that every hour is double-booked, or days where you block your entire nine-to-five in hopes of finally getting some work done, only to have your boss throw on an 8:00 a.m. call that inevitably hijacks the entire day anyway—it can feel like these systems are sucking the life from our days.

The reason these systems are so powerful is due in part to the fact that when a reminder or event appears on our calendar, there is something immutable about tending to it. Like magic (but, in fact, supported by science), if something is on our calendar, there's a good chance it's *going to happen*. The good news is that this magic can just as easily be used to make our lives more fun. An easy tactic to get started right away is scheduling time to have fun. Since we've been conditioned to view our online schedules as important, you will find that it's just as easy to prioritize things outside of work if they end up on your calendar. Like magic, that meetup with an old friend becomes immutable, too.

Since we know reminiscing and relishing the past can increase our well-being, scheduling prompts within our day for a short burst of reminiscing can be an effective strategy. Next time you do your weekly calendar, try to include a bit of time for acts of reminiscence; for example, making time to look through some old photos, reaching out to friends to let them know you're thinking of a good time you all once had, or simply scheduling a short break to relish a fun thing you did over the weekend.

Researchers have studied a few digital tools for reminiscing. For instance, to support everyday reminiscence, a group of scientists from Cornell University designed and tested a system called Pensieve that emails memory triggers to subscribers, either photos of past events they shared on social media or text prompts inviting them to write about their previous experiences (e.g., Do you remember the best concert you went to? Who did you go see and who did you go with?). They found that people appreciate spontaneous reminders to reminisce, as well as the opportunity to write about it.[10]

On a more commercial level, Facebook's Year in Review and Look Back features encourage us to remember past events, too. There is also an application called Timehop (https://share.michaelrucker.com/timehop) that collects old photos and posts from social media and redistributes them to you so you can connect with the past. The "problem" with some of these applications is that somebody else chooses which *memories* to include in your personal biography. So, Lisa Thomas and Pam Briggs from the psychology department at Northumbria University in the U.K. suggest using something like My Social Book (https://share.michaelrucker.com/mysocialbook) as an alternative. This website allows you to transform social media content into a tangible book you can save for moments of reminiscence. Thomas and Briggs found that scrapbooks were a good way to share your moments with others as well (partners, family, friends); for example, after the participants in the study made their books, they planned to show the collections to others for discussion. In contrast, consuming social media content is generally not a prosocial behavior. Thomas and Briggs also made a point of the benefits of reminiscence for all ages (since previously, it has often been associated with older age).[11] For example, my wife and I have had a lot of fun with our kids reliving our wedding through the sharing of our wedding album, as well as looking at old videos from the event. We encourage them to probe and ask questions about what took place and inquire about the friends and family they don't recognize. Often when we get to reminiscing in this way, it prompts me to check in with an old friend (a welcomed nudge from reviewing the pictures).

Strategy Four: Feed the SAVOR Loop

In training to be a psychologist, you leave your university with various tools of change that the trade calls interventions. The purpose of an intervention is to go into a domain, whether that is someone's life, or the environment of an organization, and intervene. That's not exactly what we are trying to do with SAVOR. It's not meant to be used as a blunt instrument where you start with a problem (e.g., being unhappy) and arrive at a solution (e.g., now I'm happy!). As we've learned, these types of interventions can backfire.

Instead, look to adapt SAVOR into your life as a closed-loop system—where the memories of having more fun using the SAVOR system can be used as feedback. During the time you reserve for reminiscing, use your memories as pieces of intelligence that feed and refine how you spend your time going forward.

Treating your memories as an opportunity for feedback should be performed with a bit of care. To be clear, it's certainly not something you should be thinking about when you are engaging in the act of having fun. In an interview I had with Dr. Jordan Etkin from Duke University, she put it this way, "Part of being immersed means you lose track of time, and you're not thinking about your performative or any quantitative aspects of a behavior. For instance, I am very skeptical any time people are trying to track their happiness. Drawing attention, prompting introspection about whether you're happy, it probably makes you feel less happy because, one, now you're questioning whether you're happy. Two, because taking a moment to ask yourself that question probably brings you out of a very happy experience that you might've been in."[12] Instead, when there are opportunities for contemplation, set aside a bit of extra time at the end to determine what you liked doing and what (if anything) you hope to do less of. Use this type of feedback over time to bias your actions more toward fun, as well as an act of wayfinding yourself to new organic opportunities where you are more likely to enjoy yourself.

In general, there are two primary forms of feedback: negative and positive.[13] As we look back at the artifacts and writing we have obtained or created in our Fun Habit, each item tells us something about the actions we've taken, and whether they've brought us positive or negative valance. The idea here is to use your memories as a way to develop a better instinct for what you feel connected to, or inspired by, and to use that as your guide going forward. I'm not suggesting that it's off-limits to go outside yourself to look for inspiration for new ways to have fun. On the contrary, novelty, curiosity, and discovery are certainly ingredients of fun. What I am saying is that we are so often subconsciously misguided by a deluge of inauthentic ideas that are not our own—advertising, social media, the Joneses—that we often lose sight of what we really enjoy and need to find our way back again.

When you engage in the type of reflection we've discussed in this chapter, free of self-absorption—honestly, openly looking for clues about what really lights you up, brings you joy, and connects you to something outside yourself—that's when the fun flywheel really starts spinning. In the next chapter, we'll talk about the hidden value in taking your evolving Fun Habit on the road, for fresh new experiences worthy of a scrapbook.

chapter 5

The Great Escape

Why do you go away? So that you can come back.
So that you can see the place you came from with new eyes and
extra colors. And the people there see you differently, too. Coming
back to where you started is not the same as never leaving.

—TERRY PRATCHETT

People typically speak about *escapism* in negative terms, as in, "She's got an unhealthy obsession with that treadmill, she must be running from something." Or, "He's a festival jumper because he can't handle the real world." Escapism is seen as an immature distraction. Instead of bravely changing your life's fundamentals, the narrative goes, you escape into pleasure and ignore reality.

But certain kinds of escapism—and escapes—aren't distractions at all. They are portals to a state of being with a powerful potency to improve every aspect of our lives. Such moments can provide a radical shift in perspective, one that allows you to escape *toward* a better "reality" than the one you left. In this light, escapism represents an apex of beneficial fun.

Let me show you what I mean. Consider what may be the most extreme form of escape known to humans: space travel. Astronauts literally escape our atmosphere, that thin layer that makes life and all of its pleasures and pains possible. We think of space travel as being outward looking—a voyage of scientific discovery, and in the early days, a competitive race. But time and time again, astronauts have returned to Earth reflecting on a very different experience. Their most profound moments, some discover, were not those spent looking into the infinite but, in fact, staring *back* at their home planet hanging in space. Many spend hours "earthgazing," as they call it—an awe-filled, transcendent experience. The allure of space travel is so intriguing that some of the world's wealthiest people are devoting their resources to making this dream possible. (Whether or not those resources would be better served solving problems here on this planet is an argument for another book.)

The author and space enthusiast Frank White dubbed this the Overview Effect in the 1980s, and there's now an entire institute devoted to its potential. (I might once have said this was an experience that money couldn't buy—except that in 2021, billionaires gave themselves the gift of space travel, with both Jeff Bezos and Richard Branson leaving Earth's atmosphere, though only briefly, in preparation for a new era of commercial spaceflight.)

The Canadian astronaut Chris Hadfield, profiled later in this chapter, described it this way: "You're floating weightless in a window, where you see an entire continent in the time it takes to drink a cup of coffee. Where you go from LA to NY in nine minutes, and you see all of that history and culture and climate and geography and geology and it's all right there underneath you. And you see a sunrise or a sunset every 45 minutes. You see the world for what it actually is. It has the same sort of personal effect on you, of a feeling of privilege and sort of a reverence, an awe, that is pervasive . . . You feel like you're just wildly lucky to even be there, to see this happening. And that sense of wonder, and privilege, and clarity of the world, slowly shifts your view . . . It doesn't have to be involved with spaceflight. It's more when you sense that there's something so much bigger than you, so much more deep than you are—ancient—has sort of a natural importance that dwarfs your own."[1] Hadfield says that it changes your experience of being human, helping you see through artificial biases and barriers.

What Hadfield describes seems to embody the experiential trifecta of what Dr. Frode Stenseng, who has studied both the benefits and potential harms of escapism, would describe as *self-expansion*, the "good" kind of escapism.[2] When you're in an escapist state, as described by Stenseng, you (1) become completely absorbed in whatever it is you're doing, aka *nowness*. You (2) might temporarily dissociate, which, experienced positively, can feel like being liberated from your identity, reaching what you might call *oneness*. And finally, for a few beautiful moments of time, you (3) stop judging yourself—in Hadfield's description, supplanted by a reverence for "something so much bigger than you." For anyone whose mind is frequently engaged in a litany of self-critique, you know the sweet relief of such an experience.

Most of us will never go to space (although admittedly, thanks to Virgin Galactic and SpaceX's race to commercialize space travel it's at the top of my personal Fun List). However, as Hadfield suggests, we all can—and should—experience such moments of escape. These moments have a powerful positive effect on our psyche in the moment. They allow us to be fully present, free from the "wandering mind" (or what mindfulness practitioners call "monkey brain"), which Matthew Killingsworth and Daniel Gilbert at Harvard have linked to unhappiness.[3] We float above context and judgment, utterly unable to box the experience at hand into an already-known container.

The benefits of transcending the ordinary are not experienced only in the moment. People frequently describe escapism (and fun more broadly) as putting a Band-Aid on unsolved problems. But escapism that operates at fun's peak—the state of wonder Hadfield describes above—is the opposite. It's how we solve the unsolved, and protect ourselves from "going along, getting along" when it comes to our lives.

When we are having fun, we're able to find psychological distance, or escape, from our everyday existence. And in that distance we create space, space for future reflection and synthesis, preparing us for big shifts. With distance, we come to see that "reality" is much more flexible than we may have realized. I don't mean that we start to believe we can walk on hot coals; if that's the result, it's very much the wrong kind of escape. But escapes help us, say, invent an alternative to our seventy-hour-a-week job, or to scrutinize values we've assumed unconsciously. A lot of creativity comes to us when we create time and space to expand our breadth of experience. Escapes are also a balm from the depletion we feel from monotony. We return renewed, feeling a new sense of agency, with the strength and inspiration to live ever more intentionally.

So far in this book I've focused on ways to build the Fun Habit within the parameters of your everyday life. Now that you've tasted the ways that having fun can lead to deeper life enrichment, in this chapter we'll explore how escapism can help access even higher levels of fun—helping you see daily life in the sharper focus that only distance can provide. Consider chapter 5 your first advanced course in fun.

Get Space Without Leaving Earth

Taking our cue from astronauts, one ready hack to create psychological distance is to create literal distance. Escape the world you know in order to look back at it. With a new perspective, we increase our sense of agency and gain a better understanding of what is immutable (very little) and what is negotiable (everything else). We also become clearer on our *non*negotiables, like the fish who doesn't know it needs water until it's flapping on a boat deck.

The advice on how to get this done should be astonishingly simple: Take a long vacation, preferably several. Except it isn't. First of all, at least in America, people are too busy working to take vacations, and too busy spending the money they earn on things like rent and health care. American workers had a record number of unused vacation days in 2018—768 million days—an increase of 9 percent from the prior year, according to one survey.[4] Annual surveys by Expedia have repeatedly put the U.S. dead last in average vacation days used.[5] The U.S. also shared the distinction with Thailand of being last in terms of the average number of paid vacation days—at a measly thirteen days in 2020. Elsewhere in much of the developed world, the government mandates four or six weeks at minimum.

But let's say we can take it for granted that you'll take a vacation. Will it be a true escape? It's not a given. Let's talk about Walt Disney World, to which many American families eventually make their pilgrimage. I love Disney, and have had truly great moments there, mostly watching my kids experience the magic, which is completely legitimate. Mouseketeers, Imagineers, the rides, enjoy it all ... Disney is a monument to escapism at its finest—and simultaneously, Disney is the perfect foil for an actual great escape. If you do Disney exactly the way they'd like you to, you spend dozens of hours and many thousands of dollars planning the world's most grueling schedule of standing in lines and chowing on expensive dinners with children who would rather be in the swimming pool. Meal plans, wristbands, transport, reservations—it has a more elaborate design than an army's plan for a land war, and if you're not careful, you'll take casualties. You come home drained and broke, and your kids cry when the expensive toy you bought them breaks the third time they play with it.

Disney is just an example. You've surely experienced a vacation that was crushed under the weight of overscheduling, expense, and expectation. The most important thing I can say about a vacation is this: Make sure there's protected time for renewal and autonomy—or whatever you want in that moment. Make sure there's room to breathe, or to spend three hours doing something you planned an hour for, because you're loving it.

With that piece of advice, let me offer another even more important piece: It's not an escape if you're working! The most important factor in a true escape isn't even the destination, it's the commitment to taking real time off. That means you do—not—work. *Full stop!* No email. Doing work in a more beautiful backyard is not an escape. The overall goal is psychological distance, and the instant you are chewing on a work problem, you may as well be at your desk.

Does the destination matter? In a moment I'll explore the value of what I call adventure escapes, but in the largest sense, the answer is no. The destination truly doesn't matter. Many people are so exhausted by their work and lifestyle that they go on the same vacation every year; that's what they need to relax. They rely on beach resort vacations where they can drop the kids at a kid's club and sit in a chair by the water. Pure renewal is important and worthwhile, and if that's what you need, go for it.

You won't be surprised when I tell you the single fastest way, aside

THE GREAT ESCAPE

from working, to kill the psychological distance imparted by a vacation: That's right, the *Nothing*. Social media once again threatens to engulf all that is good. Recognize that every time you open Instagram, Facebook, or whatever platform you use, you are squashing psychological distance, and are back in the gravitational force of the *Nothing*. Sharing good times with our friends and family through photographs and messages is pleasurable, and a wonderful way to savor a journey—but from what I understand, photographs can be stored for sharing later in the device that took them. Remember Nir's email tip of stopping the communication loop before it starts, from chapter 2; the same thing happens when you post a vacation photo. Someone comments, you feel compelled to respond. It can become endless. All of this takes you away from why you came. At least wait until the end of the day, or better yet, the end of the trip.

Even photography or filming may displace you. The writer Susan Sontag once called cameras "fantasy-machines whose use is addictive,"[6] and said people use them to relieve "the anxiety which the work-driven feel about not working when they are on vacation and supposed to be having fun."[7] I think there's something to that. While travel photography can be a wonderful element of fun (especially if your fun activity is explicitly photography), it may work against experiencing real-time wonder.

I often think back to taking my parents to the famous French Laundry restaurant for their fiftieth wedding anniversary. Everything about the experience encourages bliss through the escape of fine dining: the incredible quality of the ingredients and the artistry of the food presentation, served on small plates that help create a moment out of each and every morsel. The lovely setting, with crisp white tablecloths and fresh, inviting bouquets. The fact that you're there with loved ones or close friends. Even the fact that it's so expensive that you know you'll probably never experience it again. You are immediately transported.

A family friend with us that evening is a retired culinary foods and nutrition instructor. She mindfully took one photo of her plate for remembrance before turning her attention to enjoying the food. Meanwhile, on my left and on my right were groups who were constantly on their phones during the meal, taking pictures of the plates from every angle. They had already broadcast a gallery of artifacts of their visit by the time they left, but in doing so may have failed to actually experience the meal fully. They had traded, probably without realizing it, a complete sensory experience for the flat nothingness of pixels on a screen. The moment you give fun a goal outside of the relationship with the experience—whether it's the perfect photograph or a million likes—you've diluted your connection to fun.

Here are a few more ideas to consider when you're planning your escapes:

Don't break the bank. Spending years saving for your "dream vacation" means a long wait; not being able to afford a vacation is one of the top reasons Americans say they delay them. A hefty price tag also puts incredible pressure on an experience that should be the opposite. Plan a trip that fits your lifestyle and budget. Every region has its own opportunities for adventure, so you don't need a time change to be "distant." You don't need luxury, either—although if you can afford it, there's nothing wrong with being knocked out by a little over-the-top opulence. Everyone's in charge of their own fun.

Embrace the autoresponder. If you're Type-A and heavily engaged in your work, the key to leaving behind work successfully (without turning yourself into a nervous wreck) is adequate planning and preparation. Take a day or a half-day before you leave to close the loop on any open business, or better yet, delegate tasks so they're not piled up when you return. Do some contingency planning to make sure anything that comes up will end up in the hands of someone responsible and capable.

Finally, use an autoresponder—and if you can get away with it, why not make it funny, giving a little pleasure to all who receive it? You could borrow this one from Jordan Hirsch, a digital strategy consultant who brings his passion, improv comedy, to work:

THE GREAT ESCAPE

"Thank you for your message. I am traveling and will not be checking email today. If this is an emergency, take a deep breath. Repeat until you either feel better or forget why you emailed me or both."

You could also take the extreme step of fending off unwanted email by adding the note, "I will not read any email sent during my vacation so please resend your email when I return on [DATE]." Thrive Global author and media tastemaker Arianna Huffington, after a personal recovery from burnout, built an app called Thrive Away that not only sent that auto-response, but also deleted incoming messages. It's no longer available. I wonder if that's because not enough people were brave enough to use it?

Balance planning with spontaneity. Should you schedule your vacation top to bottom, or ramble where the experience takes you? To some degree this depends on your own need for structure versus freewheeling fun. Know your own needs. But you're well served by pushing your comfort zone, in whatever direction, so that your vacation becomes a blend of intention and spontaneity.

My friend Bryan Wish recently related a story about a camping trip he took with his partner. They had planned to spend a weekend in nature, away from electronics, to share a meaningful experience. One night they decided to leave the campground to find a good spot to watch the sunset over a late meal. They drove into the mountains, hit a fork in the road, and took a right. What they found wasn't a wild vista at all, but a beautifully manicured piece of land. It turned out to be an airstrip. They got out of their car to explore and found a man working in his woodshop. While asking him if they could eat their dinner on his land, they got to talking—for hours. (Imagine, for a moment, that they had crossed paths with the same man on the subway, or even in their local restaurant. There is a good chance they wouldn't have engaged him, and probably wouldn't have even noticed him because they would have been on their mobile phones or invested in their own conversation.)

The man's name was Ruel, and it turned out he had just retired from a thirty-year career as a commercial pilot. Soon Ruel was taking them on a tour of his airplane hangar, where he kept two Piper Cub airplanes from the 1940s. He floored them by inviting them to fly with him the following morning. Bryan said that flight was one of the best experiences of his life. Having looked for a sunset, he and his girlfriend instead were granted a vista of the entire area from above, gently gliding through smooth air over their own campsite. It was nothing like flying on a commercial jet. In fact, it was like nothing they had ever experienced.

Consider going solo. Don't make the mistake of thinking travel to new places requires an away team. Particularly if you're an introvert, travel without alone time to decompress can feel like a cage. Also, the logistics of traveling with a group are often more complex, potentially distracting from your adventures. Melissa, a former social worker in NYC who values her quiet time, took two trips to the tropical islands of Guadeloupe. The first trip was just okay, but not great; the second was one of her best vacations ever. The primary difference: The first trip was with a group of acquaintances, the second was with just one close friend. The group turned out to be too much social pressure, and there was a lot of bickering about where to go and what to do, with the result that no one was ever 100 percent happy.

That's a major plus of solo travel, for everyone: You've only got one person to please. But even on family or group trips, you can carve out solo time, if you're intentional about it. Consider discussing it before you leave, so there are no hurt feelings in the moment.

Level Up to Adventure

Once you've successfully developed your Fun Habit, you'll likely find you've got the energy you need to do more than reload last year's beach vacation. While it's true one can find fun anywhere, there's no doubt that traveling to a place that's completely new to you has unique benefits.

When I think about the experiences that have had the most enduring impact on me, Antarctica jumps to mind. I went there in 2005 to run a marathon. At the time I was finishing graduate school and close to getting married. I had about six thousand dollars left in my savings and I spent it all on the trip. (I was pleased to discover that there were a few others on the trip who also had more wanderlust than wealth, who had emptied their bank accounts to go; we all quickly became buddies.) When we stepped off the boat onto Antarctica for the first time, I found myself staring, gobsmacked. All I could see was soft blue ice. And thousands of penguins. There were no roads, no stoplights, no anything. Just a vast expanse of space. My brain kept trying to compare it to earlier experiences, some former memory, but I couldn't grab on to anything. Over time, my thoughts slowed down and accepted that I had no prior context. It was a completely authentic space of new experience. I let the awe and wonder engulf me—and felt my ego slip away.

You get something special from an adventurous escape. There's a reason why, in much of the world, many college students take a "gap year" or at least use their summer between high school and college to backpack through as many countries as they can afford. They return with a richer understanding of how their environment has shaped them, and head to university with a greater sense of possibility, as well as a broadened worldview. In travel, we meet people and are introduced to new influences—and experience all the wonder of a journey into the unknown.

I've had a lot of great travel experiences, but none that has stayed with me so viscerally as that Antarctica trip. And today, fifteen years later, I'm still friends with many of the people I met there. On these types of trips, I have made bonds that are as deep as relationships that have taken years to develop. The wonder we experienced together running 26.2 miles through that landscape was so profound that it changed the nature of time. There is the rush of daily life (e.g., "I feel like life is passing me by") that we're all well-acquainted with, and then there's Adventure Time, which magically expands in the same way people describe the seconds before impact in a car or plane crash as lasting "forever," remembered on a level of detail that makes a single moment a complex, textured experience—never forgotten.

In a book I love called *Here Is Real Magic,* magician Nate Staniforth tells the story of a trip to India he took to escape the monotony of his career after he had come across a book about magic there.[7] Reading about traditions such as snake charming, levitation, and fire-breathing, the description suggested "intensity, urgency, ferocity"—nothing like the routined performance he was sadly experiencing as a successful touring magician. And so, he says, he started dreaming of "a crazy, irresponsible break from the mechanized repetition of touring in America." His goal was to experience wonder like one of his own audience members, and in doing so, renew his own practice of magic.

Nate makes a case for the importance of leaving behind the safe, familiar worlds we create for ourselves: "We make our world smaller so we can control it. We make our world simpler so we can understand it. And we reduce ourselves to this diminished scale so we don't accidentally stray outside this fictionalized world and see the danger—but also the majesty—lurking just beyond the borders of our certainty . . . The danger is that over time we come to see this pale, anemic version of life as the real thing. We feel the weight of the world but not the wonder, and in time we resign ourselves to one and forget the other." The trip was so enriching for Nate, it not only elevated his craft (yes, he's still practicing magic today), it strengthened his relationship with his wife as well.

Chasing down fire-breathers in an Indian slum, distance running in subzero temperatures on a barren continent—*not your cup of tea?* Don't let me scare you off; adventure travel doesn't have to be grueling or extreme. There is some research suggesting that untamed spaces are more likely to promote fun, as well as challenge our abilities, when compared to familiar and "polished" environments. But I think it's far more important that you leave *your* beaten path than it is to embrace a Lonely Planet–style vacation in an exotic destination. Never wanting to be far from a clean toilet doesn't mean you're not cut out for travel that reaches the Living quadrant. You only need the courage to try something new, and push your own comfort zone, rather than reverting to your old standby.

THE GREAT ESCAPE

Taking a Sabbatical

Is a sabbatical just a longer vacation? Traditionally, sabbaticals have been most common in education, and are often positioned as extended time away—six months or a year—to learn a new skill or to travel. In other words, a sabbatical can be an opportunity for enrichment. Today there are many companies with shorter sabbatical policies of one to three months, sometimes paid, and usually kicking in after five or more years of employment.

That said, the majority of people I meet tell me that they'd love to take a sabbatical, or extended time away, but that it's "impossible" given their specific job or situation. I'll agree that it may not be easy, but I know it's not impossible, based on the range of people I've met who have done it. When people tell me they can't afford it, I tell them about my old neighbors Sharleen and Dan Goldfield, who both walked away from their jobs and traveled with their two daughters (ages nine and fourteen) through Australia, Southeast Asia, China, India, the Middle East, and Africa. Sharleen and Dan wanted their children to experience life outside their fishbowl, and for them to learn from diverse cultures and see "a world worth fighting for." During the 263 days of their travels, they hiked the Great Wall, camped in Botswana, and swam with whale sharks in the Maldives, just to pick a few of their adventures at random. They documented 1,510 sightings of wildlife and 780 unique species, including 70 endangered or threatened animals. When their trip was cut short in March 2020 because of the pandemic, Dan wrote on his blog, "I still can't believe it's over, how much we experienced and grew, or how much more there was to learn. I believe we drank fully from the cup of life, and it is my hope that we become better for it."

Dan was a math teacher and confident that he would find work after their return. Sharleen, who left a stable job of twenty-two years, was more nervous about work prospects upon returning, but believed the upside to the trip was valuable enough to take the risk. Sure enough, despite reentering the job market during a pandemic, Dan was able to land a teaching position in a high school, and Sharleen took a temp job while searching for something more permanent. Jaye Smith, cofounding partner of Reboot Partners, a consultancy that helps people reboot their careers and recommends sabbaticals, once told the BBC[8] that when she surveyed five hundred people who took career breaks of one month to two years, not one of them regretted their decision. They also told her that their careers were ultimately enhanced because they came back from their time away with improved attitudes.

Many people use the time between jobs to take a sabbatical. That was the case for my friend Brad Wills, who I highlighted in chapter 2.[9] Brad had an awakening one day when his six-year-old son told him he'd been collecting shells on the beach to make necklaces. When Brad inquired why, his son responded, "I want to sell them so you can work less and spend more time with me." *Gut punch.* If you're a parent who has ever worried about work-life balance—in other words, every parent—your heart just cracked open. Brad's did. He likened it to "a fast-forward moment where you are breathing your final breath and memories of your life flash before you."

Brad decided to resign from his stressful job as the chief strategy officer of a fast-rising tech company and take a six-week sojourn with his family. During that time, they went on several small trips as a family, shared many special dinners with family and friends, and generally enjoyed being together. He made more cherished memories in those weeks than he had the entire past decade. He left for the sojourn feeling burned-out and detached, and returned feeling tightly bonded with his family, with a richer sense of purpose and possibility. "I feel the fire in the belly starting to light up. Something significant lies ahead," he wrote in a LinkedIn post.

One final word of advice for anyone planning an escape, and especially an extended escape: Make sure you plan your trip centered on what lights you up. If you've already created and acted on items in your Fun File, you've been getting in touch with your own desires, and probably have a sense of the kind of experiences that are likely to shoot you to the moon. Still, it can be challenging to make decisions independent from the influence of others. The desire to impress people—whether it be your family, friends, or your thousand followers on Instagram—can sometimes crowd out how *you* really feel. Former entrepreneur turned speaker and author Derek Sivers came up with a good litmus test to figure out whether your planned trip is truly intrinsic to you (and those who accompany you).[10] Ask yourself, "Would I do this with the condition that I can't bring a camera and/or share about the trip on social media?"

For most of us, six months or a year away from our "normal" lives is going to be a once-in-a-life experience, so I don't necessarily advocate for Sivers's extremism—*please take some pictures!* It is worth getting deeply honest with yourself and your fellow travelers, however, to make sure the adventure you seek is truly how you want to spend your time.

Escaping To, Not From

You might have noticed that the escapist state as described by Dr. Stenseng can usually be found when we're having any kind of fun. Almost any time we're engaged in an activity that's extremely pleasurable, we get absorbed, enter a new reality, and stop evaluating ourselves so harshly. You might call the most superficial form of escapism *coping*. Even at this level, escapes can be significantly beneficial, a way to balance the normal discomforts that are a part of life. It might be giving yourself an indulgent treat because you soldiered through your annual colonoscopy or taking a day off work to vegetate on your couch because you've been doing too much. Remember, the PLAY Model is about having fun, not an overprescribed life. Escapes that are empowering and rejuvenating often give us the strength to take on whatever our next big challenge may be. Many of us are prone to constant self-evaluation, which causes tension and at its worst can lead to burnout, eating disorders, alcoholism, and depression. Healthy escapism can offer some respite from the assessment mode of our high-achiever mind.

Fun offers us a temporary lift; that's why we go for pleasurable activities that provide us with that feeling. Healthy, temporary escapes from the self are something we all need from time to time. The key words here are "healthy" and "temporary." We feel better when we laugh at a joke or when we build sandcastles with our kids or go for a hike. We can also feel better when we have a few drinks or gorge on chocolate.

There are important differences between pleasurable activities. While spending time with your family, friends, or in nature will usually enrich and fulfill you, drinking and overeating will often result in a feeling of eventual emptiness (and possibly sickness, not to mention other side effects). Both types of activities, however, could be classified as forms of escape.

What is important is the motivation, the deliberateness, with which we decide to temporarily transcend the "real world." Where is our mindset taking us? Are we trying to get away from present and future challenges? Or are we interested in experiencing something positive and wanting to foster positive emotions? Stenseng talks about a promotion-guided person versus a prevention-guided person. These two both enter the pleasant state of escape but from a different mindset. While the first person tries to promote his or her well-being in a healthy way through positive experience, the second one is more concerned about running away from problems and preventing any feelings of discomfort to surface.[11] As a wise man (named Ice Cube) once said, "Check yourself, before you wreck yourself."

The promotion-guided person is looking for self-development; the experience of escapism is complementary to other important activities in their life. It leads to them becoming better and more complex. Again, this is escapism as self-expansion and enrichment. By contrast, a prevention-guided person is not very likely to achieve self-development when escaping. Their aim is to direct their attention away from negative things, such as memories, worries, barriers, daily stressors. In blocking painful things from their consciousness, they simultaneously block the positive inputs as well. This group is self-suppressive. To some degree, according to Stenseng, we may be wired toward one or the other approach. He does allow, however, that context can play a role. During personal turmoil, people are more likely to seek entertainment that will take them away from their distress and sadness (self-suppression); the desire for self-development is less pronounced when we are struggling and need to protect ourselves. Also, some individuals have a stronger self-suppression tendency, which might become even stronger when they hit the rocks. In contrast, others might be more prone to an expansive mindset and will seek fun to gain positive experience, without having any alternative motive.

To parse whether your planned or habitual escapes are expansive or suppressive, ask yourself three questions:

1. What are my motivations for engaging in this activity?
2. Is my escape contributing to my long-term well-being?
3. Am I running from something, or am I running toward something?

Here's the great news: If you've followed the advice in this book so far, you've been training yourself to pursue fun in a way that's expansive, not suppressive. You've been reading the safety manual, you are buckled up, and you're ready for launch—to a space where opportunities for wisdom and self-transcendence live.

> **Hall of Fun: Chris Hadfield**
>
> Neil Armstrong may have been the first person to walk on the moon, but astronaut Chris Hadfield will go down in history as the first person to record a music video in space. He could also credibly claim to have had the most fun 250 miles from Earth.
>
> Hadfield, originally from Canada, spent almost six months in 2012 and 2013 aboard the International Space Station, and operated as its commander for the last two months of the assignment. The video he recorded was David Bowie's classic, "Space Oddity." The hit song, about an astronaut floating in space, was recorded in 1969, the same year as Armstrong's famous moonwalk. Hadfield

told the Australian news program *Lateline* that he later was able to speak with Bowie, who floored him by saying it was the most poignant version of the song ever done.

In a sign of the times, Armstrong's signature line—That's one small step for man, one giant leap for mankind—was scripted for him back on Earth. Hadfield, meanwhile, shared endlessly and candidly about everything, from how to play Scrabble in space, to how beautiful Earth looks, to what it's like to cry in zero-G. In his eyes, a patch of farms in Central Asia became "a monochromatic 3-D hallucination in the snow." The Australian Outback was a Jackson Pollock. Hadfield was a constant presence through social media accounts managed by his son Evan, who was also his partner in editing the music video. Like other inhabitants of the space station, Hadfield also conducted experiments—but his real gift to the world was taking us with him on the ride of a lifetime.

chapter 6

The Mystery

For fast-acting relief, try slowing down.
—LILY TOMLIN

During the COVID-19 pandemic I was in need of an escape. Tethered by two full-time jobs—the first, writing a book about fun while not really having much of it; the second, upper management within a company that requires wellness centers to be open in order to see any profit—I was *time* and *cash* poor. But as we've learned, you don't need a lot of money or time for escape. So, making use of my own strategies, I found my way to a bit of respite spending a single day at a hidden gem deep in the rural backyard of central North Carolina. A place called the Well of Mercy. The Well describes itself not by telling you what it is, but by telling you what it's not: a clinical facility, conference center, or meeting place. Instead, it's a little hideaway off the beaten path, dedicated to serving the individual through respectful hospitality and quiet sanctuary.

Although the Well is run by nuns, it operates as an inclusive space open to all. As such, it attracts all types, including the simply curious like myself. I spent my day at the Well doing things I enjoy. I interacted with the interesting people there, and I explored the property's amenities including amazing hiking trails and a beautiful labyrinth. But in the end, the unexpected highlight of the trip was picking up a conversation with a woman named Jane Motsinger. Jane is the head of hospitality at the Well but also provides spiritual direction for those that ask.

Jane and I connected as my twenty-four hours at the Well were ending. "Why did you come visit?" she asked. I usually don't share my problems with strangers, but in the moment I felt quite open. I explained that I'd developed some severe insomnia, probably due to COVID, but also partly due to the stress of current events, my mom's recent Alzheimer's diagnosis, as well as losing a significant proportion of my income due to the pandemic. I'd come to the Well to clear my mind because life's current pressures were also making it difficult to work. I told her about my commitment to authoring *The Fun Habit* and that the lack of sleep was making it hard to write, but that I felt driven to push through. "That sounds like an important mission. What about fun do you sense is so important you need to write a book?" For me, it was an easy question to answer.

"Simply learning to have more fun is a great thing," I explained, "but using fun to develop your curiosity turns fun's power into something amazing. A fundamental flaw of happiness is it's a subjectively self-absorbed construct. It's also contrived—in terms of subjective well-being. I've come to learn it's quite literally made up by science. We use it as an instrument to determine our *rank* in the way we experience reality. And the way many of us experience life is made up of the minutiae of where we happen to exist and the values we've developed, chosen in part from the cultural fate we're predisposed to. To evaluate one's own happiness requires an exercise in introspection, filled with questions rooted in the self and happenstance."

After a bit of back-and-forth, Jane let me continue to opine. She's an amazing listener.

"In contrast to happiness, I've come to learn fun is less *think* and more *do*. You're either having fun or you're not. Mindful of the distinction, when I see people I work with reintegrate things they enjoy doing back into their lives, it's the elixir to being burned-out. There's relief in having some protection against the things others think you should be doing. Where happiness has a lot to do about your *rank*, fun is more about finding *fit*—connecting you with what's out there. It's you and others, or you and the

THE MYSTERY

environment, interacting in a harmonious way. Where happiness is very much a *me* proposition, I've found that fun is very often a *we* proposition."

I went on to explain that the way I look at *we* doesn't necessarily mean a relationship with other people. It simply means allowing pleasure to be derived from something outside ourselves. We talked about my brother's passing and how he found his fun on the hiking trail—a relationship between himself and the wonders of nature—and other types of fun in its various forms. I told Jane I believe that at its best fun has the power to transcend us to a place beyond valence—a place where joy is limitless because it's not being fed by the self. It's being fed by the relationship you have with something else.

"That's really cool, Mike. I cannot wait to read the book," Jane said. "It sounds like you've spent a lot of time thinking about this. Are there any issues you're facing regarding this work?"

"Yes," I said. "I'm struggling to actually name this connection."

"Oh," Jane said. "Well, I'm not sure it fits for you, but a friend of mine simply calls it *The Mystery*." I left the Well feeling a lot better.

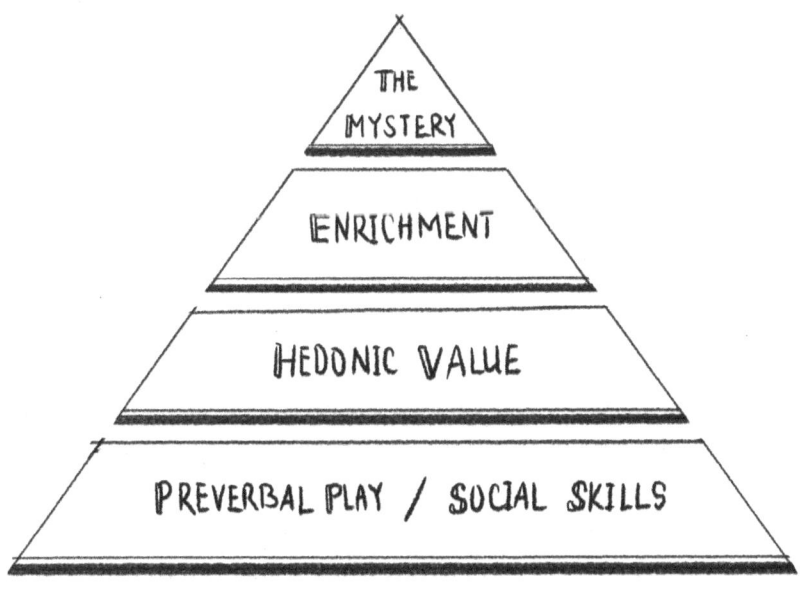

The Fun Pyramid

* * *

Not all fun is created equal. I like to describe fun's hierarchy as a pyramid. The most basic kind of fun is **preverbal**; it's the rudimentary play during which we first learn basic social skills, develop boundaries, and improve our motor skills. Whether you're observing young pups at the dog park or young humans in Central Park, it's easy to understand that fun and play are at the root of how we make sense of the world during early development.

Then there's pleasure for the sake of **hedonic value**, in part developed by evolution to nudge us toward survival, like eating calorie-dense foods (because food was once scarce), as well as make sex enjoyable to ensure our continued existence. In addition to functional pleasure, we explore fun for its own sake, too. We've already explored at length the contribution that this level of fun has on our mental and physical well-being. But as I said in chapter 1, it's at this pleasure stage that many people get stuck and exit the pyramid. At some point in life, they get busy "adulting" and either marginalize or abandon the activities that they truly enjoy. They reclassify fun as an immature distraction from the things that "really matter"—erroneously framing fun as a reckless escape, or even a runaway train to ruin.

The next level of fun is **enrichment**, a more meaningful, intentional level of fun. There's a great study that highlights why ongoing pleasure is a necessary step to this next level. Publishing in the journal *Proceedings of the National Academy of Sciences,* a team of scientists from Harvard, Stanford, and MIT looked at how (and why) people choose their everyday activities.[1] The study included a large sample of more than twenty-eight thousand people. They were asked to download a free smartphone app that prompted them to answer questions about their mood (How do you currently feel?) and activity choice (What are you currently doing?) at random times throughout the day. The researchers wanted to know what influences our choice of activities: mood or, let's say, day of the week? They were expecting to find that we are wired to look for activities that will make us feel good; that is, if we feel bad, we look for activities that will make us feel better (e.g., eating comfort food), and if we feel good, we look for activities that will make us feel even better (e.g., participating in sports). Their hypothesis assumed that people are constantly pleasure-seeking.

However, that's not what they found. Instead, people's activity choices reflected the so-called "hedonic flexibility principle." It turns out to be true that when we feel bad, we seek out pleasure to make ourselves feel better. The surprise was what happens when we're already in a state of positive valence. In the study, people who felt good were more likely to choose useful activities that weren't necessarily mood-enhancing. For example, they might choose to forgo a little lighthearted fun to sit down and write a book about it. (Or maybe that's just me. But you get the point.)

What all this suggests is that when our "fun cup" is full, we can resist the allure of short-term gains (because these types of "rewards" are already bountiful through deliberate design) and invest in long-term enrichment goals that will support our existence. However, when we are simply trying to cope, we are more likely to seek out untethered escapism.

There's a special type of fun, though, fun at the highest peak, that is seemingly initiated outside of valence. When we step into the unknown (*The Mystery*), whether that's through curiosity, surprise, or the space beyond sense-making—a place where we transcend the ordinary—it's this type of fun that often has the biggest impact on us.

The Map Is Not the Territory

In science we have a saying, "The map is not the territory," which is to say the description of some "thing" is never the "thing" itself.[2] In this way, it's important to realize a lot of the happiness "prescriptions" out there only offer you a map. When fun burns brightest, when it is supporting our growth, it is generally because we have thrown out the map in order to explore the territory. When I see people struggle to understand what this really means, I share this insight I got from observational data during my research for this book. I spent time in three different children's museums watching how kids and adults engage with various experiential play spaces. The Marbles Kids Museum in Raleigh, North Carolina, for example, has a room filled with pool noodle–like pieces and building blocks. You can basically create anything in this space that comes to mind. During my visit I watched, again and again, as kids rushed in, grabbed pieces, and went to town. Their parents, meanwhile, stood paralyzed. Waiting for their map, waiting for instructions that don't exist. They asked the attendant what they were supposed to do, struggling to understand the "point" of the game. However, once they got into the activity many of them had just as much (if not more) fun than the kids. No longer stifled by the need for a map, they were free to explore all the territory had to offer—each discovery as unique as the individual.

When fun connects us to all that's available the possibilities are endless, so our curiosity grows. Fun dips us into the unknown and we emerge each time better for it.

Before we continue exploring fun as a catalyst to connect to the unknown—to wisdom—if calling this *The Mystery* doesn't work for you, you're not alone. Perhaps why I struggled for so long to generalize a label for the top of fun's pyramid is that, ultimately, it's an injustice to you for me to assign it a label. I reached out to thousands of my newsletter subscribers trying to potentially come up with a consensus to label this phenomenon and was blown away that not a single person who responded described it the same way: *Magic, The Zone, Awe, Awareness, The Present, Good Times, The Profound, Time Control, The Wow, Joy, My Happy Place.* In the spirit of not prescribing you a map, I instead invite you (before we move on) to come up with your own meaningful term for fun's peak. Borrowing Jane's, as I have, is fine as well.

The Benefits of Curiosity

Nurturing your curiosity is one of the best ways to connect to *The Mystery*. Cultivating our sense of curiosity has been shown time and time again to increase opportunities for joy, wonder, and wisdom. Dr. Todd B. Kashdan, a psychology professor at George Mason University, believes that people who are chronically bored may lack a sense of curiosity.[3] To fight the monotony of boredom, Kashdan urges people to challenge themselves by developing a deeper relationship to what interests them. Kashdan explains

THE MYSTERY

that when we seek novelty and, as a result, get rewarded from fun and/or challenging situations, the neural connections in our brain strengthen. Practicing curiosity makes us more resilient, more intelligent, and helps our spirit stay young. When I interviewed Dr. Kashdan about curiosity, he said, "Curiosity is a form of self-expansion where your resources, your philosophies, your wisdom, your perspectives . . . grow. You get to reexamine what you view as opportunities, and what you view as threats. Some of the things you viewed as threats you now see as opportunities, some of the things you viewed as opportunities, now you kind of question yourself as you mature and value different parts of your identity."

In contrast, when we aren't motivated to seek out wonder or are not curious about discovering new things, we are more likely to deteriorate both physically and mentally.[4] Boredom has been linked to dysfunctional behaviors, mental illnesses, even brain injuries.[5] When you encourage your sense of curiosity, naturally, you are less likely to get bored. *When was the last time you flexed your curiosity?* It could be something as small as trying a new restaurant you're not sure you'll like or reaching out to an old friend simply because you're genuinely curious about what she's up to. Taking an interest in others is a great way to strengthen social bonds. Curiosity is also closely linked to creativity.[6] So, by cultivating a desire for engaging in novel activities or doing things in new ways, you are not only gaining new insight but likely enhancing your creative abilities as well.

One of my favorite ways to flex curiosity is by picking a location I've never been to (but that seems interesting), one that has a current airline mile special. I use the opportunity to go to a new locale on the cheap as the needed nudge to make the trip. Then I use some advice I got from travel hacker Erik Paquet, "I think one of the most powerful things that you can do to make a trip more meaningful is to carve out time to connect with locals and to meet people from the area. It doesn't have to be anything that's super in-depth . . . sometimes there is a breakthrough moment for many people traveling when, even if it is frustrating and hard [because of language barriers], they try to make a connection with locals." In my experience, you cannot find the best parts of any city on the map. They are only available to those who are truly curious about the territory.

Perhaps the most important part of having fun through curiosity, however, is when it helps us recognize that our ability to connect and learn from the outside world is infinite. The practice affords us the means to transcend our consensus reality for brief moments and absorb ourselves in fascination and wonder—finding beauty in accepting that we will never know everything about anything and just how amazing it is to embrace this truth.

The Benefits of Surprise

For many of us, surprises are arousing. Again, this is variable hedonics at work. We get excited when we don't know what's coming next. We try to anticipate if the surprise that awaits us is going to be pleasant or unpleasant, and that tension . . . that suspense . . . is stimulating.

According to science, surprise profoundly affects our neurology and psychology. The way we perceive surprise might be one of the keys to what makes us human.

A surprise means that we receive unexpected stimuli that interrupts our ongoing thoughts and activities.[7] It disturbs the coherence and predictability of our world. Because of the disruption, it can take us a while to process a surprise and then determine our valence, either delighted with positive emotion or dismayed with negative emotion. Drs. Marret Noordewier and Eric van Dijk from the faculty of Social and Behavioural Sciences at Leiden University in the Netherlands argue that we need to distinguish between our initial response to surprise and what comes after, which doesn't always match. For instance, even when we are pleasantly surprised, our first reaction may be negative because our brains don't like the integrity of our worldview being challenged. (I mean, who likes it when the map is wrong?)

In their article, published in the journal *Cognition and Emotion*, Noordewier and van Dijk write that "even if the surprising stimulus is positive, people first experience this brief phase of interruption and surprise, before they can appreciate and welcome the outcome as it is."[8] Our responses to surprise are, therefore, quite dynamic, and the initial response is not always the same as the subsequent response.

THE MYSTERY

We need space to make sense of the outcome before we can relish a surprise. There is a temporal dimension to our reaction to a surprise that suggests enjoyment from it doesn't always come automatically. Instead, it requires some processing and evaluation, the creation of new wisdom, which is interesting in the context of fun (which has been argued up until this point to happen in the moment).

In chapter 2, using the example of a songbird popping out of a boiling kettle, we briefly examined how we are drawn to the unexpected element of a surprise, which increases our pleasure. This is because our nucleus accumbens—a region in the brain associated with pleasure and reward expectation—responds most strongly to unexpected events (e.g., receiving a gift when it's not your birthday). The phenomenon was highlighted in a study conducted by a research group from the Emory University School of Medicine and Baylor College of Medicine.

The experiment was led by researchers Gregory S. Berns and Read Montague, who are also both medical doctors. They tested twenty-five participants who had fruit juice or water squirted in their mouth in a pattern that was either fixed (every ten seconds) or unpredictable. During the activity, the volunteers underwent functional magnetic resonance imaging (fMRI) to show brain activity.

What transpired was that activation of the brain was greater when squirts were unpredictable. There was a rush of dopamine when the juice or water was given in variable squirts. The unpredictability of the event played a more significant role than whether the participants liked or disliked the fluids.

The team concluded that our reward pathways get strongly activated by the unexpectedness of the stimuli; more so than by the pleasurability of the effect (the fact that we like something).[9] The finding of the study is somewhat logical from an evolutionary perspective. Our brain is wired to become alert during a sudden change; this takes precedence over other stimuli (such as pleasure). When our ancestors encountered something surprising, they had to act and learn from it.

Our attraction to surprise can be observed in other areas of life as well. For example, scientists found it in our appreciation of music. Vincent

Cheung, of the Max Planck Institute for Human Cognitive and Brain Sciences, and his colleagues analyzed eighty thousand chords in U.S. *Billboard* pop songs. The best ones, those that produced feelings of pleasure in listeners (as measured by an fMRI) included a good balance of surprise and unpredictability.[10] For listeners, that meant they experienced a high amount of pleasure when surprised by an event that deviated from their initial expectations.

Research shows that surprises can also help our creativity. For example, a study published in the *Personality and Social Psychology Bulletin* reported on an experiment in which the participants were shown different images and then asked to come up with innovative names for a new type of pasta. The group that was shown photos that somewhat broke the mold (e.g., an Eskimo in the desert) later came up with more original answers compared to participants that viewed unsurprising images (e.g., an Eskimo in the snow). The surprise element, however, only inspired those that were low in their need for structure. Their divergent thinking was helped by the unpredictability of the image—the prime from something out of the ordinary. In contrast, those high in need of structure experienced a decrease in divergent thinking when presented with incongruous photos, suggesting surprises do not necessarily work for us all.[11]

The Paradox of Sense-Making

It is clear fun promotes internal motivation and can be used as a path toward betterment, as well as the cognitive process of sense-making.[12] Karl E. Weick, one of America's most influential social psychologists, defines *sense-making* as an ongoing accomplishment that involves assigning meaning to experiences and creating order out of events by making sense of them.[13]

Making sense of our world is a necessary part of our development, so we spend much of our life trying to find meaning. Austrian psychiatrist and neurologist Dr. Viktor Frankl, who was a Holocaust survivor, argued in his famous book *Man's Search for Meaning*[14] that the primary motivation of a person is to discover meaning in life. Meaning is so important to us that our minds can be very creative in inventing it, from the minute details of everyday life to the grand story of our existence. Benjamin Hale wrote in his bestselling book *The Evolution of Bruno Littlemore*[15] that:

> *We do not discover the meanings of mysterious things, we invent them. We make meanings because meaninglessness terrifies us above all things. More than snakes, even. More than falling, or the dark. We trick ourselves into seeing meanings in things, when in fact all we are doing is grafting our meanings onto the universe to comfort ourselves.*

In other words, the trouble with meaning is that it is all in our heads. Further, creating meaning all the time is a taxing pursuit. To recover, we often look for ways to make ourselves feel better (without having to worry about the *meaning* of actions all the time). Would it be so wrong to proactively redirect some of our endless sense-making toward pleasure and enjoyment instead?

If the idea makes you uncomfortable, know that your instincts have likely been shaped by hundreds of years of intellectual history. Henry Sidgwick, one of the most influential ethical philosophers of the Victorian era, was no fan of pleasure. He believed that to be happy, you must commit to people and projects in a profound, meaningful way and if you have a proclivity toward pleasure, you can't do that.[16] In chapter 1, we already discussed the stultifying influence of the Puritans on the American psyche. When you're constantly trying to prove you're among the chosen, an afternoon of dreamy relaxation, or fun for fun's sake, becomes a risky proposition. It might even be proof that you're wicked. *Oh my!*

Thanks to science, we now have a more nuanced understanding of human behavior. We know that having fun doesn't lead us to reject or ignore life's more serious side. Remember the hedonic flexibility principle? We now understand that when we feel that fun is part of our lives, we can resist the allure of short-term gains (because these types of "rewards" are already bountiful through deliberate design) and invest in long-term goals that will support our existence.

The truth is, we don't have to choose one or the other. A life well-lived likely rests on a delicate balance between sense-making activities (that we choose in a rational matter) and pleasure-seeking activities (things we simply enjoy in the present).

The importance of sense-making has been long established, and this book isn't meant to challenge or defend whether part of life should be reserved for searching out meaning. The seed I would like to plant is that *The Mystery*, self-transcendence itself, might simply be the skill of truly having fun. Finding wisdom from a much deeper well than what we can create on our own. Being able to lose yourself in an experience, being able to savor the moment without attributing any context. Joy for joy's sake.

Dr. Desiree Kozlowski of Southern Cross University, Australia, talks about "rational hedonism" or the intentional savoring of simple pleasures. She argues that if you give what you are doing your full attention—be it eating a cake, playing with your kid, walking on the beach, or truly enjoying some downtime—it will enrich your well-being. The link between well-being and fun seems to be hidden in the way we make an active choice to experience life.[17] It's not so much about how much meaning something has, but whether we can transcend our ego's need for things to make sense—its need to rank our experience—its need to evaluate whether the experience makes us happier than our neighbor.

Having fun does not mean rejecting our responsibilities. On the contrary, we come with the capacity to pursue our "meaningful" pursuits with more vigor. In fact, deliberate fun might be one of the most responsible things we can do, sacrificing our ego's need for meaning and rank and simply engrossing ourselves in the wondrous gift of experience—a place true wisdom lives.

Acclaimed neuroscientist Dr. Lisa Feldman Barrett described it to me this way, "Whenever there's an opportunity to experience awe or wonder at something, I do it. Sometimes it's just looking up at the sky, at beautiful clouds, or the stars. If I were by an ocean, it might be looking out at the waves. It can even be something if I'm taking my daily walk, and I see a weed like a dandelion poking through the crack of a sidewalk, I can cultivate an experience of awe at the awesome power of nature to be unconstrained by human attempts to contain it. Or if I'm having a Zoom meeting that falls apart, because I lose an Internet connection because some satellite moved somewhere or my computer freezes or what have you. I try in those moments to remember to cultivate an experience of awe because I have to remember that even if my connections to the person who I'm speaking to in Belgium or England or China is really shitty . . . I'm still talking to somebody in England or in China, or in Belgium, and I can see their faces, and it might be blurry, but I can still see their faces. *Isn't that amazing?* Because even ten years ago, that might not have really been something that we just assumed that we could do every day. There's a lot of evidence to suggest that experiencing awe, experiencing yourself as a speck for a minute or two, really gives your nervous system a break. Because if other things are more majestic than you and you're just a speck, that means your problems are just a speck. And just for a minute, if your problems are recognized as unimportant, that actually gives your nervous system a break. It just lets you readjust and put things in perspective."[18]

In these peak moments, it is not about immediately finding meaning but about being engrossed in what the present moment is sharing with us. A study led by Professor Jordi Quoidbach of Harvard University, who also coauthored a study about choosing activities by the hedonic flexibility principle, showed that we achieve higher positive affect when we are focusing our attention on the present moment and engaging in positive rumination while experiencing positive events. In contrast, when we are distracted, our positive affect is reduced.[19] When we can transcend the need to understand our physical world through immersing ourselves with focused attention, we are truly Living.

Shortly before his death, Abraham Maslow, one of the most important psychologists of our era, amended his famous pyramid of human needs to incorporate self-transcendence.[20] In his revised model of needs, self-transcendence was added to his pyramid as the final step of our motivation, going beyond self-actualization. After studying Maslow's work and some of his unpublished personal journals, Dr. Mark E. Koltko-Rivera of New York University proposed the following description of a person who reaches self-transcendence: "Seeks to further a cause beyond the self and to experience a communion beyond the boundaries of the self through peak experience."[21] David Bryce Yaden, from the University of Pennsylvania, describes these transcendent experiences as "transient mental states marked by decreased self-salience and increased feelings of connectedness."[22] This, again, is one of the many gifts of fun: to feel free and connected to the world outside ourselves, instead of wrestling inside our own heads.

In a conversation I had with Dr. Susanne Cook-Greuter, a leading expert in mature ego development and self-actualization, she put it this way: "Freedom from constraint is not limited to early development. Anyone who has access to play, access to ideas—even access to abstract constructs—who is willing to play with ideas and constructs is going to be more likely to develop than somebody who is attached to ideas and constructs in a sort of static way, 'This is how the world is.' As soon as you open yourself up to saying, 'Well, maybe not. Maybe there could be another world, or there's another way to look at things,' you have more space, and it helps you grow. We seem to be getting more ossified . . . in what we believe, what we do, and what we see. We have no interest, no curiosity for anything else. When you are open to new things, the unexpected can happen."

Hall of Fun: Adam Yauch

For proof that you don't need to choose between a fun life and a meaningful life, look no further than Adam Yauch (aka MCA), the late prankster bassist of the Beastie Boys, a band that might have been the world's most successful joke. A band whose purpose was "really just to crack each other up," according to member Mike D's admission in the *Beastie Boys Book*.[23] The band ultimately sold twenty million records in the U.S. alone, with seven platinum albums from 1986 to 2004. Yauch was known to be the most outrageous of the group, becoming infamous for antics such as his alter ego, the fake-bearded, yodeling, lederhosen-wearing Nathanial Hörnblowér. In 1994, Hörnblowér stormed the stage of the 1994 MTV Music Video Awards, when the Beastie Boys lost Best Direction for "Sabotage" to REM for "Everybody Hurts," to protest the "outrage"—nonsensically concluding his rant with the claim that he, Hörnblowér, had "all the ideas for *Star Wars*." (Michael Stipe stood behind him, confused, helplessly fiddling with his trophy.)

Watching Yauch that evening, you might never have guessed that he was deeply engaged by then in a search for spiritual meaning. Yauch's life was changed during interaction with Tibetan refugees, people who had endured enormous trauma and suffering yet held on to their compassion and humor. In 1992, he began a lifelong study of Buddhism. Later he would tell *Rolling Stone*, "In a sense, what Western society teaches us is that if you get enough money, power, and beautiful people to have sex with, that's going to bring you happiness. That's what every commercial, every magazine, music, movie teaches us. That's a fallacy."[24] That same year, he met Erin Potts at a party in Kathmandu, striking up a friendship that culminated in the first Tibetan Freedom Concert in San Francisco's Golden Gate Park in 1996, the year that Yauch formally converted to Buddhism. Five years of annual concerts—a seamless melding of fun and meaning—raised millions of dollars and brought international awareness for the cause (to learn more visit https://share.michaelrucker.com/tibetan-freedom-concert).

On the fifth anniversary of Yauch's 2012 death from cancer, Potts wrote on Medium, "The Beastie Boys, and especially Yauch, taught me to always have fun—to work hard, to take risks, to help make the world a better place, but that you must have fun while doing it . . . and maybe even wear a fake mustache or a mullet wig. (Yauch LOVED disguises.)"[25]

An Inclusive Invitation to *The Mystery*

When we reach a certain connection with what we are doing or experiencing, these out-of-the-ordinary experiences can have a taste of spirituality, either in a secular or religious way. A study of retired ballet dancers, for example, showed that during peak moments of their dance, they often experienced spiritual feelings and altered states of consciousness, like being outside of their bodies, being less aware of themselves, and experiencing a sense of transformation and connection. Also, similar to other athletes, they talked about their feelings of love toward ballet. When they danced, they engaged in a passionate love affair; for spiritual people, this could be the love of Creation, and for nonreligious, a love of life.[26] As you deeply connect to the activities you enjoy and become a master at things you truly find fun, I invite you to use this power to grow your curiosity, enhance your creativity, surprise yourself, and gain new insight. In doing so, you will undoubtedly welcome wondrous opportunities you never before imagined, absorbing the wisdom that almost always accompanies the ephemeral opportunities for enlightenment—from the subtle connectedness a gardener feels watching their flowers blossom to the epic once-in-a-lifetime friendship that results from that one random party you reluctantly went to in Kathmandu.

We've covered a lot of ground now about having fun, from basic strategies to advanced topics. Now that your Fun Habit is coming together, it's time to talk about how important it can be to bring your friends along on the ride.

chapter 7

Friendship Is Weird

Friendship is so weird.
You just pick a human you've met and you're like,
"Yep, I like this one," and you just do stuff with them.
—BILL MURRAY

Like many people, the town I live in is not the town where I grew up. It's not the town where I went to college, or where I spent my formative years as an adult. When our family moved to Summerfield, North Carolina, we felt the pain of leaving behind extended family and many long-established friendships back on the West Coast, but we hoped we'd stay connected. That turned out to be a bit more difficult than we expected, leading to a conversation a few years after we moved about being happy in North Carolina, but a bit lonely.

Making new friends was still a slow work in progress, and keeping in touch with old friends was even harder. We often wondered: Will our friends remember us? Do they talk about us since we're not around? Then Anna came up with a fun idea to get people thinking about us—something that would definitely put us top of mind.

It happened to be time to send out holiday cards. With some simple photo editing, our family of four instantly became five, with Anna holding an unexpected little bundle of joy. We sent out our holiday cards surprising our friends and family with the ruse, and sure enough, our plan worked. Going into the New Year, our phones started ringing and buzzing with messages and texts coming in from many of our friends checking in—"congratulations, we had no idea!"—including many whom we hadn't heard from in ages. We got a lot of laughs when we let everybody in on the joke, and then had long-overdue catch-ups.

Our quirky outreach was uniquely "us," but what we had discovered is true for everybody: **We live in times that require us to be unusually deliberate about our social lives.** Just as with fun, we must fight the cultural current by carving our own path. Anecdotally and empirically, it's not easy to make and keep friendships as adults, as family and professional demands engulf us. A *New York Times* article, "Why Is It Hard to Make Friends Over 30?"[1] was so widely read and shared that the newspaper ran it twice. One person the reporter profiled was a thirty-nine-year-old woman who had hundreds of Facebook friends but not enough people in the city where she had just moved to round out a good birthday party. Another was a divorced psychotherapist who redefined being "that guy" at the local salsa class: Instead of hitting on women, he was asking all the men out for drinks. In his years as a married man and father, he had let all his other relationships go.

Some people don't have enough friends. Others only have friends-in-theory because they have no time to hang out. As comedian John Mulaney quipped on *Saturday Night Live*, "I want to write songs for people in their thirties called 'Tonight's No Good, How About Wednesday? Oh, you're in Houston on Wednesday, okay, then let's not see each other for six months, and *it doesn't matter at all.*'"

Daily life was once naturally social, when people huddled together for survival. These days we're more transient than tribal, with Amazon packages piling up on our stoops and technology providing us the means to maintain friendships (or at least a convincing facsimile) long-distance. But social networks and virtual communities do not readily provide the three things sociologists say are critical to making friends: proximity; repeated, unplanned interactions; and a setting that helps us relax and let down our guards. Cultural trends have further eroded traditional community structures. Church membership in the U.S., for example, has steeply declined in the past twenty years, with only half of Americans now belonging to a church.[2] I'm not making a pitch for the Sabbath, just noting that the community these institutions once provided is not easily replaced.

But while close social ties may no longer follow a natural progression, our nature still requires them. As with fun, flesh-and-blood friendships aren't "extras" in life. They're right up there with sunshine and vegetables when it comes to our health. One frequently cited meta-analysis established that a lack of social relationships was as bad for you as being an alcoholic or being a fifteen-cigarettes-a-day smoker, and twice as harmful as being obese.[3] Other studies have linked loneliness to inflammation and more rapid cognitive and physical decline as we age. Sure, in this era we can *survive* without friends, but it appears that life in that solitary state will be more nasty, brutish, and shorter than we might prefer.

Extrovert or introvert, you are still a social animal. You need friends—and more to the point of this book, you need friends you can have fun with. Many of the friends in your daily life today probably came to you via your school, your work, or if you're a parent, the activities of your children. You may also have very close friends whom you can count on for support, but whom you can't call up to go to the movies or to join your supper club because they live three thousand miles away. All of those existing relationships are legitimate and many of them are no doubt crucial—but because our interest is specifically to develop your Fun Habit, we're going to keep our focus here narrow.

Fun friendships are friendships organized around deliberate fun. If you're already determined to build your Fun Habit, spending time with Fun Friends isn't a distraction from your goal. You can add a friend to almost anything fun on your schedule. It's a great example of activity bundling. There's additionally something special about relationships between people who bond over shared interests. There's rarely the sense that time spent with such a friend is in tension with other things you'd really like to be doing—you're doing those things together! And when you can't be doing those things, you can always talk together about having done them, and when you'll do them next.

Hall of Fun: The Impractical Jokers

Imagine having so much fun with your friends that it earned you fame, fortune, and devoted fandom. That's the story of four men from Staten Island, New York, the stars of the TV show *Impractical Jokers*. Joe Gatto, James Murray, Brian Quinn, and Sal Vulcano were friends from high school who created a sketch comedy troupe together before shooting their pilot on iPhones and selling it to a network. It's a hidden-camera pranking show—but unlike previous such shows like *Punk'd*, the pranks ("challenges" in the show's lingo) are on each other. When one of them fails at a challenge, he's punished by the other three. And so, Sal Vulcano has a permanent tattoo of a teenage Jaden Smith on his hip. James Murray has had a number of on-screen prostate exams, one of which was assisted by his then-fiancée. Joe Gatto has crossed New York City's East River on top of an aerial tram in a Captain Fatbelly superhero costume. Brian Quinn spent twenty-four hours handcuffed to a professional mime. And on and on, across an entire decade of seasons and hundreds of challenges.

It's funny stuff, but the real engine of the show—and what makes their fans so fervent—is the palpable, relatable friendship between the guys. Their mutual affection keeps the humor from ever feeling mean, and they've got an undeniable chemistry that's fun to watch. Without the friendship, the humor would illicit cringes, not laughs, as proven by the history of a copycat attempt in the United Kingdom. When the BBC aired a licensed British version, with four comedians rather than lifelong best friends, it bombed after a few seasons. A critic for U.K. entertainment site *VultureHound* wrote, "The chemistry between them seems very forced and unnatural, sometimes verging on being a tad awkward."[4] Later Comedy Central U.K. bought and aired the original U.S. version—and the show became a huge hit.

Catch Someone Else's Fun

Fun Friends are like human growth hormone for your Fun Habit. As one study put it, "Fun is more fun when others are involved."[5] Researchers watched people play fifteen minutes of Jenga, either alone, with a friend, or with a stranger. Not shockingly, playing Jenga with a friend was consistently the most fun. But the study gets more interesting when you consider exactly *why* that's the case—and the answer provides a few hints about what kind of friends you need more generally if your goal is to ramp up the fun in your life.

One reason that friends enhance fun seems to be intrinsic. In other words, the social interaction itself is enjoyable, all the more so because we feel comfortable and at ease with friends. But the researchers also considered the possibility that the real pleasure was seeing someone *else* enjoy Jenga. You may already be familiar with the phenomena of emotional contagion and social contagion, whether by way of Malcolm Gladwell's *The Tipping Point*,[6] or perhaps the pioneering work of Nicholas Christakis and James Fowler,[7] who have shown that health issues like obesity and smoking can be contagious. Some motivational speakers might have even warned you that you become the sum of the five friends you spend the most time with.

While that tired axiom is wildly reductive, it is true that if your goal is to have fun, you need to choose your friends wisely. Not to mention, as we've already established, we cannot expand the time we have in any given week. Friends have a huge influence on how we act and feel. You've probably noticed that some people you hang out with make you playful and bouncy. You're a different person after the experience. Just seeing them and exchanging a few words can have an uplifting effect on your mood. In contrast, there are other people who can bring you down just by being in your space. Their mood, nonverbal communication, and chosen topics of conversation can have a negative effect on your own emotions and state of mind. You suddenly start feeling sad, tense, or agitated when interacting with them. We can probably all think of a few people that have this effect on us.

Emotional contagion, a concept pioneered by relationship scientist Dr. Elaine Hatfield and her colleagues,[8] means that we share our emotions with other people, both consciously and unconsciously, via verbal and physical (nonverbal) expressions, such as facial expression, posture, and tone of voice. Knowingly or unknowingly, we all have an impact on each other's emotions. Emotions flow from one person to another, and we can catch bad vibes like we catch a bad cold. Worse, unlike a cold, which often has notable warning signs, catching bad vibes usually happens without conscious knowledge.

Emotional contagion is explained, in part, by mirror neurons, which were first observed firing in the brains of macaque monkeys but were later found in humans. These brain cells, part of our frontal cortex, can't differentiate between someone else's action and our own. In other words, if you're watching someone exude joy, part of your brain experiences their emotional state like it was your own. It's a powerful effect that we're all susceptible to, for better or for worse. (It's credited as likely responsible for the evolution of modern language, however, so probably mostly for the better.)[9]

Focusing social time together on a fun activity might help protect you from "catching" the feelings of a moody or toxic friend. It might even turn their negative feelings around. That said, there's considerable upside to spending time with friends whose attitude trends positive. If they're likely to have fun, you're likely to have fun. If the environment is predisposed to having fun, you'll both be likely to have fun. Remarkably, this can be true even if you share an activity that one of you never found fun before. Researchers studying intrinsic motivation have noted that "motivation contagion" can operate as a stimulus.[10] In other words, if you observe someone who enjoys doing something, your enjoyment increases, too. For instance, even if you don't enjoy cycling, repeatedly observing a friend who does enjoy it can trigger an internal desire in you, and you start getting a feeling as if you like cycling, too. A Fun Friend might be the perfect person to help you get over the period of discomfort involved in trying something new. That said, my wife still hates camping

("Why are we paying good money to be homeless?"), so this doesn't work all the time.

That One Time at Band Camp

I'm not exhorting you to have more friends, per se. Depending on your personality and life stage, what a healthy social life looks like is very individual. The goal here is to match some of your fun plans with people who are interested. Throw out (for a minute) all those boring adult relationships where all you do is talk about the few associations you have in common. Instead, think about friendships the way kids do. They only need to know one thing: *Will you play with me?* We're discerning adults, of course, and picky about our play, so the game here is to find friends who already share our interests.

I know from experience what happens when you throw your friend net wildly, instead of deliberately. Years back when I lived in Alameda, California, I spent many a kid's birthday hanging out in a place called Pump It Up, a big indoor bounce house warehouse that became a favorite among local parents for their children's birthday parties. There was nothing inherently bad about the place, and yet every time I had to go, I found myself questioning my existence. The novelty of watching my kid jump from one piece of plastic to another waned with repetition, and conversation with many of the other parents never really got beyond forced chitchat (aka a Yielding activity for me).

Thinking maybe the stilted conversation was either because we were "on duty" or because I'm no good at polite chatter, I eventually met several of those parents out for drinks. Under more relaxed circumstances, relationships might bloom, or so I thought. *Not really.* In fact, things got really awkward because two of the parents turned out to be advocates of opposing political views. *In vino, veritas.* We didn't seem to have much in common besides our children.

When we moved to Summerfield, North Carolina, I tried again to make friends based on convenience. I trialed a few different coworking environments. Many of the cohabitants at the various locations were younger than me—much younger than me—and for the most part, my early attempts to make friends were futile.

Finally, my wife stepped in to help. She knows that some of my favorite Fun Friends have always been what I call "show bros." Guys who share my love for live music. Since we moved to Summerfield, I had gone to some shows alone, and hadn't much enjoyed it. Then Anna learned one of her coworkers liked to see bands, so she organized a blind friend date for us. We've been to two shows together so far. He's a great guy, but honestly, the best part about the relationship is having a good time around a common interest. We connect around the music, and it's more enjoyable to have a shared experience.

This is not to say that you can't find Fun Friends among the people that children and work bring into your life. After moving to a new town, my friend Meredith complained to me that the only people she got to talk to socially were "soccer moms" at her kid's sports games—but a year later, when I circled back, she told me she had eventually gotten to know some of them quite well and that a group of them had become real friends. If you both love to watch your children play sports, and get caught up in the team spirit, that commonality can be a great basis for a fun friendship. After all, it offers two of the three friendship prerequisites: proximity and a relaxed setting. And while your interactions aren't unplanned, they're definitely repeated.

The importance of proximity and repetition cannot be understated. As I know well, it is exceedingly difficult to maintain a friendship when the only way to do so is to shoehorn phone calls and Zooms into an already crowded schedule. A better approach is to make friend time the path of least resistance by merging friends and fun.

Join the Club

Have you ever heard the story about the group of friends from Spokane, Washington, who sustained a game of tag for more than twenty years? That's right—*tag*—as in, "Tag, you're it," that sturdy fixture of schoolyard play everywhere. Their game started in high school, and then was revived at a reunion almost a decade later when they decided to run a long-distance version of the game every February. One of the friends was a first-year lawyer, and drafted a "Tag Participation Agreement," outlining the spirit of the game and the rules. Everyone signed, and the cross-country game began. Instead of slowly drifting away from each other after high school, they instead found themselves more bonded than ever—sneaking into each other's homes, cars, and workplaces to tag each other "It." Their game was featured in the *Wall Street Journal*, and eventually inspired the 2018 movie by the same name.[11]

Their story, as idiosyncratic as their fun may be, illuminates three success factors that the rest of us can model to help sustain friendships in the chaos of life. First, consistency: They played the same game at the same time every year. Consistency is so important; you're much more likely to establish a habit when it's consistent. Second, accountability: The participation agreement they all signed was meant to be silly, but it made their commitment feel real. And finally, they were playing a game together—aka having fun.

If you're feeling less creative, one of the easiest ways to fulfill all those factors is to join a club. Clubs plug you into a consistent schedule that someone else took the time and trouble to organize. They build not just social interaction but accountability around your fun. You can use them to meet new friends or encourage existing friends to join to see them more.

In the past when I moved to a new city, I joined running clubs to meet people. I made lifelong friends that way both in London and Manhattan Beach, California. (You'll read about one such friend, Graeme, in the final chapter.) You can find a club, league, or team for just about any sport. But because I know not everybody is a sweat hound, I'll give you a non-sports example. Michelle is a successful freelance writer in a large American city who wanted more fun in her life. When she thought back to what had previously brought her joy, her childhood church choir came to mind. She loved to sing, and more specifically, she loved to sing with others. So, she started asking around, and soon had a list of a handful of potential choirs to join. She ended up choosing one that did benefit concerts all over the city, which allowed her to fulfill a second goal she had, to find more ways to give back. Fast-forward a few years, and she's still in that choir. They meet every Saturday. Over the years, a few of her fellow members have become her best friends.

You can also start something on your own—but do yourself a favor and keep it simple. My friend Nir, who I first mentioned in chapter 2, has a monthly event he calls the Kibbutz, the Hebrew word for *gathering*. He started the event with his wife when he realized that, consumed by professional opportunities, he had stopped spending time with his friends. Now, every two weeks, four couples get together to chew on a TED-style question over a bring-your-own picnic lunch—no prep, no mess, no fuss. Kids come along, but they play on their own while the adult conversation flows.

If a weekly or monthly commitment feels like too much, consider establishing something annual. I'm one of the sixty million or so people who play fantasy football every year. Every year, a group of my friends from high school and other walks of life and I gather in a city like Las Vegas or Lake Tahoe for our draft. We spend the rest of the year planning for it, in texts and emails that, admittedly, also involve a lot of dumb jokes and memes that I would be embarrassed to have anyone else in the world read. But it works for us and keeps alive friendships that might have otherwise faded thanks to distance and circumstance.

The key advice here is to sign yourself up for a commitment to *play with others*, whatever way pleases you.

A Counterintuitive Exception

It turns out friends don't make fun more fun for everyone. There are three groups of people who I can anticipate might have cringed during the course of this chapter. I'll address them all.

To begin, let's go back to that study I mentioned earlier, that showed people had more fun playing Jenga with friends. There was, in fact, a caveat to their conclusion: "This tendency was observed only among relatively non-lonely individuals; among lonely persons, playing with a friend produced essentially no benefit compared to playing with a stranger." As it turns out, loneliness is often not the result of social isolation. The researchers concluded, "The finding dovetails well with other research suggesting that the central characteristic of trait loneliness is the relative lack of intimacy and enjoyment in interactions with friends."

If you are someone who, right now, feels at their loneliest surrounded by people, adding just any friends may not enhance your fun. You may need time with your closest friends to unload and feel connected. That's right: "Boring grown-up talk" may be exactly what you need. That said, it's been my experience that fun time is important even for our closest relationships. Frequent lighthearted, casual interaction builds the grounding for friends to take care of each other during life's emotional troughs. I'll never forget our fantasy football draft the year my brother died. My friends knew that I desperately needed my spirits lifted. In the middle of the draft, one of them jumped up to emcee a surprise makeshift comedy show, while a few others did their best to be improv comics—the show was for everybody, but I was the primary audience. They knew my brother and I both shared a love for comedy. All involved did their best and the entire league had a good laugh, followed by a toast before we went back to the draft. Even now when I think about it, I get choked up because, aside from our shenanigans, the best part of our league is that we've been there for each other during some of life's toughest moments (and, unfortunately, this group has had its fair share).

According to British anthropologist and evolutionary psychologist Robin Dunbar's famous research on social networks, human beings are only able to nurture five close personal relationships at a time. It might be useful to identify yours, especially if you're feeling lonely, and evaluate how well you've kept up recently. If most of your contact with your true inner circle has been asynchronous or public, through social media or in large groups, try scheduling some one-on-one time, even if it needs to be virtual.

The second group of people who might cringe: introverts. According to my longtime blog editor, Hayley, "As a happy introvert, I know that introverts are inherently suspicious that people writing books about topics like 'having more fun' are just going to tell them that they should get out of the house more and do stuff with groups of people." I get it, but the fact is, social connections—and yes, fun with friends—are important for everybody. The advice even applies to introverts. It doesn't mean you have to turn every activity into a party. You may want your Fun Friend time to be in smaller groups or focused on people with whom you're already close. Hayley organizes her fun around a small, tight group of friends. Shape social interactions to fit your particular needs. But the three keys still apply: consistency, accountability, and fun. Lastly, if you are an introvert, don't let us extroverts bully you into thinking high-arousal activities are the only way to have fun. As first discussed in chapter 2, research from Dr. Jeanne Tsai, the director of the Culture and Emotion Lab at Stanford University, and others [12] has found that especially in Western cultures we're primed to believe, through marketing and social norms, that *high arousal* equals *fun* (cue the cliché Instagram influencer jumping in the air). But as Dr. Iris Mauss once told me, "This 'blind spot' can lead us to overlook paths to happiness, fulfillment, and productivity."[13] Positive emotions like peace, calm, and serenity are just as fun as anything high arousal if that's what you find pleasurable. I'll say it again, the best part about fun is it is uniquely yours to define and own.

You might also find social events focused on fun are less draining than those whose sole purpose is to yammer away. When people sign up for something activity-driven, they tend to be more accommodating of people who want to join a group but maintain some space. My brother, for example—he was introverted, but he knew he needed people, too. His solution was to join a hiking club. He loved to hike, as you might recall me relating to Jane in the previous chapter. Hiking with a group comes with an easy escape valve for introverts. If Brian wanted quiet time, he could just drift to the back. Others in the group respected that not everyone seeking camaraderie wants their ear talked off. After my brother's death, I was floored by how many people from his hiking club left messages that hinted at warm, close friendships.

And finally, let's discuss the third group: those who feel they're socially challenged. Developing relationships—particularly those you're starting from scratch—doesn't come easy to all of us. But social finesse is a skill, not a trait. Chris MacLeod, author of *The Social Skills Guidebook*, felt shy and awkward around other people until he turned things around in his mid-twenties. One tool he found helpful was Meetup.com.[14] Signing up for events there can give you a ready-made social life, one where you can practice your conversational skills in a low-pressure, activity-focused environment, surrounded by people who you know are open to making new friends. The site's online profiles make it easy to follow up with people afterward and propel friendships forward.

Finally, don't get tripped up on the idea that you're "not a people person" or "no good at small talk." This assumes that who "you" are is static—when, in fact, personality appears to be quite fluid. Consider the Big Five personality traits that psychologists say define us: extraversion, openness to experience, emotional stability (neuroticism), agreeableness, and conscientiousness. While you may have a fundamental temperament set point (and even this is debatable), researchers have found that through practice, you can change your behaviors—for example, becoming someone who feels at ease chatting with a table of new friends. You may never stop being an introvert, but with better skills, you can manage social anxiety. (If you're an introvert, you'll likely still feel drained after social events and need to recharge. *That's fine.*)

In one study, adults were able to become more extroverted or conscientious in the amazingly short period of sixteen weeks.[15] They did it by listing what they wanted to change, and what steps they could take to get there. That's a good starting place. If you want to become someone who has fun with friends, make a plan to . . . *start having fun with friends*. Pull out your Fun File, pick something, and invite someone to do it with you. Then make a list of other ways to incorporate more social fun into your life. Join a couple of meetups. Keep it going for four months and see who you are afterward. *It may surprise you.*

chapter 8

Fun and Parenting: From Bassinet to Empty Nest

On our 6 a.m. walk, my daughter asked where the moon goes each morning. I let her know it's in heaven, visiting Daddy's freedom.
—RYAN REYNOLDS

Do kids deserve an entire chapter in a book on fun? If you answer *no way*, either because you're voluntarily child-free or because—*cough*—you aren't, I hear you. I'm a father of two, and I've had my moments. All parents have. Nevertheless, I've arrived at a place where I can say with conviction that not only are kids a great source of fun, but they are also among our best teachers.

And yet: Adjacent research has found that kids can be, well, a buzzkill. Daniel Gilbert famously theorized in his book *Stumbling on Happiness* that happiness and parenting exist in an inverse relationship.[1] Children *are* the best thing in a parent's life, Gilbert told one audience at a gathering of the Association for Psychological Science in 2007, "but only because they tend to get rid of every source of joy we had before they came along."[2]

While I can't fully agree with Gilbert, I will admit that my cousin-in-law Joey and his wife, Nina, are among the happiest people I know. They resisted familial and cultural pressure to have children. Now they spend all their free hours doing what they love, which is fishing (a calm, peaceful hobby that works great with young children, for five minutes at

FUN AND PARENTING: FROM BASSINET TO EMPTY NEST

a time). Anecdotally and empirically, *not* having children is a fun option. If that's your inclination, congrats, when it comes to fun it would appear the deck is stacked in your favor.

For those who are still here: Thankfully for parents and would-be parents, more recent research has added nuance to Gilbert's conclusion. A 2016 study on the "happiness penalty" found that the culprit isn't kids themselves, but whether the parents live in a country with social programs that support working parents.[3] Or perhaps kids only make parents unhappy when they create financial struggle, as another study found.[4] As most American families know, it's hard to experience the joys of parenting when you're stretched so thin between work and home responsibilities that even an overture of play feels like it might cause the rubber band to snap. In this country, finding quality childcare is often a lonely, expensive scramble; meanwhile, we're at the mercy of our employers to decide whether becoming a parent merits increased flexibility or any other accommodation. In this harried context, it's safe to say that kids are no *surefire* recipe for happiness, or fun.

But could it be that kids aren't the primary problem anyway, but parents? Overwhelmed by the challenging demands of advanced capitalism, are we just *doing it wrong*? A team of researchers in Canada found that amongst all the beleaguered parents out there, there is one happy group that may be beating the odds. These parents report that they are deeply fulfilled by their children. Where the parents in the 2004 survey (we discussed in chapter 2) had rated time with their kids and housework as about the same amount of fun, the parents indicated in this study couldn't get enough.

What was the difference? Did these parents manage to carve out space to satisfy their own needs? Did they resurrect their passions or find some artful balance that eluded the rest of us? *No.* The defining factor of this group of parents was the opposite. What they shared was a deliberate and unwavering focus on their children's well-being. The study termed these people *child-centric*: "parents [who] are motivated to maximize their child's well-being even at a cost to their own and are willing to prioritize the allocation of their emotional, temporal, financial, and attentional resources to their children rather than themselves."[5] They put their children's needs before their own—and the result of all this selflessness wasn't less happiness but *more*.

I don't want to overplay a study that involved a relatively small sample group. Neither do I want to tackle the undeniably worthwhile question of whether a selfless life is a more satisfying life. But I'd be lying if I said I thought there was nothing to the notion of "child-centric" parenting. It resonates with what I've discovered as I've explored fun with my own family. It's key to recovering the blessing from the burden—whether with our kids, our grandkids, our nieces, our nephews, or any tiny human with whom we want to have fun and make happy memories.

Any good chapter on "fun" parenting needs a horror story, and I'm happy to take the fall. When my daughter, Sloane, was three, I had a genius idea. We would go on our first solo father-daughter road trip together to attend the Rise Festival, an annual event where thousands of people gather in a dry lake bed off Interstate 15 near Las Vegas to release floating lanterns into the night sky. I was all-in for the quasi-spiritual vibes, and my daughter would get to experience a scene from one of her favorite Disney movies, *Tangled*, which features a lantern release. It was a total win-win, and I would get a kick start on my plan to go down in history as the Most Fun Dad *Ever*.

Admittedly, the plan wasn't perfect. To get to the festival, we'd have to drive most of the night from Los Angeles, get some sleep in a roadside hotel, and then kill the better part of the day in what seemed to be our most "kid friendly" option in Vegas, the Circus Circus Hotel & Casino. When we finally left Vegas and got ourselves situated at the festival after a long walk from the parking area, it was all I had hoped it would be. The music—amazing! The sky—enormous and beautiful! Everywhere you looked, you were met by a profound feeling of collective effervescence. We threw our mats down and I settled in, prepared to vibe and soak it all in until the big release. Sloane, of course, did *her* version of fun—she went extrovert. She ran around the perimeter of our staked-out plot, stomping on our neighbors' blankets in the process, getting in the way of the delicate preparations required to release thousands of candlelit lanterns safely.

FUN AND PARENTING: FROM BASSINET TO EMPTY NEST

That was the moment I should have changed my attitude. Only one of us could reasonably control ourselves and adapt to the whims of the other, and that person was me. *The adult.* Instead, I was stubborn. I let my irritation grow minute by minute. While others were entertained by her antics, I became increasingly drained from the sense of duty to police her behavior. After a couple hours of waiting, we finally released our lantern. I sensed the awesome beauty, sure—but through a fog of frustration. To finish the scene, our lantern was barely aloft when Sloane chirped, "I want another one! I want another one!" I captured the moment on video and later shared it on Facebook, where a friend quickly razzed me, "Typical kids want more . . . Ha-ha!!"

Afterward, we were both starving and needed to eat. So did everyone else, and accordingly the concession lines were endless. (If my wife had been there, she'd have been smart enough to have brought snacks.) Finally, we were nearing the front of the line. I smelled the savory goodness of food truck cuisine. I saw the whites of the cashier's eyes. And then—I heard Sloane's little voice: "Papa, I need to go pee." Inwardly, I groaned. When I looked down, her eyes told me it was serious. Normally I would have bailed out of the line. But because of how everything had transpired up until that point—the fact that things hadn't broken the way I'd planned, the fatigue from the long drive, the need to eat, and the feeling that we were trapped in an impossible situation—I said the tragic words: "Just. Hold. It."

I'm sure you see what's coming a mile away. She peed her pants, moments before it became our turn to order. Thankfully, she wasn't too upset. If anything, she was indignant. I was the upset one, because I suddenly saw the truth. I wasn't the *Most Fun Dad Ever*; I was the *Worst Dad Ever*.

I had broken what I now recognize as the two cardinal rules of having fun with children: First, **follow their lead.** Time with children needs to be child-centric, and a slew of doctors and child psychologists back me on this. We have to meet children where they are—and that means embracing *play* wholeheartedly. If you're an adult with a fun-for-fun's sake deficit, it is likely that play does not come easy to you. But trying to squelch the play out of children is not just developmentally inappropriate, it's a recipe for disaster. Play may be typically seen as the wheelhouse of young children, but it's also a great way to connect with tweens and teenagers. The trick is to find a way to be more than a spectator in your child's fun. I can remember hearing some of my friends at college talk about their fathers playing video games with them or taking them to the golf course. They were inevitably the kids who went home during holiday breaks, instead of staying on campus. (And just as it is with small children, it really doesn't work if you don't let them take the lead.)

But there's also a second, less well-known rule of parenting: **Play isn't play if you're not both having fun.** I broke that rule, too. I created a situation where I put Sloane's fun and my fun at odds with each other, ruining it for both of us. That was my mistake—because while the two rules may seem in paradox, they're not. At least, they don't have to be. This chapter is all about setting the conditions to make both possible.

In the line for our food, my daughter's pants soaked, I took a deep breath. Sloane agreed we should get our food, so we did. Then I began to make amends. I gave her a big hug and hoisted her wet little body onto my shoulders so she wouldn't have to walk the uncomfortable two and a half miles back to our car. It was a bonding moment for both of us, as we ate and relished the experience on the long walk back. And so my fondest memory of the Rise Festival isn't the festival itself, it is instead walking back to the parking lot, saturating my shoulders in my daughter's urine, and sharing some subpar French fries. And despite the challenges, we both remember the event as a lot of fun.

Prepare to Course Correct

If you're a parent, you may already be familiar with the science and reasoning behind the advice to let children lead in play. Play is generally defined as "an activity that is intrinsically motivated, entails active engagement, and results in joyful discovery."[6] Play is voluntary, fun, and often spontaneous. Research suggests that when adults fail to let children lead, instead directing play—e.g., "it's better to do it *this* way"—it limits children's joyful discovery, and play's developmental benefits are minimized. Play often ceases to be playful when it gets an extrinsic push. In one experiment led by Dr. Elizabeth Bonawitz, in the psychology department of the University of California at Berkeley, preschoolers who were told a function of a toy, focused mainly on that function. Meanwhile, those kids who received no instructions explored and discovered other ways to have fun with it.[7] More broadly, so called "child-led play" empowers kids, keeps them engaged, and allows them to express their full creativity. *All very important!*

The trouble is many parents have taken this message to the extreme. When their kid says jump, they say how high. They don't express preferences. And so the parent finds themselves on, say, their thirteenth game of Candyland, taking orders from a tiny tyrant whose demands never stop and who is a very poor loser. As a result, the parent dreads playtime and checks out, constantly sneaking glances at their phone. Or they avoid it outright. Neither is good for either party's fun.

If that experience sounds familiar to you, a corrective is desperately needed, hence the importance of our second rule: *Play isn't play unless you're both having fun.* The insight comes from Professor Peter Gray,[8] one of many psychologists who emphasize the importance of play in children's emotional and intellectual development. As such, he's also taken on the pressing question of how to make playtime more fun for parents.

As Gray sees it, reaping the benefits of play for both parents and children requires negotiation and compromise. Look to your child for direction, but don't be afraid to cocreate playtime so that you're doing something you both enjoy. After all, if your child were playing with a friend, their friend wouldn't be shy about letting their desires be known.

Hardly Strictly Bluegrass Festival, San Francisco, California, 10/2/2016

After having a year to recover from the Rise debacle with Sloane, I decided to take my son, Archer, then one and a half, to the Hardly Strictly Bluegrass Festival. I was choosing the activity, again—but this time, I committed to enjoying the event on his terms. He was a toddler, so we toddled. We never stayed still. As a result, I didn't get to do everything I wanted, but I also did some things I didn't expect to. Letting him roam freely meant we engaged with a lot of interesting people who got a kick out of his toddler enthusiasm, for anything and everything. I came home feeling happy that we got to hear some great music and that I had given my son a great experience, heart filled with the realization that his presence had made the festival even more awesome. Choosing to center the day on him, in the context of an experience I had chosen and knew I'd enjoy, proved to be the sweet spot for memorable fun and meaningful bonding.

Fun, you might recall, requires autonomy. And maybe that's the real takeaway of that child-centric parenting study—that what set those parents apart wasn't so much their selflessness, but their *self-direction*. They consciously chose to prioritize their children, making every interaction with them an expression of their own desire, whatever the activity.

Take the Pressure Off

Does the idea of cocreating, or expressing your own preferences to your child, make you feel nervous, guilty, or selfish? Perhaps you'll feel better knowing that your anxieties are the product of a very modern lens on how to be a parent. A coworker recently told me she was fatigued from seemingly endless hours of what she perceived as obligatory play with her young son. Needless to say, she wasn't having fun. The comedian Maz Jobrani has a great bit about the tyranny of modern parenting research and expectations, which result in you singing and dancing a ninety-minute Broadway show every night to get your child to brush their teeth and clean their room.[9]

Jobrani and my coworker, it seems, are both feeling the sometimes frustrating constraint of what anthropologist David Lancy of Utah State University calls "the modern neontocracy"[10]—in which children dictate the lives of adults.

With anthropology as his guide, Lancy argues that the entire idea of playing with your child—whatever that looks like—is uniquely modern and Western. Far from a fundamental of raising children, it's a privilege earned by rich, industrialized, educated societies. Most of the world, for most of time, has seen parents' chief responsibility as loving and protecting, not serving as twenty-four-hour playmates or surrogate "BFFs." In centuries past—or even decades past—grown-ups did grown-up things while children played with other children. Lancy calls this hands-off approach *benign neglect* and sees some benefits—for example, preventing the emergence of "kidults." Benign neglect has made a comeback in recent years in the form of the free-range parenting movement, in which some renegade parents allow their children a greater degree of independence, earlier, to build resilience, confidence, and capability. And, in fact, elsewhere in the world, behavior that many Americans would call neglect—for example, not knowing where your elementary-age son goes after school or sending your children to the playground alone—is still normative behavior.[11]

I share this point of view not to argue for it, but to suggest that it can help bring our expectations back into balance. I want to relieve you of the feeling that playtime is an obligation—which, as we know, rapidly squelches autonomy-loving fun. Somewhere between casting your six-year-old out into the street with a baseball bat to fend for themselves and never leaving their side, lies a happy medium. If you're killing yourself trying to spend every moment you can bonding with your child, you can ease up. Play with them, but also let them spend time doing their own thing. My coworker ultimately realized that she could spend quality time with her son while encouraging him to make his own play. They finally started to enjoy the summer weather in their backyard—him engaging in solo water play with the hose, her reading a book.

Once you take the pressure off yourself, you may start to see playing with your children for what it actually is: a voluntary choice, not an obligatory burden. A privilege, even. That mental shift alone can be transformative. A relief from duty and an invitation to actually have fun.

Recognizing that play with our children benefits us as much as them isn't just mind games—it's what the science tells us. Michael W. Yogman, M.D., assistant professor of pediatrics at Harvard Medical School, is an authoritative voice in behavioral health. Dr. Yogman's research highlights the value of play for parents; namely, rejuvenation and a comforting reconnection to their own childhoods.[12] It's also a great way to have a more satisfying relationship with your child: to get to know them better, to see the world from their perspective, and to enjoy their individuality and sense of humor. Further research also indicates that playing pretend with your child or reading together can reduce parental stress and improve parent-child interactions.[13]

As parents, *we're so hard on ourselves*, which is of little surprise given the pressure of a parenting culture that can make you feel like you're failing if you're not providing live, Muppet-level entertainment to your children every waking moment. The more we cast aside those expectations,

FUN AND PARENTING: FROM BASSINET TO EMPTY NEST

the more our children's requests to play become welcome invitations for delight.

Become a Better Player

There's more to many parents' resistance to play than the weight of obligation. Otherwise, hearing the words "Will you play with me?" wouldn't be right up there with "I think I accidentally wet the bed," at times. The truth is, there's a reason we're not that interested in the unstructured play that children love: Our play muscles have atrophied. Just as the experience of a game like tennis improves when we build muscle and increase our skill and comfort on the court, so it is with play. Many parents are rusty. Remember my experience watching parents befuddled by pool noodles in the children's museum? These parents certainly weren't unique in their confused resistance to a free-play environment. Well-meaning attempts to guide our child in game play all too often end the fun. Stephanie Shine, assistant professor at Texas Tech University, and her coauthor Teresa Y. Acosta observed similar scenes at the Austin Children's Museum (now known as Thinkery). Rather than following their kids' lead and jumping into play, parents tended to prompt and observe. Shine and Acosta found that parents were often too concerned about what their children would learn, so they didn't relax and immerse themselves in an imaginary scenario. They wanted to guide kids toward "real life experience" and prosocial behaviors, so they made suggestions, narrated, explained, taught, and structured.[14]

Just as many of us adults lose the ability to enjoy fun for fun's sake, so it goes with play. We try to impose meaning on play or force it (and our children) to serve our understanding of reality. We can be tyrants ourselves, burdening play with our grown-up priorities—say, to keep things neat, or to provide dictated learning experiences.

Not only does play suffer when we lose our ability to engage with the world in a childlike manner. *We* suffer. That insight comes from the paradigm-shifting psychoanalyst Eric Berne, who developed a behavioral change method called transactional analysis in the 1950s. Berne summed up all adult human behavior as emerging from one of three possible ego-states: the Parent, the Adult, and the Child. This "ego-state model" helps explain how people behave and relate to one another. In the Parent state, we mimic our parents' (or an influential figure's) reactions that we have experienced in the past. For example, we scold someone, or shout to get our way (if that was the pattern in our family). But the Parent state isn't necessarily negative; it's also the state that ensures that we act in a morally acceptable way and follow society's rules.

The Child state returns us to the way we behaved, felt, and thought as children. For instance, if we get a negative evaluation at work, we might cry or lash out in a tantrum. The Child state also has positive implications. According to Berne, this ego-state is the source of our emotions, creativity, recreation preferences, spontaneity, and intimacy.

Finally, the Adult state develops as we mature, and helps us process information and see reality through a filtered lens.

According to Berne, the way we communicate with each other depends on our current ego-state. For instance, it's not uncommon to see a married couple that talks to each other as if one were a child and the other one the parent. Our ego-states affect the way we interact; Berne talks about "transactions" between people. Even as equal adults, we don't always relate to each other as adults. Berne considers unproductive transactions as problems within the ego-states.

Although the Adult is seen as the most mature of the three states, Berne is clear that we need all three of them. A well-functioning person needs to be able to separate the three, however, and recognize when a state isn't serving us, or alternatively, when we've suppressed a state that we need. Operating from only one ego-state would make us incomplete.

For instance, Dr. Thomas A. Harris, Berne's friend who wrote the self-help classic *I'm OK—You're OK*[15] based on transactional analysis, argues that a person who blocks the Child state will likely not enjoy life. Partly, because to really enjoy play, we need access to our Child ego-state. The Child ego-state also releases the emotions and creativity that aren't bound by our thirst for sense-making. If, in contrast, we are always relating as the Parent during play (directing, controlling, suggesting), we're less able to let loose and enjoy the interaction, and the same goes for our kids. Being in the Parent ego-state can be appropriate in many situations, but it's a wet blanket at playtime. *What's the fun in that?*

While the word *play* might not light up your insides yet, how does *liberation* sound—liberation from the dull conformity of the adult world. Reconceive play with children as a beautiful and rare opportunity to stop worrying about how you look and what others think. Kids are among the cherished few who won't judge you for being kooky, wacky, or nutty. In fact, much of the time, they're wishing you were all three.

Try One or More of These Strategies to Support Flexing Your Play Muscles

Develop a transition ritual. In *The Alter Ego Effect*,[16] Todd Herman includes a story about a father who was in the military. This dad really struggled with his children; his impression was that they didn't like him. Working with Herman, the dad came to see that he was playing the same role at home as he played at work: drill sergeant! No wonder his kids didn't enjoy his company. Many of us working parents suffer from a similar problem when we return to our families after a day on the job: We have left work behind physically, but we haven't really left work behind mentally. During time reserved for the family, we're still churning on problems of the day, and checking in via our mobile devices. We might even walk through the door on a call. How we connect with our children improves dramatically if we instead have a clean transition between our work role and our family role. Some therapists use what they call a *transition ritual* between clients, so that they show up for each one present and open. You can use the same tool. Before you walk in your home's front door (or leave your home office, if you work from home), take a quiet moment to center yourself and mentally switch roles. You might even want to take a few deep breaths to clear your head before entering the house. Sometimes I'll turn my ball cap around backward. My wife's friend lives by her work calendar so methodically that her cue is Outlook literally alerting her at 6 p.m. that it is "family time."

Practice story editing. Don't get stuck on the notion that dedicated playtime is the best or only way to have fun. Instead of pressuring yourself to create "quality time" or enrichment, edit your story to create playful fun in everyday life. Inject some silliness into chores together or turn dinner into game night. We've had great success with this in my family. For example, at one point we had come to think of the twenty minutes before everyone left for school as one of the worst parts of our day. To beat the ticking clock, my wife and I had effectively banned fun. We were completely task focused and impatient with the kids, who only became more adversarial as a response. In adults vs. kids, there are rarely winners. Finally, my wife and I decided to edit the story. We would turn getting ready into a game. The first step was to start the "getting ready" part of the morning a bit earlier, so that it was no longer a mad, stressful dash. Then we mixed up the environment and injected silliness into the routine to change the energy and mood. Objective reality did not change. I'm not going to embellish and say the kids got ready any faster. But subjective reality certainly did. We got out the door around the same time each morning all a heck of a lot happier. It's not bulletproof. We still have mornings where things go off the rails, but now we have more enjoyable mornings than not, simply by having a bias toward fun—a welcome change. (**Pro tip:** As long as you're okay with childish humor, start your kid's morning with kid-friendly songs from Matt Farley's the Toilet Bowl Cleaners. In my experience, it works better for boys than girls.)

Destress learning. To help her six-year-old grandson confront challenges with a playful spirit, Susanne Cook-Greuter invented a game called *Missed*. When something doesn't go right, she doesn't correct or admonish him. They celebrate it: "Hooray, missed!" "The learning opportunity becomes fun rather than this pressure to have it done right," she told me.[17] Adults, unlike children, have a well-developed Judgment Habit, notes Dr. Cook-Greuter. We judge experiences reflexively through the lenses of language and culture. Many of us have been conditioned to believe that there's nothing more important than getting the right answer, because our parents and teachers rewarded it in the past. If we rewrite the rules, celebrating both the hits and the misses, we free children to follow their curiosity without fear of judgment.

Get physical. Physical activities such as wrestling and rough-and-tumble play can also be developmentally beneficial. Dr. Yogman (the Harvard professor introduced a couple sections back) notes that such play can give children many useful experiences, from improved agility to taking risks and learning about boundaries and empathy.[18]

Studies also show that when parents play and interact with their children, oxytocin gets released—that's the hormone first name-dropped in chapter 1 that promotes social bonding and empathy. An Israeli study, for example, found that fathers' oxytocin levels increase when they have playful interaction with their kids.[19] In this playful state, the research shows, there is an immense amount of positive mutual exchange, uplifting the well-being of both parent and child. Rambunctious, rough-and-tumble play isn't every parent's cup of tea; 70 percent of the time, it's fathers who engage in this kind of play, according to one of Dr. Yogman's studies.[20]

In my house I love to blast music with my kids and race them around the house in a game we call *Tickle Monster*. My wife and I have an agreement: I keep the chaos to one floor, so she can go upstairs, shut her door, and enjoy some peace and quiet while we're given a temporary hall pass to be lawless. The ice packs and superglue are applied before she comes downstairs, so our antics have little impact on her desire for order.

Relish *Their* Play. When you can't play anymore, take a break by watching your child play. In *Savoring*, Fred Bryant writes, "Untapped ways to enhance savoring include becoming more childlike, humorous, or aware of coparticipants' joy."[21] Passively watching your child might also help you warm up to your child's approach to play, in the same way that being around a friend who enjoys cycling can "rub off" on you over time, as we discussed in chapter 7. It can also be a huge win for the child being watched. Bruce E. Brown and Rob Miller of Proactive Coaching LLC conducted an informal study, asking hundreds of college athletes to think back to what their parents had said to them that had amplified their joy during and after sports games when they were kids. Overwhelmingly, their response was, "I love to watch you play." Author Rachel Macy Stafford wrote what became a viral blog post[22] about the deep and immediate emotional impact those words had on her daughters, initially spoken after swim meets and ukulele lessons. The impact was twofold: Watching her children perform with those words in mind heightened her own joy, and then hearing her say the words heightened theirs.

The Trouble with Toys

You're possibly already familiar with the abundant research showing that experiences make people happier than possessions. You can apply the same wisdom when it comes to boosting your family fun factor: Skip the toy aisle in favor of creating memories together.

I used to travel every six to eight weeks for work. Early on, I followed the advice someone had given me to sweeten the bum deal for the kids by bringing back a present each time I returned home. The concept seemed reasonable on paper. It reduced the kids' apprehension of me leaving and increased their excitement of my return. The first couple of times it worked as intended, my kids were super excited to see me—and then also happy with whatever toy I offered. It was fun for all of us. But as the months passed, their excitement became more about the toy than about my return. Their desires for the external reward associated with my return also grew sophisticated over time, with them telling me in advance what they wanted with the help of Amazon research. Finally, things flew off the rails completely when I came home with Caitlin (a streamlined engine from the world of Thomas the Train) for my son. He frowned, dropped his shoulders in disgust, and told me it wasn't what he had asked for. (He had asked for a more expensive Caitlin, a model with an additional axle. *He was three!*)

The hedonic treadmill once again rears its ugly head! Kids are as susceptible to it as adults, particularly when it comes to material possessions. As soon as they get one thing, they want the next—bigger, shinier, different. Soon every room of your house looks like a landfill, which is exactly where all that stuff is going, eventually. Having more toys doesn't mean better quality play for your child. A recent study at the University of Toledo found that when a toddler is given four toys to play with, they'll play with each toy longer and more creatively than if they're given sixteen toys.[23]

FUN AND PARENTING: FROM BASSINET TO EMPTY NEST

There's more at play than hedonic adaptation when it comes to the superiority of experiences in providing lasting, meaningful fun. The degree to which we enjoy a thing—whether it be an experience or a new car—is enhanced by the degree to which we're able to relish it after the fact. Discussing the phenomenon in *Savoring*, Fred Bryant and Joseph Veroff quote French writer François de La Rochefoucauld to simplify what they found when they looked closely at the role of savoring in happiness: "Happiness does not consist in things themselves but in the relish we have of them."[24] This is true for experiences as much as for gifts—both are enhanced by our ability to relish them afterward. But while children burn through gifts, experiences create rich and indelible memories that provide fun when we reminisce about them, long after the event has ended. Better yet, shared experiences have the added bonus of strengthening your relationship every time one of you says, "Remember that one time when . . ." and you reminisce about the memory together.

In my case, I didn't cut off the toy spigot entirely. I shifted to experiential gifts—puzzles and games, or toys that we can assemble together. My arrival at home now signifies the opportunity for a novel and fun family activity, and we all enjoy it. And the games get used a lot more, and longer, than the toys ever did.

Hall of Fun: Caine's Arcade

If you need more proof that children don't need toys—or adults—to have fun, check out Caine's Arcade. In 2012, Caine Monroy was nine years old and facing a summer vacation spent kicking around his father's auto parts store in East L.A. There weren't a lot of toys at the store, but there were a ton of empty cardboard boxes. In Caine's creative hands, those boxes became the makings of an elaborate arcade. Game by game, the arcade took over the store. Caine built a claw machine, a basketball game, a soccer game, and dozens of others. He made tickets, business cards, and a staff T-shirt. Customers were hard to come by—until one day a film-

> maker walked into the store and became the first customer to buy a 500-game fun pass. Nirvan Mullick spread the news of Caine's achievement via Facebook—and with the help of Caine's dad, surprised the arcade creator with a flashmob of excited customers. The story became a viral news sensation and Caine's fans raised $242,000 for a scholarship fund. Caine ran the arcade for two years, delighting thousands of customers, before "retiring" to junior high school. To see it yourself, check out the short film *Caine's Arcade* (or learn more by visiting https://share.michaelrucker.com/caines-arcade).

The Fun-With-Kids File

As we already know, increasing our options increases our likelihood of fun. If you have children, it behooves you to have some fun ideas in your Fun File for your kids as well. Here's some ideas to get you started:

- Take a class together, of their choosing
- Grow a pizza garden together, with all the herbs and vegetables you like on a pizza
- Scour Meetup.com for events and clubs you might both enjoy
- Attend a free community concert
- Volunteer together, for example to clean up a local beach or park
- Make short films with your smartphone, re-creating scenes from your favorite movies
- Visit an experience museum, such as the Sloomoo Institute in New York
- Have a game night: puzzles, board games, or charades
- Take a hike or spend time in nature
- Build things together or attend a Maker Faire

FUN AND PARENTING: FROM BASSINET TO EMPTY NEST

You Time Is Still a Thing

No matter how "good" you get at calling forth your inner child, no matter how satisfying the interactions, face it: You also need time off, time when you're not actively parenting. Time doing exactly what *you* want to do. Most of us developed our preferences for fun twenty, thirty, or forty years before we had children. Centering our lives around our families doesn't mean we throw all that out the window, or, per Gilbert, "get rid of every source of joy we had before they came along." It *can't* mean that. If we empty ourselves of everything that came before, what's left won't stand on its own, let alone provide the strength needed to be a great parent and partner.

The key is finding ways to fit old passions into a new lifestyle. Adapting your favorite activities to include your kids is a great approach, but not always the best one. Sometimes it's more rejuvenating—and more fun—to reconnect with the "before" version of yourself. Give yourself space to rock out, or renew, whatever fun is for you.

A friend of mine did that literally. If you google *Darren Pujalet*, you'll find pictures of a well-groomed real estate agent in conservative Manhattan Beach, California. But if you google *Darren Pujalet—drummer*, you'll get a very different search result. You'll find tons of references to a drummer in the jam band Particle, one that played world-famous music festivals such as Bonnaroo in Tennessee and Coachella in California. It's the same Darren Pujalet. One is Darren before kids, one is Darren after.

As a drummer, he had played 1,300 shows in ten years across ten countries. For Darren, for various reasons, being a touring musician was incompatible with having a family, so he ultimately left the band. Unfortunately, leaving the band meant giving up the thing that lit him up more than anything else in life (other than being a husband and a dad, of course): playing in front of a live audience of high-energy fans.

While Darren's story is extreme, many parents feel a sense of loss, and a splintering of identities, as they adapt to new responsibilities. Darren became very successful in a new career he enjoyed, and he loved his family. Nevertheless, over time, the trade-off wore on him. Parenting began to feel like drudgery. He thought he had abandoned his old life, but, in fact, it was casting a dark shadow over everything else. Fearing that he was nearing a breakdown, he finally sat down with his wife. "I need to start drumming again," he told her. Together, they came to see that his two selves—drummer and dad—weren't as incompatible as it had once seemed. Sure, he couldn't be a full-time musician, but he could still play music and even perform. With his wife's support, Darren started to reconnect with his old bandmates, indicating that he was keen to play in one-off gigs. Soon, he was traveling back on the stage, carrying the energy of those gigs into every other interaction he had. Because he felt more like himself, enjoying time at home with his family became rejuvenating instead of depleting. And in those moments when caring for small humans began to feel Agonizing—we all have them—he had more strength and patience to carry on, with love.

It's important to bring up again the data suggesting that although we modern dads continue to improve our contribution of sharing parental duties when compared to previous generations, the balance of opportunities for leisure still favors fathers (specifically those in heterosexual partnerships). No matter what type of family partnership, the goal should be keeping opportunities for fun equitable. For instance, Darren supports his wife's passion for yoga, taking over parental duties during times she needs a reprieve, which sometimes includes yoga retreats away from home.

If you have a spouse, make it a point to support them—and ask the same of them. If you are a single parent, you may feel like taking time for yourself is impossible. But you almost certainly have friends who would act as surrogate aunties and uncles while you're away; some might even be willing to sign up for a regular gig so that you can make indulging your passions a habit, rather than a black swan event.

You time is so important—and for parents who are married or have partners, so is *us time*—time to relax and reconnect with each other, away from domestic life. If you do nothing else after reading this chapter, sit down with your partner and schedule a date night in the near future.

Then, find another family to swap childcare with. Don't be shy: Tell them the date you'd like to go out, then suggest three dates when you could reciprocate. Babysitters are great, but they're expensive, and the cost puts a lot of pressure on your evening. Plus, agreeing to a childcare exchange is a great way to build a closer relationship with another family while creating some (literal) free time for grown-up fun.

The Long View

For most of us, families are a lifetime commitment. That doesn't mean they don't change dramatically over the years. What was fun a year ago might not look the same next year, let alone a decade later. This is more obvious when it comes to little kids, but it can be harder to keep up with as parents and children age. From the independence desired by most teenagers, to the warranted angst of the sandwich generation, to the loneliness and grief felt when the nest goes empty, there is truth in the expression, "the days are long, but the years are short." If your relationships with your partner or children aren't what you'd like them to be, now is a great time to start doing things differently. It is up to us to seize opportunities for reinvention—to throw out the old Fun File, as it were, and start fresh.

Cindy Myers, fifty-seven, and her husband, Mike, sixty-nine, together experienced the profound and unexpected joy that can greet us if we have the courage to make big changes. For thirty-five years, since she was in high school, Cindy had been living in a town called Ridgecrest, California. Ridgecrest is an isolated, conservative community where most residents work for the government. Cindy and Mike both had good government jobs that afforded them a nice home, as well as resources to travel—and yet Ridgecrest was like a glove that never quite fit. Still, they stayed put, stuck in the security of the status quo, despite an uneasy feeling that life wasn't as satisfying as it could be. They stayed "mostly out of obligation and a lot of fear," Cindy told me. Her daughter and her daughter's children, and Cindy's mother and ninety-eight-year-old grandmother, all lived in Ridgecrest. That made it even harder to leave.

Over the years, the close proximity of her family had helped keep Cindy from feeling lonely when Mike was traveling.

In the years following Mike's retirement at sixty-four, their situation changed. Mike had been an extremely active physical thrill seeker all his life, and it had begun to take its toll. Gradually he had to stop doing some of the things he loved, like rock climbing the Sierras. One passion that Mike's health still allowed for was boating—but Ridgecrest was landlocked. Cindy and Mike decided that the answer was to uproot themselves from the home they had lived in all those years and move to the Pacific Coast. Says Cindy, "My personality was not very open to change. *Ever.* And I didn't have a lot of confidence about who I was or what I wanted in life. But finally, the clock just said, *Get your shit together or else you're going to miss it all.* I knew it was either now or never. So, we powered through."

They faced their fears one by one. Some of them proved unfounded. One was that they'd have to leave their grandkids. Instead, once they shared their plans, they learned that their daughter and son-in-law were interested in a parallel move. Also daunting was downsizing decades of belongings from a large house—but it was undoubtedly worthwhile. "I can't tell you how freeing it was to finally settle down and realize that we weren't encumbered with all of that crap," Cindy says.

Finally, they made the big move, from Ridgecrest to the Puget Sound on the coast of Washington. Now, fun in their life has an entirely different landscape: Cindy wakes up every morning to a view of the Cascade Mountains, and enjoys watching the dolphins and sea otters play. Extroverted Mike, meanwhile, has found a whole new community of friends and fellow adventurers on the docks. Because Cindy is an artist who had a home studio in Ridgecrest, she initially thought she'd spend all her time once they moved in the neighboring Port Townsend, where many artists have studios and galleries. Instead, she has found she is most excited to simply explore her new territory. "Every road I take is a new adventure. I don't know anything about this place, so it's fun," she told me. She and Mike also spend plenty of time together on their boat, a cabin cruiser—"basically an RV on the water"—exploring new horizons and ports nearby.

FUN AND PARENTING: FROM BASSINET TO EMPTY NEST

Cindy doesn't just feel renewed, she actually feels like she's a different, and better, person than she was before the move. She feels calmer and more relaxed, and more confident in what she thinks and feels. Best of all, she has a better relationship with her family. Her daughter found a place twenty-five minutes away, a distance Cindy calls, "a blessing in surprise." They now see each other once a week, forcing them to be more intentional with their time together and giving Cindy the space she needed to set up her own life in retirement. Her relationship with Mike has also changed in surprising ways. After so many years of them both working, "the first year was pretty rough, just us getting to know each other once again." But now Cindy and Mike have built a new, closer relationship—all afforded by the chance to start over in a new place, rebuilding all their old routines from scratch, while still enjoying the heck out of their grandchildren with the benefit of an expanded purview.

chapter 9

Bring Your Fun Habit to Work

*If your boss is getting you down,
look at him through the prongs of a
fork and imagine him in jail.*
—RICKY GERVAIS

Set aside all the typical ways employers may have pitched you on "fun at work" in the past. Forget, at least for now, the awkward happy hours, the free pizza, or the contrived company-sponsored social events. Throw out the birthday cakes, the Ping-Pong tables, and the giant jars of M&Ms. Ditch the kooky sock contests. Throw out the "fun culture," the casual Friday, the freedom to "be yourself." The tiny desk concerts. (Okay, maybe keep those.)

Also set aside the idea that fun at work must rest on "pursuing your passion" or achieving your fondest ambition. Go ahead and give up on the popular notion (*for at least a minute*) that work can or should be pleasurable.

Nothing is wrong with all that stuff. I like Ping-Pong. But manufactured fun at work typically suffers from three things. One, it's forced, and that's never fun. Two, it's one-size-fits-all. And three, no matter how it's packaged and sold to you, it's still work (e.g., there is an argument to be made that the office Ping-Pong table is really just there to keep you at work). And yet, if you can swing it, there is tremendous benefit to blending actual fun, recognizably different from productivity, into your workday. Fun doesn't distract us from work, as was long thought. It helps us get the work done. Science supports the idea that everyday enjoyment helps us accomplish long-term goals; the fun stuff makes the hard stuff easier. Drs. Kaitlin Woolley and Ayelet Fishbach are two researchers who have repeatedly demonstrated these links. In one research project on academic achievement and study time, they showed that bundling fun elements with the act of studying increased persistence in schoolwork among high school students.[1] Their studies have also revealed that people tend to underestimate the power of short-term rewards—and even if we go into an activity motivated by a delayed reward, an immediate reward is often more motivating.[2]

But let's not get confused about what an employee's workday is for: productive, often demanding, labor in exchange for pay. I lived through the dot-com era, that brief, confused moment when tech companies thought work was about who could throw the biggest parties and buy the nicest chairs, and we all know how that ended. Yes: Work is, well, *work!* Meanwhile, the vast majority of us need to work to survive, and—depending on the economic environment—we may not always have our pick of opportunities. Given these realities, we have to look at what fun means in this context a little bit differently. We need to do more than shoehorn in ad hoc leisure activities or install tropical Zoom backgrounds.

Here's your new measure of success for bringing your Fun Habit to work. Ask yourself:

Am I finishing the day on time and energized?

When you can answer yes, I guarantee you'll not only be kicking ass at work, you'll also likely be maximizing the fun potential of each and every day. (And if you don't finish your workday at all, we have to solve that problem, too. Burnout is a real challenge for so many people, in our always-on, "give 110 percent" professional climate.) What we want to avoid at all costs is the kind of work life where you faceplant into your couch at the end of the day, too drained to enjoy yourself in the hours you're not working.

Let's start with a radical proposition, for anyone who feels that professional success defines their self-worth: Can you take your work less seriously?

For many, it's not easy. Simply finding and keeping a job, any job, that pays well enough to live comfortably is an inherently serious challenge. And beyond financial security, the old Protestant work ethic might raise its ugly head. The deeply ingrained belief that work defines our identity, materially and spiritually, affects people who work in big offices with multiple bosses and HR managers, as much as it does entrepreneurs and solopreneurs.

Would it make it any easier if I told you that engaging with your work more playfully could have a powerful effect not just on your energy, but on your performance? I'm not talking about how you present yourself at work; taking on a more playful persona might benefit some but backfire for many—for example, those at the early stages of their career seeking to establish credibility and capability. I'm talking about the mental game of how you approach and execute the tasks of your job. In the 1970s, Donald MacKinnon produced some groundbreaking research studying successful people considered the most creative in their fields. MacKinnon wanted to know if some inborn trait, like high IQ, set these people apart. As it turned out, it wasn't an inherent trait. What he found was that they had developed a "way of operating" that allowed them *to engage with work as play.* He didn't call it a Fun Habit, but that, in essence, is what it was—just applied to work. And because they had this habit, their work output was more interesting, and they were more invested in it.

You, too, can develop a new way of operating at work—whether work is in a corner office or the corner of your bedroom—that allows your Fun Habit to flourish. The timing is great, since technology, despite its challenges, has brought unparalleled flexibility to the world of work. Every day, fewer and fewer employees go to an office. Many workplaces have gone remote or allow employees to float, with flextime increasingly accepted. Many other workers are freelancers, lone wolves who step into and out of teams, or gig economy workers. We've gone from kooky sock contests to working in our pajama bottoms. Even for those workers whose jobs are tied to a physical space, this shift toward increased autonomy and choice is bound to have an effect. There's no better time to be bold in designing our attitude and approach to our working lives.

BRING YOUR FUN HABIT TO WORK

Fun at Work's Secret Ingredient

In 2020, Drs. Erik Gonzalez-Mulé and Bethany S. Cockburn released an intriguing study called "This Job Is (Literally) Killing Me."[3] The researchers sought links between work and mortality—in other words, they wanted to know what kind of conditions on the job might tax your physical and mental health to the point of increased risk of death. You might guess that demanding, and therefore high-stress, jobs were the killers. Not the case. In fact, under certain circumstances, demanding jobs were linked to *better* health outcomes. What twenty years of health data across more than three thousand workers revealed was that your stressful job is more likely to kill you when it is also *lacking in autonomy*.

Human beings crave autonomy. We need autonomy. People think of professional ambition as being driven by the desire for power—but it's a mistake to think the ambitious want power over others. As a review of nine studies by researchers from the University of Cologne, the University of Groningen, and Columbia University concluded, "People desire power not to be a master over others, but to be master of their own domain, to control their own fate."[4] Further, autonomy plays a central role in motivation. Self-determination theory,[5] developed by Dr. Richard M. Ryan and Dr. Edward L. Deci from extensive research, suggests that both motivation and learning peak when we're fulfilling three basic human needs: autonomy, competence, and relatedness (i.e., a feeling of connectedness that is absent of ulterior motives).

When we have greater control over our work, we're healthier, we're more motivated—and there's yet one more major benefit. Perhaps most importantly for our Fun Habit, we come home less likely to be drained of energy and inspiration. Self-determination theory goes beyond simple motivation and learning and is, in fact, the key to vitality—our lust for life. When our needs for relatedness, competence, and autonomy aren't satisfied, we feel used up and empty.

What all this points to is yet another reason why we've mentally divorced work from fun: During those forty (or likely more) hours of your life, someone else is telling you where to be, what to do, and maybe even how to do it. If you're someone who feels like your job or work is not any fun, ask yourself:

- Do I feel a sense of autonomy during the workday?
- How often does my job make me feel competent?
- Who at work do I relate and get along with?
- Can I freely express my opinions and ideas?
- Am I aptly applying my greatest skills and talents? Why or why not?
- How often (and to what degree) do I feel camaraderie connected to my work?
- What are the satisfying areas of my work I can celebrate?
- Are there opportunities where I can learn and engage further, that I will likely find fun and interesting?

Then troubleshoot from there. For now, let's focus on shifting the lever on autonomy. Technology has provided opportunities to retake autonomy that past generations of workers never had: the ability to work from home, or from a beach in Bali; the ability to communicate asynchronously, via a variety of devices; the ability to provide services such as therapy, training, and coaching remotely. The COVID-19 pandemic accelerated these trends, leading many companies to do what may have previously seemed impossible: find ways to keep business moving full-steam ahead with 100 percent remote workforces. Employees who never thought they'd be free from the cubicle were suddenly retrofitting their apartments into the corner office. We may now be responsible for more work than ever, with painfully blurred boundaries, but at least we have the trade-off of increased flexibility.

Meanwhile, thanks to research, such as the studies mentioned here, managers—at least, the good ones—are awakening to the benefits of putting as much control into the hands of workers as possible. This isn't only true of knowledge workers. Workplaces such as hospitals and factories are finding that problems are more quickly surfaced and resolved when they move away from command-and-control policies to empower the front line.

Whatever kind of job you have, you are likely in a position to increase your autonomy. You might just need to be proactive about it.

Strategy One: Retake Your Break

Work breaks aren't just a pause in your work tasks. They are your chance for total autonomy during that time . . . *if* you resist the social pressure to drift into idle watercooler chatter. Relatedness (connecting with others) and autonomy are both linked to vitality. And yet, it turns out that using your breaks to enjoy autonomy is far more important to your well-being than using them to socialize. This was the conclusion of John Trougakos and his colleagues, who found that **relaxing activities that provide opportunities for high autonomy during lunch are the best way to recover from work stress.**[6] They speculated that this is because socializing at work requires self-regulation—carefully controlling your behavior—which is often enervating rather than relaxing. After all, you can't guarantee that hanging with colleagues will produce feelings of relatedness; autonomy, however, is fully in your hands to enjoy.

In the studied group, it was not so important what people did during the lunch break, but the fact that they chose it themselves. In other words, the watercooler is a perfectly fine *choice*, if that's a fun, restorative activity for you. Even working through a lunch break turned out well for those in the study that had done so *by choice*. Also, having lunch with your two best friends might differ from having lunch with a random coworker. In the latter example, you'll probably need to be more self-regulating, potentially leading to fatigue.

The bottom line is: Your lunch and break time should be yours to spend as you please. Be deliberate about what you do during that time, so that you return renewed (rather than further depleted).

Strategy Two: Define Your Creative Space

Even when we're in control of a project, we don't always feel autonomous when we sit down to do the work. For one, we know someone will one day judge it, therefore we have the thought of our boss, manager, or client sitting on our shoulder. I remember, as the young cofounder of the marketing company Zugara, what a thrill it was to come up with online creative campaigns that the team knew were going to be used by juggernauts like Disney and Sony. Our digital art, *seen everywhere*! And yet, our excitement and enthusiasm were at times tempered by the awareness that legal teams and brand standards would ultimately tell us what we could and couldn't do anyway. Any type of constraint can be a fun killer. As well, workplaces, whether we engage with them physically or virtually, often bustle with stress, anxiety, and sometimes even real fear. Most of us are working in a domain created by others, which again makes it harder to feel in control. This affects our well-being as well as the quality of our work. When we feel out of control, our sympathetic nervous system can take over and fool us into thinking that a wrong move might literally kill us. How fun-loving are you in a state of terror? *Not much?* Me either.

Help overcoming this challenge comes from an unlikely source: comedian John Cleese, of Monty Python fame. In a now widely circulated lecture,[7] Cleese explained what he sees as the secret to the unusual creativity of his scripts, even when compared to his talented Monty Python colleagues. Consistent with Donald MacKinnon's findings, Cleese said his results weren't superior because he was more talented, but because he was willing to sit longer with the script, noodling until he produced the most original material possible. After relating this story, Cleese did something spectacular: He offered his version of an "operating system" to engage with our work more playfully, with an open, relaxed mind.

Cleese says you need three things: space, time, and confidence. While Cleese doesn't frame it this way, I see these three things synergistically creating more than space, but a fortress, inside which you have ample autonomy surrounding whatever challenge is on your desk.

First, *space*: You need to be able to enter a comfortable space that you control. This is how you get psychological distance from your boss, your coworkers, and all the controlling aspects of work that lead to your thinking being hampered by stressful deadlines, judgment, and fear.

Then, *time*: You need to give your "play" session a clear beginning and end. Cleese quoted the early twentieth-century Dutch historian Johan Huizinga to explain why this is so important: "Play is distinct from ordinary life, both as to locality and duration. This is its main characteristic: its secludedness, its limitedness. Play begins and then (at a certain moment) it is over. Otherwise, it's not play." In other words, if you want to engage your work more playfully, you have to separate it from business as usual by giving your playtime a beginning and an end. You create a unique space in time that sits outside the impending traditional linear timeline that races toward a deadline.

And finally, *confidence*: If you can't trust yourself, at least trust your process. Cleese says the easiest path to quick confidence is to tell yourself that when you're in this state of play, there's no such thing as a mistake. No one can judge you. You can take the work you create and rip it into a thousand pieces and never share it with anyone.

This is your space, your playtime, and you are in control. For these moments, your job is to play and have fun with the work task, using rules of your own creation.

Strategy Three: Ask for It

Here's a hard truth: If your boss is overly controlling, it's a sign he or she doesn't trust you. You could be defensive about that, or you could take proactive measures to build trust. Approach your boss (or client) and make sure you have clear, mutually agreed-upon expectations and priorities. A memorable professor of mine, Dr. Barry Grossman, said your stakeholders should always have a sense of confidence and control, and one begets the other. Let your boss or clients know you'll be providing updates on your progress at set intervals. Finally, the most important piece: Keep the updates coming on a consistent basis. I use this method myself, after reading Kate Frachon's post about it on Kate Matsudaira's

Ink+Volt website,[8] and I encourage employees to do the same. Trust me when I say no boss—or at least, very few—likes to micromanage. It's exhausting and time-consuming. What bosses and managers really care about is a quality outcome delivered on time. When an employee steps up and shows they're ready for autonomy, leadership is generally happy to provide it, if it's been earned.

Strategy Four: Tame Your Scarcity Mindset

So-called "eff you" money isn't in the reach of most people, no matter how many lattes we pass up. We need our jobs. That said, the more financially secure you are, the more your work feels like a choice rather than indentured servitude. Finance affects autonomy for freelancers and entrepreneurs as well. If as a freelancer you don't plan well, your dwindling bank account can become a far more tyrannical keeper than your office boss ever was. As for entrepreneurs, keep in mind that you're only your own boss when you're self-funded. The moment you take on investors, you are, on some level, beholden to someone else's demands. If you're a small business owner or solopreneur who is of the mindset that success requires relentlessly growing your company, Paul Jarvis's *Company of One*[9] is a great read that might change your mind.

Because the need for job security is real and fear-inducing, many reasonably find themselves tethered by a scarcity mindset, which prevents them from taking charge of their career or current position. You might think, "Jobs don't grow on trees," and—depending on the economic climate—you may be right. However, thinking within that paradigm can prevent you from discovering those opportunities that do exist, or even creating them. If you find yourself struck by a scarcity mindset, try creating an inventory of your *nonfinancial* wealth. That list would include things like the unique skills or qualifications you have to offer an employer, and the friends and family who might support you in the search for a new job. Knowing you have options can help offset the fear of taking risks at your current job, as well as empower you to look for another job that is more fun, pays better . . . or hopefully, *both*!

Hall of Fun: The Beer Pong Barons

Following your passion may have pitfalls—but those who successfully surf the wave of entrepreneurship have undeniable fun, especially when their business allows for that magical combination of autonomy, competence, and relatedness. Two of my favorite examples are Nate and Jeremy Fissell, two brothers from my hometown who took Jeremy's passion for tinkering and Nate's fun-loving persona and combined them to build a beer pong empire. Fun is literally their business. It started when Jeremy, who had already been importing and selling glow sticks, realized he could snap one of his sticks under the rim of a modified cup. Several patents and innovations later, the Glow-in-the-Dark Party Cup was born.

He pulled in Nate, and together they applied Jeremy's new invention to the popular beer pong party game and developed an entire GlowPong line. Next, they tricked out a party van with neon images of people playing the game, then debuted the product in places like Isla Vista, California, home of UC Santa Barbara, where Nate had attended school. "I got mobbed in Isla Vista because everybody saw the van," says Nate. "People were on their bikes following me down the street, yelling, 'Bro, can I get another one?' I literally had to hide the van." After attending a trade show in Las Vegas, they soon inked a partnership to sell their game in all of Spencer's gift stores, and more recently, they opened their GlowPong storefront on Amazon. Nate says, "The way we branded from the beginning was to try to establish a vibe. Get crazy, be wacky. Dress up in your team color. Be the red team with the red cups against the blue team with the blue cups. We sold that fun, summer, California vibe, and it really paid off over the years."

Jeremy's the kind of guy who's all-in, whatever he's doing, which he refers to lovingly as "his disease." He's a guy whose side hustles spawn side hustles of their own; GlowPong is one of several businesses built on the back of his inventions. But he's also a collector, with a 2,500-square-foot warehouse operating as a makeshift museum. He has every Walkman ever made, eleven BMX bikes, a wall of vintage OP ski jackets, a massive collection of boom boxes, and—the jewel in the crown—a pre-World War II train collection housed in a double-sided display case, nine feet tall and twelve feet wide, that he hand-built. "People come over and they just trip out," he says. "My prewar O-scale train collection rivals the Sacramento railroad museum's. So, I do stuff like that. I'm sure into whatever I'm doing, and I'm passionate about it." His other life passion, his two sons and wife, serve as a balance, getting him out of his workshop.

Nate is the operator and salesman of the pair. "Half of my day is managing what's going on, emails, anything in the morning. And then I usually go to the warehouse. I get some physical labor in. I'm putting some stickers on some boxes to ship out, managing our imports. It sounds like it could be a drag, but I actually really enjoy it." Autonomy is an undeniable part of the appeal. "I can break up any day of the week any way I want. It's the ultimate freedom." He takes advantage of it, traveling frequently with friends, on adventures that take him all over the world. "I have to bounce, or I go crazy," he says with a chuckle.

Manage Your Arousal

Many of the autonomy strategies described in this chapter have an additional benefit—they all help in managing arousal. I'm not talking about sex. *Arousal* as a psychological construct of emotion refers to the level of stimulation (or enervation) a particular activity has on our energy state. Many workplaces—sometimes deliberately, sometimes not—encourage a constant state of high arousal. You've probably experienced something like this at some point walking into a trendy clothing store. They pump buzzy music and bright lights that are meant to pep up both you and their employees. It's manufactured fun, and they're hoping that however you walked in, you'll finish your visit motivated to buy, buy, buy. In an office environment, high arousal isn't likely to be generated with music and lights. More often, it's the result of emails constantly flooding in, or apps like Slack pinging you with nonstop notifications. Authors Adam Gazzaley and Larry Rosen wrote an entire book called *The Distracted Mind*[10] about the stress and anxiety induced by digital messaging because of the heightened arousal it continually produces. For sales organizations, it might be the ringing of a bell after every sale. Meetings scheduled back-to-back. Aggressive targets and the relentless communication of high stakes.

What's important to understand is that all of this arousal isn't necessarily bad—it might just be bad for *you*. The nuance here is that some people perform well in high-arousal states, while others crumple. Whatever your level is, when it tips toward too much, you do crappy work, are robbed of competence, and finish the workday feeling like something a dog left behind.

Work becomes more fun when we become better observers and managers of our own arousal. We win in two ways. First, we become more productive by working smarter. We get more done, feel more capable, and reap the rewards of both. And second, we finish the workday with more vitality, both because we've felt more capable and because we have taken some of our precious energy off the table for ourselves.

This is a new concept for most people, but there's one group who have fine-tuned the relationship between arousal and performance: athletes. Since arousal affects each of us differently, high-arousal states can be helpful or hurtful. Some athletes, just like some workers, thrive on adrenaline and nerves. Others do best when they're relaxed and not feeling pressure. For decades, coaches have been using a model developed by Russian sports psychologist Yuri Hanin for finding that sweet spot for performance. Once an athlete becomes aware of their Individual Zone of Optimal Functioning (IZOF), the emotions and arousal level where they perform their best, they can set conditions to get into the right zone when they need to.[11]

To do this for yourself, think about the times when you've done your best work. Find two to three words that describe your emotions in those moments. Then think about the times your work has suffered and identify two to three emotions associated with those moments.

Example of Hanin's IZOF Profiling

Helpful Emotions	Unhelpful Emotions
Excited	Unwilling
Energetic	Tired
Motivated	Uncertain
Confident	Bored
Easygoing	Tense
Satisfied	Nervous
Overjoyed	Dissatisfied
Pleasant	Angry

Based on the emotions that resonate, you can begin to understand where you sit on the spectrum of low to high arousal. Then think about how you can reshape your work environment to better match your Optimal Arousal Zone. For example, say you're someone who picked "Excited" and "Energetic" as your helpful emotions, and "Angry" as unhelpful. These emotions suggest you may perform well amidst high-arousal states. If you're doing all your work in the quiet solitude of a home office, maybe it's time to experiment with working in a coffee shop or a coworking space. Or, say you're someone who does their best work when they're feeling "Pleasant" and "Easygoing," and you're working in an open-space office. When you know you need to perform, try booking a quiet conference room for an afternoon, taking a walk to center yourself, or asking for time to work at home.

The point isn't so much to define yourself as one way or the other, but to increase your awareness of what ratchets up your arousal, the resulting emotions, and how they affect your work, so that you can make tweaks to your environment and take on challenges in your best state.

Potential Arousal Boosters
- Fun and invigorating workouts and body movement (e.g., group exercise class at lunch, walking meetings, etc.)
- Great cup of coffee or tea
- High-arousal entertainment (e.g., high-energy music, inspirational talks, etc.)
- Flexing creativity and curiosity (e.g., brainstorming, mastering a new skill, etc.)
- Friendly competition
- Adequate hydration

Potential Arousal Tamers
- Reading
- Time with pets
- Aromatherapy
- Proper lighting
- Caring for plants
- Meditation and mindfulness
- Journaling
- Walking
- Naps

So now we know we are each tuned to perform best at a certain level of arousal. It turns out that *what* we're doing matters, too. Some activities will be completed more successfully in a state of high arousal, others low. Research psychologists Robert Yerkes and John Dodson first established the link in the early 1900s when they sought to train mice to enter a particular box, using electric shocks when they chose the wrong box.[12]

When the task was easy, the mice improved their mastery most when the jolts were the strongest. But when the task was hard, the strongest jolts slowed their learning. Arousal was helpful—but only to a certain point, after which performance hit a wall. (We're not mice, and yet, who doesn't identify?)

Researchers have built on Yerkes and Dodson's conclusions in the years since, and now generally agree that complex tasks or new learning are best approached in a state of low to medium arousal. Familiar tasks, not necessarily easy but often repeated, are best with medium arousal. And finally, easy tasks may be best performed by inducing a high-arousal state.

What does this all mean? Whenever possible, reshape your environment and the task itself to match the desired arousal level. Two tips to get you thinking:

- When it makes sense, do your most difficult work first, before the cognitive noise of the day starts to impinge, and when you have the least time pressure. If you are a night owl, the opposite likely applies.
- If you've got something boring and administrative to work through, ratchet up the arousal by racing against time: Can you finish by x o'clock? Or purposefully schedule it at the end of your workday, so that you're motivated to finish and get out the door. If it won't introduce mistakes, make things more fun using activity bundling (e.g., coupling repetitive work with high-arousal music).

The Trouble with "Being Yourself" at Work

Relatedness—the degree to which we feel connected to others—is another huge factor in determining whether we leave work energized or depleted. Relatedness at work is no simple thing. For one, time spent socializing with work colleagues is no guarantee of renewal. In John Trougakos's study about work breaks mentioned earlier, employees were better off *working* through lunch than attending a mandatory company lunch. That's how much people dislike being forced to socialize.

Even voluntary socializing at work may drain you. Think about the time you spend with friends outside the workplace. It's fun and renewing because you can relax and be yourself without worrying about judgment or offense or hidden agendas, which is not always the case at work. Maybe you're lucky and also have colleagues that make you feel that way. *Great!* Still, at work you've got your credibility to maintain, and depending on how weird you are in your natural state (me: *very weird*), that creates a certain amount of risk and tension.

There's another challenge, too, with socializing at work. Part of being a good colleague is helping create an environment where everyone feels comfortable and included. We know that this is often *not* the case at work, particularly for anyone outside the majority, whether due to their gender, sexual orientation, race, or ethnicity. Fun at work requires establishing spaces where everyone feels safe, and many workplaces have yet to achieve that goal. Figuring out how to get there is far outside the scope of this book. Plus, there's no quick or easy solution, and current efforts to find one often put undue stress on already marginalized employees. A personal example of this comes from my wife, who is of Pacific Island descent. When the Stop Asian Hate rallies took place in 2021, she was encouraged to openly share her perspective for a company-wide webinar as part of her work's ongoing DEI (diversity, equity, and inclusion) efforts. Sharing her personal experience with colleagues has led to crucial and needed conversations within an organization that doesn't have many AAPI (Asian American and Pacific Islander) employees, and she is supportive of her company's effort to help others understand each other. And yet, she admits the experience of sharing and reliving painful memories centered on her race was an Agonizing experience, and something she wouldn't have volunteered to do.

Is all this enough to make you want to limit social interactions at work to the bare minimum? For some people, that may be the right answer. Others may still find themselves craving opportunities for human connection during their working hours, or even after work. For the latter group, here's some insight.

1. **Forced social interaction is rarely fun or renewing.** This is so important for everyone to understand, but leaders in particular. Such events don't even have to be mandatory to feel coercive. After-work happy hours are standard fare in many companies, but we're only beginning to understand how harmful they can be. No matter the good intent, what they do is extend the workday. People who don't drink are immediately alienated, and those who do can easily find themselves in a vulnerable state, their credibility or even their safety on the line because they had one too many. **The bottom line is:** If you need your employees to be drinking to have fun together, the fun probably isn't worth having in a work setting. Skip these events if you don't enjoy them, and lobby for alternatives. Complaining may feel stressful at first, but you'll feel the opposite of alienated when you become a beacon for people who feel the same way.

2. **Follow your affinity.** Affinity groups have been the go-to for many large corporations looking to create safe and supportive social spaces for individuals from underrepresented groups, bringing people together up and down the organization and across functions. The same thinking can be applied more broadly as you seek out friends and allies in your professional environment. Don't be constrained, or even guided, by your function or your company's organizational chart. Instead, look for people with whom you have natural affinity and shared interests. Look for activity partners, like someone who might want to take an after-work bike ride. If restorative social interaction is the goal, you're probably better off pursuing relationships with the people you work with the *least* closely, since the professional stakes are lower (as long as you are considerate of not abusing a power dynamic). You might find that you get more energy hanging out with, say, the lobby receptionist than you do with the people on your own team.

3. **Bring your friends to work.** If you crave relatedness at work but aren't finding it, use your breaks to connect with friends from your life outside of work. Go to lunch with your oldest friend or step outside and call them in the sunshine. Skip the office happy hour in favor of friend time, or even try inviting your friend along as a wingmate.

BRING YOUR FUN HABIT TO WORK

For freelancers, entrepreneurs, and the like—really, anyone who controls their own schedule, collaborators, and location—this is all even easier. If your relatedness quotient is low, pick a few outreach activities to commit to, for example:

- Every week pick a professional contact you haven't caught up with in six months to reach out to
- A weekly in-person lunch with a contact you genuinely like, or think you'd like if you knew them better
- A monthly activity date with a friendly colleague, like an exercise class or museum visit

And by all means, if you're lonely working at home, chat up your local delivery people. *Why not?!?* People underestimate the potential of surprise connections and encounters as a source of fun. That's what Nicholas Epley and Juliana Schroeder found when they asked a group of bus and train commuters in Chicago about conversations with strangers.[13] Most of the commuters said chatting with a stranger would lead to the least pleasant commute. The researchers then randomly asked a subset of the group to do exactly that and sent everyone on their way. Every single bid for conversation was accepted, far beyond what the commuters predicted beforehand. And the kicker: Afterward, it was the people who spoke to strangers who reported having the most pleasant commute.

Take your blinders off when it comes to whom you're willing to connect with (in situations you feel psychologically and physically safe, of course). Take advantage of serendipity. It's a great way to build surprises into every day, which we know (from chapter 6) invigorates us in ways that the same old routine never will.

Learn to SAVOR Your Work

I've now given you a toolkit to energize your work based on the available science and my own experience. Now it's your turn. The highly individual nature of fun (and work) means you'll get the best results experimenting on your own. Ask yourself: What can I do to increase my sense of autonomy, competence, and relatedness when it comes to my work? What can I do to wrangle more fun out of the hours in my workday? As a final step, **try applying SAVOR.**

Story Editing: What stories are you telling yourself about work that might be undermining you? Get clear on your personal priorities and values and see whether your actions are aligned. There's nothing more draining than fighting your own instincts.

Story editing can also help you on a more practical level. According to Kaitlin Woolley, whose work on the links between pleasure and motivation I cited earlier, shifting your focus at work from the aspects of your job you don't like to those that you do, can make a difference. To increase the perceived pleasure of any work task, Woolley suggests asking yourself, "Are there aspects that I inherently enjoy about this activity that I can focus on?"

Activity Bundling: Activity bundling when it comes to work can be wonderful—or it can go sideways quickly. For example, watching TV while you plow through paperwork might seem like a great idea—until you later realize you did a sloppy job and meanwhile can't remember anything about the episode you just watched. Bundled activities should enhance each other, not degrade each other. Try pairing uncomplicated tasks with pleasurable activities (e.g., listening to music). You could also think about bundled activities as rewards: If you spend an hour doing something difficult and concentration draining, you could follow it with something relaxing and fun from your Fun File.

Variable Hedonics: Is the repeated monotony of your work life getting you down? One obvious way to juice things up with variable hedonics is to mix up your schedule. Shift between tasks, switch the order you normally do things, flip a coin to see what's

BRING YOUR FUN HABIT TO WORK

next, etc. But here's a crazy idea: Take that approach and reverse it. Instead of injecting novelty into your work by doing many things, find many ways *to do the exact same thing*. When it comes to grueling, tedious, or boring tasks, approach the situation playing the role of researcher—dig deep and unearth discoveries that make the task interesting again. Finding new approaches becomes a rousing game, played against yourself. Looking at this another way, even the most repetitive tasks become fun when you elevate them to an art form. Embrace the spirit of that famous Martin Luther King, Jr., quote—"If it falls to your lot to be a street sweeper, sweep streets like Michelangelo painted pictures, sweep streets like Beethoven composed music . . . Sweep streets like Shakespeare wrote poetry." That's a potential recipe for feeling engaged at any job, so long as your focus is on the activity itself, and not solely driven by the desire to be recognized for your good work.

Options: Whether you're employed or self-employed, you may have settled into a clear, rigid job description. All that rigidity is probably somewhat imagined. Your work life most likely provides many options that you've never explored, whether it's lending a hand on a colleague's project, or what I call "working the perks." To provide one simple example, how many events related to your industry or profession have you attended in the past three years? Conferences and events are great opportunities to jump out of the mental, physical, and social groove you've worn for yourself at work. Don't wait for someone to invite you—do your own research and take the initiative to ask for the budget and time off to attend, especially events that not only allow you to flex your curiosity and grow professionally, but also have outside opportunities for fun. I'll never forget the time my shy but beer-buzzed colleague Brady Tuazon got the attention of Dave Grohl at a Foo Fighters concert at the E3 trade event in Los Angeles. When Dave asked the crowd what they wanted to hear, Brady yelled "Play Zeppelin!" Although Dave wasn't going to appease Brady's request that day, he did invite him up onstage. After a bit of playful banter, Brady realized this was his one opportunity to engage with the Foo Fighters. What did it take? *Brady simply asked.* Dave responded, "This freak wants to play some Zeppelin! All right, Brady, let's see what you got." And just like that, Brady was onstage with the Foo Fighters, Dave Grohl's guitar in his hands, playing "Whole Lotta Love" in front of the entire crowd. After his solo he shared a Crown and Coke with Dave onstage.[14] The dude was walking on air for weeks after that. *Legend.*

The point is this: Look for opportunities to step outside your role, environment, or comfort zone (if the payoff is fun). Think of your work environment as your playground. What equipment haven't you tried? What territory have you yet to explore? What friends can you rally with? Be creative in creating options for yourself, beyond your work description.

Reminiscing: My inspiration when it comes to reminiscing at work is behavioral change expert BJ Fogg, a social scientist who urges people to embrace the "superpower" of being able to make yourself feel good at any given moment. Fogg emphasizes the importance of celebrations. "In my research, I've found that adults have many ways to tell themselves, 'I did a bad job,' and very few ways of saying, "I did a good job.""[15] You don't need a manager or client to recognize you. Find a colleague, friend, or loved one to celebrate meaningful, authentic milestones with you, both big ones and small ones. Who you celebrate with doesn't really matter, so long as they take the celebration to heart. A prized artifact of mine is a trophy my writing buddy Ryan McFadden gave to me when I told him this book got a publishing deal. A big marble sign of the horns trophy that says *Kick Ass* on it. It may sound silly, but having a fellow writer I admire gift me with a physical object freed me to celebrate something otherwise intangible that I'd worked extremely hard for. Selling a book has so many milestones that it's easy to get caught up, never stopping to say, "Wow, *I did it.*" Ryan's thoughtful trophy made that possible. Even today, when I look at it, I'm able to reminisce about the win and relish the feeling all over again.

If you want to be celebrated, start by celebrating others. You'll find out quickly that the positive energy you flow out inevitably flows right back to you.

Three Shortcuts to Immediately Improve Your Work Life

To those of you who are still thinking, "Playing at work may be possible for some people and some jobs, but not mine," I want to introduce you to Judy Cornelison. Judy works in a place widely considered to be where fun goes to die. She works in a dentist's office. She's a dental hygienist. In fact, she's my dental hygienist. Judy didn't grow up dreaming of being a hygienist. She chose the work pragmatically, when she found herself needing a career after raising children and going through a divorce. A career counselor suggested it, and a four-day workweek job, with decent pay and free dental, sounded pretty good to someone who had spent most of her life as a mom and a volunteer at her kids' schools. And she, personally, had never had a negative experience at the dentist. So, she busted her butt to put in the necessary training and started a new career. But pretty soon she discovered something a little depressing: Most people hate going to the dentist. They didn't want to be in her chair. She hadn't really thought about the fact that her new line of work made her what clients perceived as the worst part of their day. Judy was an extrovert and enjoyed connecting with people, so all these unsatisfying interactions were cumulatively draining. Work was tolerable, but it wasn't fun.

So, Judy found a solution. She stumbled into it, really. A patient gifted her one late December day with funny Happy New Year glasses. After he left, she had the impulse to keep wearing the glasses. *Why not?* When her next client walked in, Judy looked up, prepared for the familiar *ugh, I'm at the dentist* expression. Instead, the patient saw the glasses, had a moment of confused surprise, and then flashed a giant grin. The glasses had broken the ice. So, the rest of the day, Judy kept wearing them, except when she was actually cleaning patients' teeth. And the rest of the day, she was the recipient of smiles and laughter.

That evening, she decided she would wear something special every day. Sometimes it would be an accessory, sometimes a full costume. There was a flamingo hat and glasses; a shark hat; blinking Christmas lights; a head-to-toe, one-eyed, one-horned flying purple people-eater costume. You name it, Judy has worn it. Twenty-eight years—and thousands of outfits later—she hasn't missed a day, and her decision has transformed not just her job, but the experience of everyone she treats. Because of Judy, visiting the dentist isn't just the highlight of my day, it's the highlight of my week. From a distance, maybe it sounds corny. But it goes beyond the outfits themselves. It's the pleasure of meeting someone who's decided to embrace something a bit wacky, solely to help people relax and smile in a stuffy, clinical medical office.

Her performance art has real impact. Judy tells me that she has patients from before her costumed days who asked for nitrous before they'd let her clean their teeth. Now they don't need it, "because I was willing to do something that put them at ease." Patients love to bring her fun items they find shopping or traveling to add to her kit. Her kids sometimes get embarrassed by her silly costumes, especially when clients post pictures of her on Facebook, but not Judy. "It doesn't bother me a bit. I enjoy it. It's become my signature in life."

You probably wouldn't have put *dental hygienist* on a list of "passion projects"—but that's what Judy made it. You have to be passionate to persist as long as she has, and to create as much joy as she has. And in there is an important takeaway, one that you may need to hear if you still believe there's no possibility of fun in your workday: We hamstring ourselves when we think of passion at work as being about *what* we do instead of *how we do it*. Bringing passion to work is a choice you can make today, a choice that has the power to turn drudgery into fun.

High-performance psychologist Dr. Michael Gervais, an early mentor whose work has profoundly influenced me, has taught me and others about the dangers of the "passion trap," the idea that there's some singular passion you must discover and achieve in order to become happy.[16]

It's another facet of the happiness trap, aka the hedonic treadmill. Once again, you're pinning your enjoyment on some improved future state. So, what's the here and now? *Chopped liver?* An inevitable disappointment? If life is what happens while you're making plans, *bam!*—you just determined your fate.

We can get much better results, immediately, by refocusing on how we are experiencing our *now*. If that sounds familiar, it's because it's what we've been up to all along in building our Fun Habit. Now we're applying the same strategies and tactics directly to work. Stop thinking that professional gratification will come someday, with *X* career move or *Y* milestone. Leave that BS for the Joneses. Instead, ask yourselves the more immediate question: **How can I increase my enjoyment in the work I am doing today?**

In short, I'm asking you to give striving a break. Is that easy? *No way!* Hustle culture and our own cognitive bias have us relentlessly focused on future states—and, worse, on outliers whose outcomes are very likely never going to be ours. Let me burst your bubble: Whatever Nike might have said about it, you are not going to be Tiger Woods. Or Elon Musk. Or whoever sits at the tippy top of your professional skyscraper. No amount of hard work or hustle is likely to produce that outcome—and yet our biases warp reality. Our minds seize upon the outliers and disregard the average cases. We grossly underestimate the amount of work it will take to get from point A to point B (see https://share.michaelrucker.com/planning-fallacy). The time and energy some people pour into their careers is the equivalent of spending your entire paycheck on Mega Millions lotto tickets, an asinine strategy that essentially does not improve your odds of winning. Most of us would never throw away that much money on such slim chances, but the uninformed among us are more than willing to throw away something much more valuable: *their time.*

I'm not saying that there aren't jobs for which it's worth trading short-term happiness for long-term outcomes, or that pursuing a professional passion is meaningless. If your dream is to be a doctor, *go for it.* The world needs more good doctors, and unless medical training goes through a radical overhaul, there's really no other way. But many of us are working with abandon without carefully considering what we really need and want out of life. Many of us are following a script someone else has written, only to take notice when it's too late to create a meaningful story line for ourselves.

I'm also not making a pitch for professional mediocrity. You can pursue professional excellence without having work define and subsume your entire life. Remember the research on elite violinists that Malcolm Gladwell made famous? Suddenly everyone became focused on the idea that becoming great at anything was a pure function of time, and a lot of it—ten thousand hours, as you may have heard. The trouble is, the study wasn't looking at what it took to become a great violinist or even an excellent one, but *one of the world's best* violinists. How many of us really need or want to hit that high a watermark in our own careers? The other trouble with the study is that many people focused on the number of hours and missed the more important point, that how the time was spent was the real distinguishing factor. The elite performers were extremely disciplined, consistent, and deliberate, and when they weren't practicing, they left it behind. *They relaxed.* Their success resulted from focused effort over time—*deliberate practice*—not from cramming practice into every waking hour.

We all have times when we're more focused on the future we want than the present we have. But if you find yourself stuck, here are three ways to reawaken your Fun Habit at work right now:

1. Ask yourself often, how can I have more fun at work *today*? This is not a rhetorical question. This is you, whipping out a piece of paper, and coming up with three ideas to bring passion and fun into your next workday or week. If you feel stuck, evaluate your work calendar event by event just like your personal revolution in chapter 2. For example: Meeting with a couple fun colleagues? Take it out of the conference room and bundle it with something more interesting.
2. Don't work when you're not working. Sounds easy, but in practice, it's so hard, for all the reasons we've already discussed. But

it's worth being deliberate about shutting down: Studies show that people who detach from work and pursue deliberate leisure (read: Pleasing and Living quadrant activities) in the evenings come to work the next day in better spirits than those who fail to detach from work.[17]

3. Repeat after me, when needed: *Passion (and fun!) is not limited by what I do, but how I do it.*

chapter 10

The Pleasure of Hard Fun, or How to Accomplish Almost Anything

*Thirty ways to shape up for summer.
Number one: Eat less. Number two: Exercise more.
Number three: What was I talking about again? I'm so hungry.*
—MARIA BAMFORD

In the last chapter, we questioned work hustle and learned innovative ways to have more fun at work. We needed to do that, because so much striving in the professional sphere is not only not fun, but also harmful. It's often extrinsically motivated—by your boss, by cultural pressure, by those famous Joneses everyone wants to keep up with.

But there is a good kind of hustle. It's the striving that comes from an impulse deep within, sometimes referred to as *hard fun*. It's motivated by the fundamental human desire to level up and learn new things. When life is in balance, striving with intention is healthy. Striving to get better at something, or master something new, makes us feel alive.

When we over-index on easy, pleasurable fun, one of two things can happen. First, we can get bored. Imagine that you're lucky enough to be trapped in one of those gated beach resorts where all there is to do is to lie on your beach blanket for a week. At first, it's great. But after a few days (maybe weeks for my low-arousal friends) you find yourself feeling itchy. Suddenly, climbing into the mouth of a volcano or swimming to the bottom of a cave seems like a great idea, so you sign up for an excursion, and off you go. Alexandre Mandryka, the video game designer I first

THE PLEASURE OF HARD FUN

mentioned in chapter 2, puts it this way: "Boredom is your DNA telling you, 'Move on, you're not learning right; you're losing your edge.'"

There's a second possibility. You get itchy and your brain tricks you into thinking the only way to scratch the itch is *more pleasure*. So, you add more drinks and more food and then some more drinks. You become like the rats in a famous study, where the scientists hooked wires into the rats' pleasure centers and gave them a button to push to experience pleasure. The rats quickly became so addicted to pushing the button that they stopped feeding themselves. They were happy to starve if they could just have that blissful surge. Pleasure—feeling good—became unsustainable and destructive.[1]

Most of us enjoy a life balanced between easy and hard fun. When our "easy" cup is full, we find ourselves seeking challenges, or betterment through growth and learning. Goals, and the work we put toward them, give spice to life.

And yet: Hard fun is just that, *hard*—at times even grueling, uncertain, terrifying, and rendering us vulnerable to embarrassment. That's why many efforts at self-improvement fail. Things get tough, or we don't see the results we want, and we give up.

Fun to the rescue! In this chapter you'll learn how to apply your Fun Habit to even the biggest, hairiest, most audacious of goals so that you stick it out and achieve whatever you've set your sights on. More importantly, you will learn that when our goals have a bias toward fun (i.e., our motivation is pleasure), rather than being rooted in explicitly stroking our self-esteem, or coming from a place of necessity, pursuing goals makes us happier.

Ever heard of the Ironman? It's the famously grueling endurance triathlon requiring participants to swim 2.4 miles, bike 112 miles, and run 26.2 miles, within seventeen hours. Participants go to extremes to finish fast. They train hard, and they race hard. They optimize their gear and apparel hoping to shave off precious seconds. Some are so fixated on a fast finish they don't even stop to urinate, they just let it out. There are elite athletes who have had to crawl over the finish line. People have died in the Ironman.

Me? When I was thirty-one, I finished the New Zealand twentieth-anniversary Ironman wearing board shorts and a Hawaiian lei. I bicycled with external speakers attached to my bike, blaring a curated playlist I crowdsourced from friends' suggestions that powered me through. My prerace prep was to shave my hair into a mohawk (circa P. Diddy at the 2003 New York City Marathon).

Was I the twelfth-to-last person across the finish line? *Why yes, I was.* Did I achieve my own personal record? *Why yes, I did.* And now for the rest of my life I can say I am an *Ironman*! There were so many wins. I started my seventeen weeks of training overweight and arrived in New Zealand forty pounds lighter. Through some creative crowdsourcing (way before GoFundMe was a thing) I essentially bet a bunch of friends I could finish, and plenty of them liked the odds that an overweight beer-drinker would likely fail. Ultimately, after finishing and collecting the purse, I used the funds I earned to fulfill my dream of opening a burrito shack. (ROCKiT Burritos was open for exactly one night with the help of my friend Patrick Fellows, during which we hosted a charity event—but, alas, that's a story for another book.) Throughout the experience I created some amazing memories, most especially the one of my parents,

20th Anniversary Ironman New Zealand,
Taupo, New Zealand, 3/6/2004

brother, and girlfriend (now wife) cheering me on at the finish against the backdrop of beautiful Lake Taupo.

I was able to do all those things because the goal and the process to achieve it was, at every step of the way, designed by me to be pleasurable. My desire, my motivation, my rules. That's a theme you'll see running through much of the advice here around how fun can help us with those big hairy audacious goals: Do it your own way, for the right reasons. Part of why we so enjoy leveling up is that we're flexing those autonomy muscles. We're taking control of our own fate. Even when you're sweating, with your muscles seizing up, vision blurring, suppressing the urge to vomit—nothing feels better.

Make It Your Game

If you have ever worked on setting goals before, you've probably been told in the past to make sure they are "SMART": **Specific, Measurable, Achievable, Relevant, and Time-Bound**. But probably no one ever told you that one of the best reasons to make them SMART is because, done right, it can make them more fun, too.

Alexandre Mandryka was the one who really clued me in to the fun connection here. When we spoke about video game design, he said that humans are creatures who crave learning and challenge, and video games provide a ready opportunity to do that. So does life, of course—but video games have a special feature. Unlike real life, they also provide something we're all frankly desperate for—a clear and unambiguous feedback loop. In a video game, you beat the boss or the level's objective and move up to the next level. Or . . . *you die.* (Did you just hear the sound of Pac-Man dying in your head?)

Adult life on the other hand? "Reality, worst game ever," as summed up by a popular Internet meme. Real life is excruciatingly wishy-washy when it comes to feedback about whether we're moving in a positive direction. Say, for example, you pick between two jobs. Did you pick the right one? *Who knows?* Even worse, you'll never really know. With twenty years of hindsight, it might still be fundamentally unknowable. Life isn't totally without feedback loops, of course—especially negative ones, like getting fired or dumped. On the positive side, promotions are a potential indicator we've leveled up. But there are so many factors outside of your control affecting whether you receive one that to rely on a signal like this as feedback is a recipe for frustration.

Enter the simplicity of SMART goals, a productive opportunity to give life the clear stakes and thrills of a video game. (If you have never heard the term *SMART goal* before, a quick overview is available at: https://share.michaelrucker.com/smart-goal.) When you set a specific and measurable goal, you create an unambiguous opportunity to level up. You either achieve the goal, or you don't.

The *achievable and relevant* parameters in SMART goals speak to another favorite friend of fun, autonomy. Is the goal in your control, and is it an outcome that really matters, not to just anyone, but to *you*, specifically? (More on autonomy later in the chapter.) Finally, *time-bound*. Earlier in the book I mentioned the benefit of setting a period of time that defines when you're playing and when you're not. So it is with goals, too. An effort with an end point looks like a playful experiment, instead of a never-ending slog.

Before we get into goals and measurement in more detail, I need to strike two cautionary notes. One, in Alexandre Mandryka's words, "Fun is the fuel of the machine." When it comes to gamifying life through goals, never forget that *it's not a game unless it's fun*. Your goal can be genius-level SMART, but you still need to find ways to enjoy yourself along the way. Delay all your gratification until the future state—the achievement of the goal—and you've put yourself in a precarious place. *Life's too short for drudgery.* Plus, you may lose motivation and quit. Two, when it comes to increasing your well-being through fun—using the same logic we did with escapes in chapter 5—make sure your goals are set up to move you toward something rather than being motivated by avoidance or protecting your ego. Dr. Christian Ehrlich from Oxford Brookes University has extensively researched the science behind the *why* and *how* we strive for goals. Over the past decade, Dr. Ehrlich has refined a framework of goal-striving reasons and has found that our happiness is best supported *when* (1) our goals are pursued because they are pleasurable, or (2) they help others (as opposed to when they are formed out of necessity or to solely feed our ego), or (3) *both* (which we explore in the next chapter).[2]

It took me a long time to learn this lesson personally. As you now know, sports and sports training have been a source of hard fun for me throughout my life. Despite my whimsical Ironman approach, I spent many years after that training with the "no pain, no gain" mindset. Looking fit fed my ego, so I hired gritty personal trainers who gave me exactly what I wanted at the time. They pushed me to grind out arduous workout regimens, with a relentless focus on algorithmically improving my numbers. And although it's not fair to say I didn't derive enjoyment from some of the sessions, I often didn't look forward to going. You might identify with the pattern I fell into: I'd train hard for a few weeks or months, then burn out. Eventually I'd decompress from the prior experience only to essentially repeat the experience because it required starting all over again at square one.

For a study as a doctoral student, I researched this same phenomenon with CrossFit zealots. If you have never heard of CrossFit, it is a form of high-intensity interval training known for its rigorous workouts. It has developed a cultlike following, and "CrossFitters" use acronyms like AMRAP (As Many Reps/Rounds as Possible) and ATG (Ass to Grass, meaning during squat-type exercises you should be getting as low as possible) to show the uninitiated that CrossFit is not for the faint of heart. Initially, almost all the CrossFitters we surveyed loved the social dynamics and the competitive atmosphere, despite the grueling nature of the workouts. However, a majority of them (in the small sample group of our study) ultimately deemed the practice unsustainable, and some even sustained injuries that forced them to stop working out altogether. There have even been accounts of CrossFitters getting rhabdomyolysis, a condition where your muscles cannot be repaired because you've literally destroyed them by working them too hard.[3] There are also plenty of accounts of folks who really enjoy CrossFit—but for some, sustainability and longevity are an issue.

Finally, in my forties, I began to be less concerned about looking good simply to feed my self-esteem; plus, I'd become a lot wiser about exercise physiology and the long-term consequences of overexertion. Accordingly, it was time to take a different tack with my fitness efforts. I relinquished all the old algorithms. I hired a trainer, Jessie, not because she made some promise about giving me a "beach body," but because she has a dynamic personality that I correctly guessed would make our workouts fun. And because they were fun, for the first time in my life, I trained consistently for a solid year. And at the end of that year—wait for it—I was as healthy as I've ever been! The goals we did set, I exceeded, almost accidentally. The entire time I believed that I might be lowering my bar when it came to fitness — and it led to what? *A better outcome.* It turns out *consistency* was the piece of the fitness equation I was missing, and it required fun to attain it.

Never forget that whatever your goal, you're in trouble if you don't find ways to keep it fun. With that in mind, let's move on to measurement. Quantifying your progress is undeniably part of the picture of leveling up—but we need to do it in a way that doesn't squelch your fun.

Make It Yours

Before you continue, pause to think about a SMART goal for yourself. It might be something you've been considering for a while. Or it might be something inspired by your new Fun File. It could be a learning goal, a performance-related goal, or yes, even a professional goal. Don't feel like you have to be 100 percent committed to moving forward with it, but it will be helpful to have a goal in mind as you continue to read the chapter. By the end, your SMART goal will be fully charged with fun.

How to Make Quant Work for You

Although I am a big fan of Gary Wolf and the Quantified Self movement, I have also been critical of the quant approach to self-betterment at times. By *quant*, I mean the awareness of *self* through data, with countable steps, minutes meditated, calories consumed—you name it—that can, in theory, be used to help motivate behavior change. The market has responded to the quant movement with a CES (Consumer Electronics Show) trade floor of new tools for biofeedback, with the Fitbit and Apple Watch probably the most widely known.

To be clear, I'm not anti-quant. Done right, data can be eye-opening, and useful. But I also see an underappreciated *downside* of quantifying life. I already shared in chapter 1 how focusing on quant sapped my experiential pleasure of using a meditation app. But my real awakening to the dark side of quant arrived years before, and still gives me the chills—a story I'll relate in a moment. In the years since, I've learned I'm not alone in questioning quant, or experiencing its potential ill effects.

Jordan Etkin is one researcher investigating quant's downside. (I referenced Dr. Etkin already in chapter 4, questioning the value of tracking happiness.) In her paper "The Hidden Cost of Personal Quantification," she reports on the result of six experiments looking at its effects.[4] For example, in one, Etkin asked a group of college students to spend the day walking with a pedometer; another group also walked but did not measure their output. The study supported what we already know, that measurement can lead to short-term behavior change. The students with the pedometer did, in fact, walk farther, without being asked to. But Etkin also found an unfortunate downside: They enjoyed their walking less than the folks who didn't measure their output. What could have been pleasurable, instead was experienced as work. Long-term, that will negatively affect your motivation, as was the case with me and personal training until I was lucky enough to find Jessie. These findings were replicated again by Rachael Kent, who looked at fitness professionals who tracked their progress through Instagram.[5]

The real trouble is most people seem to be very Pollyanna when it comes to quant. "They don't see a downside, and typically, they think it will benefit some aspects of their experience," Etkin told me. Given the proliferation of quantified feedback tools, "It's potentially a recipe for some really unhappy times," she added. Dr. Etkin's work taps into foundational ideas from social psychology suggesting that when you artificially create extrinsic motivation (meaning the factor that causes one to act is an external reward, trigger, or outside pressure, rather than an internal desire like pleasure, pain avoidance, or something that supports your identity) it can undermine intrinsic motivation.[6] The trouble is, intrinsic motivation appears to be much more sustainable than the extrinsic kind. In a very famous study of schoolchildren (cited more than four thousand times), a segmented research group of preschoolers were rewarded for coloring, then compared to a group of children who colored just because it was fun. Then, researchers took away the extrinsic reward—and the children in that group found coloring a lot less enjoyable. Meanwhile, the children in the intrinsically motivated group continued to enjoy the activity.[7] In my own experience working with health clubs, it is not uncommon for me to see members realize they forgot their activity tracker, one that rewards their effort with some sort of contrived incentive system (e.g., points for heart rate, steps, etc.), and simply leave the club without exercising—because why exercise if it's not going to count, *right*?

Still, even Etkin allows that quant can be useful when applied to "something you really want to move the needle on"—like, say, a SMART goal. For example, "If you are trying to improve as a runner—or even maybe not actively trying to get faster, but just trying to understand factors that might affect your performance across days—then tracking can provide useful information because you're trying to learn or change that thing."

Ultimately, quant can be a powerful tool with a very sharp edge that we should all be mindful of. It tightly focuses your attention on whatever you've chosen to measure—which *can* be a positive, provided you're measuring something meaningful and appropriate to your goals. If you're not, it can create a huge setback in your health and happiness. I saw that play out in real time when I was conducting an early pilot program to test a variety of health tracking devices.[8] My collaborator and I randomly gave a small group either an activity tracker, a wireless weight scale, or a blood pressure cuff and asked them to track their data. We were hoping it would lead to more healthy behaviors. It had never occurred to us that the data could lead to *unhealthy* behaviors, but that's exactly what happened to one participant. This participant was an amazing cyclist—super active, always out on her bike, fit and happy. She was not a person who needed to lose weight. Unfortunately, she was randomly assigned the scale, and during our mid-study check-in with her it became clear she was perseverating on the thought she should lose weight. Dismayed, we almost pulled the plug on the program. Since then, I've been increasingly concerned with overly leaning on quantification as a tool for changing behavior.

To summarize, if you're going to take a quant approach, be incredibly intentional about it—and make sure you've got the right key performance indicators, or KPIs. KPIs are often used in business as a way to define, measure, and track the success of a project, initiative, or campaign. They answer the question: What indicators should be used to effectively tell us whether an area of performance was a success? Which begs the next question: How do you figure out the right KPIs for you?

Rig the Game in Your Favor, aka Finding the Right KPIs

A little-known fact about the Ironman: In the earliest days of the competition, participants weren't as oriented on setting records for time. In fact, there was no seventeen-hour time limit the way there is today. Some of the participants completed the events over the course of a weekend, stopping to socialize during transitions. In the very first Ironman race in Oahu, Hawaii, in 1979, the lead competitor for most of the race ended up in second place because his crew ran out of water and instead gave him beer for hydration, causing him to stagger and stumble into cars.[9] The winner finished the race in 11:46:58. (They added the seventeen-hour limit in the 1980s, and things began to shift—another great example of the mesmerizing effect of quant? We'll never know.)

When I entered the race, the culture was very different. Most who enter were looking to earn personal records or were competing to win. As an out-of-shape 255-pound man, I knew I'd need to think differently. I would focus on two things: enjoying myself and finishing the damn race. I threw out my ego and admitted that for me, those were the achievable goals that mattered. If I had focused on improving my time throughout my training, I would have likely talked myself out of the entire adventure.

What I didn't realize was that in being so intentional and honest about what KPIs mattered for me, I was unconsciously rigging the game in my favor. That's what meaningful, personal KPIs do: They set you up to win. Thinking back to the SAVOR system, this is a form of story editing. You're reframing your goals and achievement strategy so that they appeal to your own idiosyncrasies.

There's a terrific model out there for choosing your KPIs, and it doesn't come from elite athletes or their coaches. It comes from clinical psychologists working with people to make what may be the most difficult behavior change imaginable: getting off alcohol or drugs. I first learned about the model back in 2011, when I was doing coursework for my doctoral degree, and made several friends at school who were addiction therapists at Kaiser Permanente. They were having (and continue to have) crazy success using an approach called motivational interviewing. The central focus of motivational interviewing is putting the patient in charge of the process. The more in charge they are, the more the motivation to change comes intrinsically (from within), instead of being something pushed on them by family, health professionals, or society. And the more motivation comes from within, the more likely it is to have staying power.

This isn't much different for addicts than the rest of us. You've got to make a goal 100 percent yours. Otherwise, it's not that fun, and even with the best of intentions, most of us abandon what we don't enjoy. Motivational interviewing is a collaborative process led by a clinician, but there are insights that you can apply to your own individual process.

First, identify your personal motivation: Shove to the side all the virtuous reasoning that is supposed to motivate you to improve your behavior. Instead, own your true desires. The process won't work if you're so self-critical that you suppress, ignore, or fail to identify the feelings that will really propel you forward. To give a recognizable example, consider the person who wants to lose weight. Do they really care what their BMI is? In my experience with health and wellness, most don't. What's really motivating might be their upcoming high school reunion, where they'd love to cruise in with a body that's at least reminiscent of their teenage self. Is this a bit vain? *Maybe*. But is it more motivating than some arbitrary number? If yes, use it to frame the goal. While a doctor might assign a KPI in terms of a target weight or BMI, the person in our example might be better served by using pants or dress size as a KPI, or even an outfit that's initially too snug to fit into. Better yet, use a personally derived scale from one to ten measuring how pleasurable the reunion would be for you if various sizes are achieved. We've all got our quirks, might as well put them to work. If they're deeply personal, even better—those can be the most powerful. You don't have to share with anyone. Use them as your unique secret superpower.

Being motivated by the thought of impressing your old classmates does have some shortcoming—namely, it's ego-driven, with all the inherent weaknesses of that kind of goal. That doesn't mean you have to ignore it. But digging deeper, do you have any altruistic reasons for losing weight?—for example, being able to race your kid on the playground and actually enjoy it. Understanding your own motivation from many angles can help you develop a really healthy set of KPIs that will support you in going the distance.

And don't just *think* about what motivates you. Write it down, read it. Make sure your reasoning resonates. If it ceases to resonate, rethink it and reinvent it.

Own the "how": Once your motivation is front and center, you can move on to consider the how—the actual steps you'll take and the milestones you'll set to measure your progress. When it comes to the how, give yourself freedom to do it your way. Whatever your goal, there's almost surely an industry and community of people who will tell you what they think is the best way to achieve it. Don't be afraid of their advice, but check it against your own preferences. I like to call this, "pulling the meat from the bone." Be realistic about your habits and lifestyle. This is your Fun Habit in action: *Your desires and enjoyment matter!* Love writing but hate getting up early? Don't schedule time for working on that manuscript in the morning—no matter what that guru tells you. Do you hate the treadmill? Try running outside or hiking instead. Hate cycling outside? Get a Saris indoor bike trainer or try out a virtual indoor offering like Peloton.

In short, *increase your level of fun, so the work gets done*. When it comes to measurement, never forget your motivation. A friend of mine told me she wanted to get in better shape and had therefore purchased a new scale. I asked her why she wanted to get in shape. She needed more energy, she told me, and wanted to feel physically and mentally strong and capable. In her mind, getting in shape meant losing weight, with daily weigh-ins for feedback. We thought together about her authentic intent, and she realized that exercise would contribute more, and more quickly, to her goal than dieting. She wasn't unhappy with how she looked, she was unhappy with how she felt, and had seen in the past how quickly regular exercise changed that. So, instead of focusing on weight loss, she decided to indulge her competitive side by training for a ten-kilometer race. Her plan looked something like this:

SMART Goal: Run a 10K within three months
Motivation: Increase energy levels
KPIs: Completion of training plan; finishing race; tracking energy and enjoyment levels before, during, and after workouts

Some Final Considerations with KPIs

Try to include at least one KPI focused on increasing fun, whether during the time you put toward your goal or more generally during your big push.

- Make sure your KPIs are fully within your control. Let's use weight loss again as a negative example. Your weight is controlled by many factors, including genetics, age, and hormones. You can do all the "right things" and still end up stymied with that as your measurement of success.
- Keep your KPIs as far in the background as you can. Etkin suggests figuring out the least-frequent interval in which you could receive feedback and have it still be meaningful to help you course correct and stay motivated. Don't check the data

more frequently than needed. A number of wellness products reflect the wisdom of this advice, including the Shapa scale, which doesn't tell you your weight, only whether you're trending in the right direction. Sam Harris's Waking Up meditation app was built to include a streak counter, but in a recent update his development team has hidden this feature in the hopes of reducing the motivation to meditate for an artificial virtual currency, or what he calls, "spiritual materialism."

When the Going Gets Tough

Let's stay real here: Not every moment of pursuing a goal is like a thrilling video game. There are low and painful moments; days when you'd rather not bother. Fun can come to the rescue. What follows are some ideas based on my first Ironman experience—and, of course, some current behavioral science—that can help you make the truly hard stuff as fun as possible.

Activity bundling, aka *lures*: I'm a big fan of the idea of *nudges*, popularized in behavior change by Richard Thaler and Cass Sunstein in 2008 in their book *Nudge: Improving Decisions About Health, Wealth, and Happiness*.[10] Nudges are small changes that lead individuals to make better choices. In 2009, Volkswagen took the idea and added a key ingredient: *fun!* You may remember seeing some of the viral videos for the campaign they called Fun Theory. In the most famous example, they asked the question: "Can we get more people to choose the stairs by making it more fun to do?" They then transformed a subway staircase in Stockholm into piano keys that pedestrians would "play" by taking the stairs and filmed the results as people overwhelmingly chose the stairs over the escalator. (You can check it out here: https://share.michaelrucker.com/fun-theory.)

Volkswagen, like Thaler and Sunstein, was primarily focused on behavior change at the public health level. More recently, authors such as BJ Fogg in *Tiny Habits* and James Clear in *Atomic Habits* have popularized the idea at the individual level, refocusing self-improvement efforts on tiny changes that make positive behaviors the path of least resistance. To use Fogg's most iconic example, say you start with a goal to run every day. Scratch that, says Fogg. Think tinier, much tinier: Set a goal simply *to put on* your running shoes every day—and then watch the magic happen as you end up running more than you would have with your original goal.

Because we're all about the proven powers of fun, I suggest a twist—not a nudge, but a *lure*: a thoughtfully applied dose of fun to help pull you as you move along the steps toward your goal. It can be tiny; for example, working out in clothes that give you pleasure. For me, that meant loud board shorts for my Ironman training, instead of the Speedos and expensive bike shorts that signified, to me, a nasty combination of extravagance and humiliation. It could be using your favorite song as your alarm to wake up in the morning or cutting your children's carrots into star shapes. (Fancy-shaped food delicately arranged on toothpicks isn't simply performative parenting. Many studies show that what foods look like has a major impact on how much gets eaten, particularly when it comes to children.[11])

Lures can also take the form of activity bundling. The hardest part of my Ironman training was the cycling, my weakest and least favorite of the three triathlon sports. So, instead of cycling on the road, I got a CompuTrainer that turned my bike training into a game. Lured to something more fun, training became enjoyable. I went from hating it to looking forward to it. During the race itself, which was at times truly grueling, my lure to completing the cycling leg was outfitting my bike with speakers so that I could listen to songs my friends picked for me before the race. Hearing the songs not only lifted my spirit during the most difficult stretches, but since each song was as unique as the friend who picked it, it was like having them right there with me cheering me along (something that in reality was not practical given the race took place in New Zealand).

Name your goal: Shakespeare was a great poet and playwright but a shoddy behavioral scientist. As it turns out, a rose by any other name might *not* smell as sweet. For example, a study showed that we significantly increase our choice of healthy food when those choices are labeled with "indulgent descriptors"—labels as whimsical as "twisted carrots" and "dynamite beets."[12] Language matters, so give your goal or project a name that you love. I didn't refer to my Ironman training as Ironman training. *Yuck!* I called it the Burrito Project, because of my plan to use the loot from my friends' wagers to open my beachside burrito joint. It was a name that matched the entire spirit of the endeavor and made me smile whenever I thought about it. It also connected my training to my *motivation*, which was to give myself the momentum to start my next big project. Give your goal a name that lights you up. It might be funny, it might be whimsical, it might even be serious. *You decide.*

Reward yourself: As we learned from Woolley and Fishbach, immediate rewards are more motivating than most of us give them credit for. Consider rewarding yourself every time you cross a major task off your list or hit a milestone. Write down a list of small indulgences (feel free to pull from your Fun File) and pick one when the time comes. Just ensure the reward is in line with your long-term goals (e.g., if weight loss is your ultimate goal, don't reward burning three hundred calories with six-hundred-calorie smoothies).

When the day of the Ironman arrived, the alarm clock woke me up at 4:00 a.m. and all I could think was one thing: *What if I fail?* All the self-doubt I had done so well to suppress came crashing down on me and I felt panic set in. Then I remembered an email I had gotten from Dave Scott, a local legend from my hometown of Davis, California, and the first person ever inducted in the Ironman Hall of Fame, due to his success with the sport. "It's just an Ironman," he wrote. *He was right!* What would happen if I didn't finish? It would be embarrassing, but I'd get over it. All the stakes involved were of my own design, and could be reimagined if the bottom fell out from under me.

It's a fine line: We have to take our goals seriously in order to commit to them, but if we take them too seriously and don't have fun along the way, fear and pressure can overwhelm us. This is especially true when, as adults, we are trying something new that makes us feel awkward and vulnerable.

Constantly reminding ourselves to frame our goals inside of fun puts us in a safer space. When I was reminded that the whole point of my Ironman adventure was to have fun, it mattered a whole lot less if I actually finished the course. That thought was enough to get me out of bed and into a car to drive to pick up my best friend Micah. Which brings us to the final ingredient for bringing your Fun Habit to your biggest, hairiest goals: *people*.

Hall of Fun: 43 Things

The early social experiment 43 Things was a website created in 2005 that quickly became popular for the fun way it enabled easily sharing goals with others. The site prompted visitors with a question: "What do you want to do with your life?" In answer, you listed up to 43 different goals. (The founders picked 43 because it seemed manageable; it was less than 50 and a prime number.) You could also check out others' lists and cheer them on. The site engaged and inspired millions of users before going offline at the start of the year in 2015. While the most popular goal on the site ("Blogging") was revealing of the cultural moment, others were recognizable classics: lose weight, stop procrastinating, run a marathon. Still others were poignant: kiss in the rain, love myself, stop caring what other people think of me.

Cofounder Daniel Spils shared that he personally completed more than five hundred goals using the site, "everything from 'eat a banana' to 'start a company that survives two years' to 'get married.'"[13] But until 2016, there was one particular goal that had gone unfinished: "record an album in my basement." (Since 1996, the multitalented Spils has played the keyboard in the Seattle band Maktub.)

THE PLEASURE OF HARD FUN

> After hearing that a former colleague had passed away, Spils found himself reflecting on "the fleeting nature of our human connections and the things we aim to achieve." So, he pulled out his old list and decided to finally check making an album off his list. He and his wife, Brangien, became a band called The Argument, and together released eleven songs, all recorded in their basement.

Make It Social

Take it from an Ironman: To accomplish the impossible, it helps to have spectators. If you've been to a big race, you know that the best spectators aren't passive at all. They scream and cheer. They pass out snacks and extra water. They wave creative, funny signs that make you laugh when you're hurting. They grab you when the race is over, kiss you, and give you a burrito and beer. (*If they're my wife, anyway.*)

I can honestly say that I wouldn't have finished the race without the people who supported me. Mohawk and board shorts are great, but having family and friends there was what made it truly fun and created the most indelible memories. During the Ironman, I hit the wall just after passing 100 miles on the bike. My quads seized up with cramps, and I had to get off the bike. I thought that would be the end, that the cramps would never stop. But miraculously, they did, and I came into the last transition with five minutes to spare. From that point, my memories are sweet—despite a damaged knee, exhaustion, and everything you'd expect after swimming 2.4 miles and cycling up and down 112 miles of rural roads.

The marathon was my comfort zone, and I had just over six hours to finish it, which helped. But what really made it great were the people. My parents were there, my mom cheering me on as I was one of the last people to wheel myself into the transition tent before the bike cutoff. About five miles into the run, I got to slap hands with Micah, who was already on his second loop and would go on to finish in less than thirteen hours. After seeing him and feeling the exhilaration of knowing he was already cruising to the finish, I felt my knee start to loosen up and picked up my pace. I noticed spectators recognized me because of my mohawk and cheered loudly—and then even louder on my second loop. A Kiwi family followed me the entire final two hours of the race, bringing me a lei because of my crazy board shorts. A quarter mile from the finish, my father popped out of nowhere and congratulated me. From there to the finish line, I had a ridiculous grin on my face. At the official time of **16:38:49**, I had done it! *I was an Ironman!*

Typical advice regarding making goals social has mostly focused on accountability. People like Tony Robbins urge you to put your goal out there in public because you'll not want to live down the shame of failure. But is shame really that motivating to anyone? To me, that completely misses the real magic of inviting others into your goals. The reason to do it is that your goal immediately becomes more fun. That fun factor solves the accountability problem handily. Do you really need to be held accountable to doing something enjoyable with people you like? *Probably not.*

You can see this shift in thinking playing out in fitness trends. In the '90s, boot camps were all the rage, with a focus on friendly hazing and tough love. Today the trendiest players in social fitness are SoulCycle and Peloton, cycling classes that harness big group energy and positivity to help people get and stay fit. I have several favorite Peloton instructors, but the one whose classes most rely on fun's fuel is Jess King. King positions herself as the host of a party that's always there for you. Her classes can be challenging, but you don't care because they're fun. If you look at the web page for the Jess King Experience, you might not even know it was for an exercise class. There's no mention of calories, fitness, or feeling the burn. Instead, you're invited to "a party of the people" with a mission to inspire a "sense of togetherness," a "moving, musical, immersive experience that our Members are inherently a part of." (If you find Peloton as fun as I do, let's connect on the platform. I ride as **Cr8Fun**.)

Finally, remember that friends are more than supporters or ride-or-die buddies. They're also incredible resources as you seek to learn and master new things. The most literal example of this I've seen was on a friend-of-a-friend's Facebook feed. Carrie had developed a list of things she wanted to learn how to do or to get better at—everything from making a soufflé, to learning to play the theremin, to writing a book. She put the entire list in a Google spreadsheet and shared it, saying, "This is my way of reaching out to all the people with whom I've not spent enough time in the past twenty-five years." She asked people to sign up on the spreadsheet to teach her what they could during a Zoom meeting. She also encouraged people to add their names if they saw something that they also wanted to learn, so that they could do it together, or to add an item if there was something she could teach *them*. The spreadsheet had 131 learning goals, and three weeks later, about thirty of them had volunteer teachers or learning partners from among Carrie's Facebook friends. Her first Zoom was with an old friend who taught her how to juggle.

We already know the powerful positive influence our friends can exert. When leveling up, you benefit from that influence even more. Who in your circle might be up to join you for some *hard fun*?

chapter 11

Fun Is a Force for Change

Some people see things that are and ask, why?
Some people dream of things that never were and ask, why not?
Some people have to go to work and don't have time for all that.
—GEORGE CARLIN

In 1986, five million adults and children joined hands to form a 4,125-mile-long chain across America. Anyone old enough likely remembers the day. For fifteen minutes, the country deliberately united. Participants held hands and sang "We Are the World" and "America the Beautiful," along with a song written specifically for the day. The event raised $53 million in aid for Africa while making a powerful statement about what collective action can accomplish—and how great it feels. To stand together, whether gripping the hand of your best friend or the hand of a stranger, was like a magic portal to the transcendent fun we discussed earlier.

If you've participated in collective action of any kind, you've no doubt experienced this feeling, whether by handing food to someone in need as a volunteer, marching for social change, or rallying around a political candidate who you believe will really make a difference. Joining forces for a cause presents a beautiful opportunity to step outside of yourself, into something bigger—something hopeful.

Perhaps that's part of why pursuing goals that help others boosts our well-being, as we learned in the last chapter from Dr. Ehrlich's study of how the *why* of setting a goal affects our happiness. In the past, most academics have focused on how well goals serve the "*I*," highlighting the benefits of goals that strengthen our sense of autonomy. Ehrlich's goal-striving reasons framework both expands the frame and tightens the focus, so that we can home in on the well-being effect of goals pursued with purely altruistic, outwardly focused motivation. What he found was that individuals benefit when their goals have been chosen with the "*we*" in mind. *Being* the change you want to see in the world (e.g., helping others, making the world a better place) has also been identified by Ehrlich as one of the key ingredients to positively supporting our subjective well-being.[1] In other words, being a force for good is a great way to make yourself happier. It's yet another chance to use fun to transcend the *me* and jump to *we*, connecting us to something bigger than ourselves, and maybe even allowing us to catch a glimpse of *The Mystery*.

Now coming full circle, collective action is a natural fit within the definition of fun you may recall from the first chapter. Collective action and fun are both:

Biased Toward Action
Both get you off your proverbial couch and out into the world. Instead of worrying about the weight of the world's problems, you're out there doing *something* to make things better. It's a relief from the powerless feeling that comes from digesting the endless disheartening stories fed to us from news outlets and social media.

Prosocial
Both get you outside of your head. Instead of feeling alone, you are connecting to something other than yourself. You're shifting from *me* to *we* thinking, and you stop taking yourself and your own problems so seriously.

Best When Autonomous
Choosing the way you will help others feels completely different than being guilted into doing something because it's your "duty." When we're feeling judged or pressured, we tend to become our

least charitable selves. I'm reminded of a *South Park* episode where the animated character Randy Marsh declines to give a dollar to charity at the cash register. Then, in order to complete his purchase, the Whole Foods cashier forces Randy to say into the loudspeaker, "I'm not giving anything to the hungry kids," after haranguing him about his decision. "So, with the ice cream, the vodka, the pizza pockets, and nothing for hungry kids, that's $37.83," says the cashier loudly while everybody in line watches. Albeit satirical, it's funny because it draws on the true discomfort we experience when we feel coerced.[2] (To see the clip yourself, visit https://share.michael rucker.com/donation-shaming.)

Did you include activities inspired by altruism, volunteerism, or activism in your Fun File? Perhaps not. At times I've been in that camp myself. The reasons vary. We are time poor, working too much, and therefore want the freedom to use the rest of our time for personal pursuits and moments of spontaneity. In the West, we are steeped in a culture that positions prosocial activities as distractions from the *really* important things, like individual success.

Further, anyone who has committed themselves to a cause knows that not every moment is pleasurable. The struggle to get ahead of any significant problem or social issue can be painful and exhausting. It can feel like two steps forward, one step back. It can force us to get intimate with the omnipresence of pain and suffering, both our own and others'. For those who commit deeply, it can mean long hours and real sacrifice, sometimes even danger.

Fun, the Underutilized Ally

Successful changemakers are wise to the fact that blending pleasure with activism sustains and grows movements. It's **activity bundling** at its most impactful. Think, for example, how musicians have propelled social change by making their music the soundtrack of a movement. I already mentioned "We Are the World," as well as Adam Yauch and the Beastie Boys playing to giant crowds to help free Tibet (in chapter 6). Music played a huge role in the fight against Apartheid in the 1980s. And it's not just music. Other forms of entertainment—humor, theater, fundraising galas—provide the energy needed to sustain a movement and make an impact. Fun attracts people who might not have otherwise contributed their time. Simple pleasures can be a footbridge into deeper commitments.

Whether or not you see giving back as a moral imperative, it's a wise addition to any Fun Habit. Because you know what's not fun? Feeling the burden of the world's problems and *not* helping. Most of us feel a draw to contribute to the greater good in some way but end up drowning in the abundance of societal ills, frozen in so-called *choice fatigue*.[3] You might recall the science of choice fatigue from the Fun File exercise in chapter 2. When there are too many choices to comprehend, we become paralyzed and dissatisfied, sometimes even anxious. With so much collective trauma coming at us from all angles, it can feel like we're carrying the weight of the world's problems on our shoulders, especially when we feel like we are contributing *nothing* to make things better. *Nothing*, there's that word again. Worrying obsessively or posting another "supportive" meme only feeds the *Nothing* more.

I am not trying to villainize sympathy; it is certainly a better option than apathy. However, by definition it lacks empathy, and it certainly lacks action. Instead, let fun and compassion be natural allies that move you toward collective action. Fun is a great way to get yourself started on the path as a contributor and changemaker—and a great way to keep you moving forward even at times when the process is arduous.

The Personal Benefits of Giving Back

If the massive global challenges facing humanity have you feeling uneasy and anxious, collective action is almost guaranteed to pick you back up—especially if you choose your point of entry with fun in mind. PlayBuild is a great example of a nonprofit that uses fun as the fuel for community contribution and social impact. Founded in New Orleans by Angela Kyle and Charlotte Jones, the organization is devoted to changing children's lives through play. The first PlayBuild site was created in

2013, when Kyle leased a thirty-by-ninety-foot lot in a blighted, predominantly Black neighborhood of New Orleans and transformed it into an ingenious, colorful "design playground." Story editing at its best, PlayBuild reshaped a dilapidated environment into one that provides an inviting, inclusive fun space to play. In a neighborhood that has few parks or playgrounds, the PlayBuild installation provides visitors giant blocks, tubes, and Rigamajig Builder kits to create imaginary additions to their neighborhood—houses, castles, stores, you name it. Fun is obviously an important outcome, but the mission runs deeper: to help kids see that they can be agents of change in their own community, or as Kyle once put it, "to put them directly in touch with the transformation of the built environment so that they see the opportunity to be *agents* of that transformation and not just passive observers as whole blocks morph into something different [post-Hurricane Katrina]."[4]

PlayBuild seeks to give more kids, adults, and volunteers the opportunity to learn so that they can actively shape their environments and become conscientious stewards of their neighborhoods, cities, and the planet. Put in terms psychologists would use, this is a means of building *self-efficacy*, the belief that you have what it takes to face any challenge. As Angela told me, "Having community volunteers engaged in the movement has been really powerful because it empowers them with authority, ability, and the capacity to have their voices heard. In an area where people of color are being hurt by gentrification, by advocating for something that's very important including issues of safety, mobility, and accessibility, these volunteers become an active part of the community planning process."

Participating in collective action appears to produce similar results for teenagers and adults building new and better "structures" in the real world. Worrying about the world's problems may be overwhelming, but digging in with others to make positive change is not. In fact, it appears to produce the opposite effect, a stronger sense of self-efficacy and self-awareness, according to one study of teenagers across the United Kingdom.[5] Sharing a purpose with others also boosts *relatedness*,[6] which we discussed earlier as being a primary building block of well-being.

FUN IS A FORCE FOR CHANGE

While research on the psychological benefits of political activism is somewhat limited, there is a large body of study linking service work, or volunteering, to improvements in physical and mental health. Volunteering your time to help others inevitably provides opportunities for community and connection—which has been shown to have major health benefits, including alleviating depression,[7] lowering blood pressure,[8] and improving longevity.[9] Even donating money to charity has been shown to improve health,[10] suggesting there is more at play than simply the act of being out there in the field.

At PlayBuild, the "work" itself is fun by its nature, making it a win-win proposition for anyone looking to renew themselves through community engagement. Angela says, "The intergenerational aspect of play is great, too. Kids and grandparents in the neighborhood coming together. We'll host an Easter egg hunt or a picnic in our space where it's not just kids. It's kids, it's parents and grandparents and aunties and uncles, and everyone's coming together and playing together. It creates an alternative mode of communication because the environment is different, and that can be really powerful."

Own Fun as a Starting Place

You may feel the urge to judge yourself for putting fun at the top of your criteria as you seek opportunities to serve. But immediate gratification can open up options to get you started, and then help you move iteratively to more challenging work, or deeper commitment to an issue—and if not, at least you've contributed something. One of the pervasive themes of this book applies: When it comes to fun and more serious pursuits, one doesn't need to be at the expense of the other. In the language of improv comedy, it's not "either/or," it's "Yes, and." (This phrase has traveled from the stage to mainstream conversation as shorthand for the value of an expansive, growth-minded attitude.)

One inspiration of mine for fun-focused activism is Graeme Staddon, the friend I mentioned in chapter 7 who I met as part of the Serpentine Running Club when I briefly lived in London. (We bonded over trying to find quality chips and salsa in the U.K. Alas, we failed, but had a lot of fun trying and enjoyed some good beer in the process.) Sadly, Graeme lost his father-in-law to prostate cancer in 2016, and then in 2017 his father was diagnosed with breast cancer (yes, men get it, though very rarely). His father survived. Graeme decided that he wanted to do something to help save others from suffering. He announced in early 2020 that he would run twelve marathons that year, with a goal to raise £5 for every mile run, or £1,572. If a marathon a month sounds crazy to you, consider that Graeme was fifty-one years old and had only recently taken running back up. Nevertheless, he threw up a donation page on a fundraising platform and got started. His first two marathons were self-organized, and the third was the Larmer Tree Marathon in South Wiltshire, England, which he ran with his wife. He had planned to run a mix of solo and organized runs—and then, the pandemic hit. England, like so many places, imposed a strict lockdown. No more group marathons.

Many people might have quit. Graeme didn't, and the reason he didn't underlines why fun activism has real staying power. First, Graeme chose a small set of issues he was personally invested in and deeply committed to. Second, the medium for giving back was an activity he loved and held in deep regard. He knew how to plan a running course and organize his own support. Meanwhile, England's lockdown still allowed people to exercise outdoors (as long as the act of social distancing could be maintained).

His amazing solo commitment made for a good story, and the local news quickly ran with it. He was on the radio, and his donation page was shared far and wide. The months ticked by, and as December approached, he decided to up the ante by finishing his project with a double marathon in December—52.4 miles from West End in Southampton to Sandbanks in Poole, which he planned to run in ten to twelve hours, starting and finishing in the dark. Instead, he finished the course in 9 hours and 59 minutes—bringing his yearly mileage total to 2,127 kilometers (1,322 miles), with a total of £5,692 raised, almost quadrupling his initial target.

Running may often be a solitary sport, but his experience creating the fundraiser was anything but. In a post on Facebook, he said what amazed him most was all the conversations his effort created, both in person and online. People shared their stories about loved ones with pancreatic or breast cancers. Others told him that he had inspired them to get active.

Many people around the world experienced 2020 as lonely, uneventful, anxiety-inducing, or even depressing. A year with little to no options. Graeme, meanwhile, was living his best life, inspiring others, and contributing to cancer research all while doing what he loved. *It's an easy sell, isn't it?*

If Graeme could raise money running marathons during the pandemic, a period during which *nobody ran marathons*, imagine what you might do if you set your mind to unleashing your own interests and creativity in service of a cause. What can we learn from Graeme about getting started? Being thoughtful about how you direct your community engagement can produce an experience that satisfies the three basic psychological needs of the self—autonomy, competence, and relatedness (e.g., feeling connected to others)—and at the same time, expansively connects you to so much more.

- **Pick a cause that's personal:** Giving back expands your sense of autonomy when you're doing work that's uniquely meaningful to you, rather than work chosen because it's popular or guided by social pressure. With your mind open, try to discover what's calling you. Then, be intentional about where you direct your altruistic energy. There are a million different problems to solve and ways to help. Direct your energy toward what resonates. You're much more likely to sustain the commitment if it intrinsically motivates you and makes you feel good.
- **Find a way to participate that fits your personality and skill set:** Being active for a cause doesn't mean you have to be in the front row of a rally. Organizations need help with everything from spreading information, to preparing meals, to raising money, to building houses. If you feel like you're exercising your unique gifts in the service of others, you will enjoy a feeling of competence that could even invigorate other areas of your life, professionally or otherwise.

- **Spread the word:** When done from a place of authenticity, sharing your community engagement with others is a great way to relish the experience and deepen your commitment. This is an opportunity to enhance your sense of relatedness, by forging a deep connection with the work itself and potentially drawing in other interested people to join in the fun.

In short, shift your motivation from reward-based and egocentric lures ("I'll participate so that I can get the incentive/impress my friends/be left alone") to more intrinsic, compassionate lures ("I'll participate because it lights me up inside/because doing good, feels good"). This shift produces the best experience and the best outcomes. It's also motivation that lasts.

To inspire you further, here's another example. Noah Kagan, the founder of AppSumo, is someone who wanted to organize a fun event for his community, while also doing something good. The event he developed, the Sumo 50 Charity Ride, was custom-fit to create camaraderie and joy, not just for him, but for the community of entrepreneurs he's forged over the years. I can state this from experience because I attended the ride. Whether he knew it or not, he offered me (and others) the perfect combination of rewards-based and intrinsic motivations to attend. He had Lance Armstrong's organizer design a twenty-five and fifty-mile course for the event, so we all knew in advance it would be an enjoyable, possibly challenging course. Before the actual ride, he planned a great party with an epic magic show by Jonah Babins (who is an amazing magician, check him out here: https://share.michaelrucker.com/jonah-babins). After the ride, we enjoyed tacos (Noah is infatuated with tacos), margaritas, and live music. To influence people to give more, Noah offered various incentive options including personal business coaching sessions for those that met specific donation thresholds. Meanwhile, every $300 the event raised provided a laptop for a child whose family needed the help. The inaugural Sumo 50 event netted fifty laptops for children in need.

Living in a rural section of North Carolina during the pandemic, I saw firsthand the impact not having a computer had on underprivileged kids who face numerous burdens regarding the challenges of virtual schooling. I'll go back anytime Noah has the event. It's a great time, with good tacos and (more importantly) really fun people. But, of course, it is not just for the fun—attending means more deserving kids will continue to get the tools they need to succeed.

Fun Together for the Greater Good

Noah's story is a great example of how contribution and service are easier to build into your life if you invite your existing community to enjoy the ride with you. This includes your family, whether that means your kids, your parents, or . . . your chosen family—whomever you spend your quality time with.

One of my favorite childhood memories with my dad is participating in an annual event called the Great American River Cleanup. My dad used to be an avid scuba diver. He and many other divers would suit up with scuba gear, while the rest of us would board rafts and operate as support crew. The divers skimmed the bottom of the river for trash, while those of us on the rafts waited excitedly to see what they dredged up. There were prizes, like an award for "Most Keys Found," claimed one year by a guy who pulled up an old typewriter.

The event itself was a lot of fun—in part because it was a family affair. A few years back, I participated in a beach cleanup at Crab Cove in Alameda, California, with my daughter. We both care about the ocean, but the honest truth is that we never would have woken up early on a Sunday to wear plastic gloves and do the tedious hustle of picking up trash if it hadn't also been a great way to entertain ourselves on a weekend morning. The organizers were smart and conceived it as a fun family event, with various activities for the kids. We knew other neighborhood kids would be there, too, so that made it even more fun. Even without the festivities, we probably would have enjoyed being out in the sun and the fresh air, with old friends and new faces. Nevertheless, the lure of some organized fun is what got us out of bed.

Children who volunteer and engage in impactful work receive a boost in self-esteem while building real-world skills.[11] The kid-oriented social impact network Katamundi offers a turnkey opportunity to get started. The platform lets you find a cause, develop a way to contribute, then build a team to accomplish your goals. Yvette Hwee, the founder of Katamundi, put it to me this way: "After three years of doing social impact work with family and friends, I can positively say that our biggest benefit is having fun together as we work hand-in-hand toward our common goals. By being part of a team, not only do we find the service work socially gratifying, but we also enjoy a sense of belonging and purpose."

Another seamless way to get involved in a cause is to find an opportunity through your employer. If you work for a large organization, they likely have corporate social responsibility (CSR) programs and one might resonate with you. Can you join an existing initiative—or if not, can you start one? The founder of Marathon Tours & Travel, Thom Gilligan, has woven philanthropy into everything his company does. You might recall in chapter 5 I mentioned running a marathon in Antarctica. Marathon Tours & Travel was the means, and our trip (all of Gilligan's Antarctica marathons) raise money for Oceanites, a nonprofit scientific organization that monitors Antarctica—and the planet—for negative impacts from climate change and tourism. Almost everywhere Marathon Tours & Travel has a marathon, they find a way to contribute. The Maasai Marathon in Kenya raises funds to pay high school tuition for Maasai women. In Madagascar, Marathon Tours & Travel is helping fund a local health clinic, and at home in the U.S., Gilligan's company has organized an annual Boston Marathon fundraising team (going on two decades) that has raised more than $635,000 for the Charlestown Boys & Girls Club of Boston. Gilligan and his colleagues see marathoning not just as a physical challenge, but as an opportunity to improve the human condition. Their unique activity bundling of marathons with extreme travel adventure and philanthropy elevates fun to its pinnacle.

Marathon Tours & Travel isn't a nonprofit, it's a for-profit business. It supports the livelihood of Thom Gilligan and all of his employees. All of these anecdotes highlight that you do not have to have a special tax status or even a formal organization to wield the power of fun to do good. Fun, creativity, intention, and follow-through are all it takes.

Fun, Easy Options to Get Started

And the more you train yourself to look for options to give back, the more easily you'll find them.

Fun, Easy Options to Get Started

If you don't yet have impactful activities in your Fun File, take some time now to add them. Below are some ideas to get you thinking:

- Sign up for a cause-based fun run
- Buy tickets to a gala or other event supporting a cause that interests you
- Participate in a community cleanup or planting event (or organize one on your block)
- March for a cause—and have fun making signs with family or friends beforehand
- Track your movement with the Charity Miles app (https://share.michaelrucker.com/charity-miles), which connects you to corporate sponsors who make charitable contributions based on your mileage; invite friends to sponsor you in a challenge
- Make your next vacation a service trip
- Monetize a hobby (e.g., pottery, crochet, jewelry) and donate the profits to the charity of your choice
- Raise money for a cause using your birthday party as the impetus (an idea made popular by Charity: Water)

Once you have enough options, don't forget about the value of variable hedonics. If you are already passionate about a cause, this bit of advice isn't meant to derail you. You're already there, *so stay the course*. However, if you're looking for a great way to kick-start kindness into your Fun Habit, integrating a series of small random acts of kindness to get the ball rolling can be an effective strategy. Dr. Juliana Breines put it this way for *Greater Good Magazine*, "Intentionally practicing kindness in our everyday lives, even on days when we're not in a particularly generous mood, can go a long way toward turning kindness into a habit. That's largely

THE FUN HABIT

because of the way kindness breeds happiness: The good feelings serve to reinforce our kind acts and make us more likely to want to perform them in the future."[12]

Hall of Fun: The Ice Bucket Challenge

Remember the national viral phenomenon known as the Ice Bucket Challenge? It began when Pat Quinn and Pete Frates, both young men who were living with the neurodegenerative disease known as ALS, challenged each other and others to dump a bucket of ice water on their heads and make a donation to the ALS Association. The craze spread rapidly, ultimately enlisting thousands of volunteers, including many celebrities, from Bill Gates to Leonardo DiCaprio to George W. Bush to Oprah. The videos and the scenes behind them were the epitome of fun, in all the obvious ways—and a few more subtle ones. For instance, the campaign gave participants total autonomy. Quinn, Frates, and the ALS Association didn't publish rules about what your video should look like or what you had to say. People could tell their story however they liked. That made the videos more fun for people to produce, but also more fun to watch. As the campaign continued, participants got more and more creative so they could break through the noise. One popular video featured an entire wedding party doing the dunk in their formal wear. Aside from the fun of watching celebrities and friends alike react to freezing cold water, the challenge aspect (aka edgework from chapter 2) also added a level of intrigue. It's fun to both engage in, as well as watch someone respond to, a dare.

Whatever was fueling the fun, it worked. At the campaign's peak in 2014, the association's website visits peaked at 4.5 million per day, up from 20,000 before the challenge. In its busiest night, the organization pulled in $11.3 million, and the campaign generated $115 million overall.[13] At the time, there were critics who worried that the silliness of the effort would undermine the seriousness of the cause. The concern seems a little absurd, particularly given that both founders of the challenge have since passed away, Frates in 2019 and Quinn in 2020, both under the age of forty. No one can mistake the seriousness of this terrible illness.

Frates and Quinn, at least, died having seen the tremendous impact of their commitment to fun even in the worst of circumstances. In 2019, an independent research organization reported that the donations raised by the challenge had enabled the ALS Association to increase its annual funding for research around the world by 187 percent. It funded research that led to the discovery of five new genes connected to ALS, while also funding clinical trials of potential treatments.[14]

Fun may seem light as air, but it is a surprisingly powerful force. The Ice Bucket Challenge was a massive mainstream turning point inspiring a new generation of philanthropists to reinvent the staid old model of fundraising (big parties for rich people; shame ads serenaded by Sarah McLachlan) through fun.

Altruism and Reminiscing

Just as reminiscing is a powerful tool in your personal SAVOR system, reminiscing is equally, if not more, powerful when it comes to the reward of making an impact. Researchers Kellon Ko, Seth Margolis, Julia Revord, and Sonja Lyubomirsky randomly assigned participants either to perform prosocial behaviors, recall prosocial behaviors, both perform and recall prosocial behaviors, or do neither (the control group). The participants in all three groups (other than the control group that did nothing) felt comparable positive gains in well-being. *That's right*, the group that simply reminisced about a previous act of kindness got about the same lift as those that took action.[15] Passing along this knowledge to you shouldn't inspire you to do the least possible and then simply recall it when you need a boost. *I sure hope not!* However, it is the perfect reminder that fun and kindness have uniquely powerful benefits, long after the act, if we are intentional about relishing these memories when the time is right.

A Final Word About Self-Compassion and Renewal

May 8, 2020, was a dark day for me. We were on lockdown during the early months of the pandemic. I'd recently been made aware my mother had been diagnosed with Alzheimer's. The health club industry I work in was imploding, with businesses around the country closing their doors and going bankrupt. Every company meeting felt like a fight to choose between a rock and a hard place. My brain and my body seemed to be betraying me, saddling me with headaches and brain fog. Whether due to stress, the onset of long-haul COVID, or likely the combination of both, I was acutely aware health was failing me, but until this day I had been hiding it well.

Amidst all this, I was one of many white Americans engaged in a personal reckoning, awakened by the Black Lives Matter movement. And so, on May 8, I took what I hoped would be a very small but meaningful action. I joined a virtual group committed to each traveling 2.23 miles to honor the life of Ahmaud Arbery, a Black man who was shot and killed while jogging near his home in Brunswick, Georgia. As I began to walk the distance alone in my neighborhood, my heart was heavy with the reality that so many of the freedoms and opportunities that I took for granted were, in fact, privileges denied to others. I knew other people were out there walking and running for Ahmaud, too, but all I felt in that moment was very alone, which ultimately led to a panic attack while attempting the gesture. When I went to bed that night, I tossed and turned, gripped by the onset of severe insomnia that would last for months.

My effort, sadly, was a "what not to do." As I set off to participate that day, I knew deep down my tank was empty. But I thought that maybe that was what was required of me—to just do *something* instead of the dreaded *Nothing* we've talked about throughout this book.

FUN IS A FORCE FOR CHANGE

I was just one privileged white guy trying to complete a couple miles, so I hear you if you're playing the tiny violin. But burnout is a documented challenge for those involved in all types of service (those doctors I told you about in chapter 3 were all initially drawn to the profession driven by a passion to serve—*each one!*), and a threat to the sustainability of social movements, empathy, altruism, and the greater good in general. It can lead passionate people—those contributing because they believe in a better future—to abandon the work altogether. One study found that the pressure to contribute may lead individuals to struggle with saying no, even as their tank approaches empty; they might also feel shame that the work is weighing on them, which can lead them to isolate and ignore their own care.[16]

What could I have done differently? For one, I could have found others to join me—and afterward, sat with them and unpacked some of the complex emotions of the moment. Even if we hadn't talked at all, showing support shoulder to shoulder with friends or even strangers would almost certainly have left me feeling less lonely and overwhelmed.

But perhaps more importantly, I could have changed my behavior in the months prior. Looking back, I realize that I had stopped really having much fun. I should have known better. Veteran activists understand that many individuals (including themselves) may not see the end of the struggle. The change you seek may happen incrementally, over years and decades. Like a research scientist, you'll be lucky to experience a single groundbreaking achievement. And so, if you want to be in the game long enough to make a meaningful contribution, your devotion to the cause can't consume you. *You won't make it.*

Wanting to make a difference doesn't mean being angry all the time. Comedian Trevor Noah said something similar when an interviewer from the *Guardian* questioned why he wasn't angrier, or perhaps more polemic in his comedy, given that he is a biracial man who grew up under Apartheid in South Africa, and whose childhood was marked by violence and political unrest. He was also abused by his stepfather. Noah explained his good humor this way: "What is the point of existing in a feeling that does not move you forward? Because now what's happening is you're stewing in your own anger and resentment and bitterness, but the system you're trying to go up against doesn't feel any of that. It doesn't even know. So you're wasting that energy." He credited his mom with showing him that love and laughter were the primary emotions they needed to process life: "We turned our situation into something we could laugh at."[17]

Your emotional response may not feel like something you can control, at first. But you can start by giving yourself permission—in fact, ordering yourself—to renew your bias toward fun. We weren't built to fight all the time. Think about it the way I and many others approach personal philanthropy: You can make a meaningful contribution by giving a dedicated amount, consistently over a lifetime. *No one's asking you to give it all away.*

At the end of 2020, I opted to take a dose of my own medicine, as mechanical as it felt at first. That was how I ended up on the retreat that led to the writing of chapter 6, one of a handful of steps I took to bring myself back into balance.

Don't defer fun until the world's problems are solved, because they never will be. We each have the responsibility to create space for renewal, celebration, connection, and joy—for ourselves and, even more importantly, for each other. This is yet another way to make a case for the importance of a Fun Habit—and here you start to understand that yes, it takes discipline to bias yourself toward joy when the world has so much darkness. I don't know Trevor Noah's mom, but I would guess that her disposition toward love was a conscious choice, and not always an easy one.

While fun is a starting point for contributing to a better world, the end point is up to you. The more you take care of yourself, energizing your psyche with acts of pleasure, compassion, and contribution that inspire you, the more you may find you're able to lean into the occasional discomfort that comes with the need for growth. If you can keep it up, the reward may be the discovery of unparalleled connectedness, satisfaction, delight, and joy . . . and sometimes even a soul-satisfying step into the wonder of *The Mystery.*

Conclusion

Finding Ultima

I do have a "belief system," but that belief system comes down to what Michelle always said, which is, "It's chaos. Be kind."
—PATTON OSWALT

As a kid I really enjoyed Choose Your Own Adventure books. In my neighborhood a bunch of us traded these easy reads like playing cards. It was fun to compare our unique endings with each other, sharing a completely different story even though we had all read the same book. I liked almost any title I got my hands on, but one in the series was a standout, *Inside UFO 54-40*. In the story, "you" are the protagonist. The tale begins aboard the Concorde, the luxury supersonic jet, on a flight from New York to London. While airborne, you are abruptly abducted by aliens and find yourself teleported aboard a cigar-shaped spaceship. As the first pages unfold, you quickly find out you're no longer within the realm of Earth—and the adventure begins.

Readers of this genre are used to a mixed bag of possible endings—some good, some bad, some that finish in a compelling twist. Not *Inside UFO 54-40*, however. Uniquely in this one book, all the available endings are unhappy or strangely unsatisfying. As the story progresses, you are teased with the existence of a utopian planet called Ultima. Ultima sounds amazing, yet there are no story lines based on the choices available in the book that get you to this magical place.

A few of us in the neighborhood that read this book around the same time literally mapped out each decision tree, looking for paths that would lead to Ultima. After careful study, analyzing every possible outcome, *we had the data*—Ultima was an impossible destination.

Or so we thought. One day I sat down and, ignoring the book's convention, read it page by page from beginning to end. Hidden within the pages of the book, *there it was*: Ultima! Available to anyone willing to dare sidestepping convention and choose to simply *arrive*.

Although puritans might consider this cheating, I don't look at it this way. *Not at all*. I cracked the code. **The beauty of finding Ultima is that no specific set of choices get you there.** There are no conventional paths. Yet, hidden within the middle of the book, there Ultima sits, for anyone to discover.

Fun is our Ultima. It's been hiding in plain sight this whole time. So easy for you to find, it's a wonder why it ever seemed elusive. Someone can lure you in the right direction—but ultimately, it's your choice to be curious and use your agency to arrive.

All Good Things Come to an End

There is only one thing I can accurately predict about each and every one of you reading this book: At some point your life will come to an end. (A book about fun can't include a chapter on death, I've been told, so I had to sneak this bit into the conclusion.) For some of us, like my brother, the end comes too soon. If you've made it this far in the book, I hope my message has resonated. I hope when you are faced with the decision of having to mortgage having fun for things that are not thoughtful priorities, you now deliberate more critically about the toll you're paying. Rooted in the cliché that you can't take anything with you in the end, there is a universal truth: *Life is both total and finite*, so you should prioritize and plan to make the most of it. Yet, that's hard to do because most of us live like we have no expiration date. In fact, we are wired not to think about our end. This has been thoroughly explored in the book *The Worm at the Core*[1] by researchers Tom Pyszczynski, Jeff Greenberg, and Sheldon Solomon, who have coined this *terror management theory*. Since most of our internal systems have been built to help us with self-preservation, we quite literally get terrified by the cognitive dissonance created when we contemplate that ultimately, these systems will fail us.

Memento Mori

Instead of being terrified by death, what if we embrace it? Have you ever had an experience that woke you up to the reality that your life could end tomorrow? For me, that wake-up call was the sudden passing of my brother. For Ric Elias, the CEO of Red Ventures, it was a goose.

January 15, 2009, was a pleasant afternoon in New York. For Ric Elias, there was nothing extraordinary of note as he caught U.S. Airways Flight 1549 home to North Carolina. At about three thousand feet into the trip, Ric and his fellow passengers heard an explosion. Flying geese had knocked out all engine power to their plane. Two short minutes later they were told to "Brace for impact," as their plane began its crash course into the Hudson River.

Confident that his life was over, various thoughts went through Ric's mind as the plane descended. Many of the thoughts were rooted in the regret of all the opportunities for joy he had postponed in life up until this moment. He coined this failure, "I collect bad wines," as a strong metaphor for all the delayed, "unopened" experiences he'd miss out on if he did not make it out alive. Ric also realized how much time he had wasted on negative energy because he had not been mindful of its collective impact.

The good news is that Ric and the rest of the passengers survived. Ric emerged from the "Miracle on the Hudson" a changed person. Ric's personal runbook now has a new script: "If the wine is ready and the person is there, I'm opening it. I no longer want to postpone anything in life. And that urgency, that purpose, has really changed my life."[2] None of us really knows when our time will be up, but we can learn from those that came close and benefited from being able to foreshadow their regrets.

A *memento mori* is an object used to remind us of death—but we can just as well use these artifacts to remind us to enjoy the gift of life as well.

Ric's memento mori is his wine cabinet. Mine is a picture of my brother and me waiting in line for the Kingda Ka on our last adventure together, sitting on a copy of Randy Pausch's book *The Last Lecture* on the desk in my office. When I'm traveling, it's the saved voicemail of my father calling to tell me of Brian's passing. When I feel like I need to renew my bias toward fun, I at times rely on one of these artifacts. The voicemail is especially useful if I'm in a town where there is an opportunity to link up with an old friend but I'm feeling a bit lazy. If you're looking for your own memento mori, a countdown timer is an effective option. I have one that you can use for free, available here: https://share.michaelrucker.com/memento-mori. Look at it whenever you need a reminder that *now* is the time to say yes to fun.

Why is the acknowledgment of death such a potent tool in having a bias toward fun and removing all the "might-have-beens" in our lives? Accepting the notion of mortality pushes us; it is a driver to express ourselves before it's too late. Some people become very prolific as they realize their end is near. David Bowie, for instance, had a remarkable eighteen-month run before his death in 2016.[3] We start appreciating life more, enjoying ourselves more, having fun with others.

But why wait until someone has penciled in the end to have a relationship with death? Why delay fun for the end when it can comfortably coexist with life's responsibilities, both mundane and profound? When we acknowledge that life is time-bound, we grant ourselves the agency to live our lives accordingly.

Pain is an ingredient in the human condition. Whether we like it or not, it's part of the journey. I once thought there ought to be a way to "hack" life such that unpleasant stress could be avoided. Now I see how wrongheaded that is: Denying its place in the natural order only seems to amplify its effect. Pain and loss are inherently part of our design. We will see loved ones die. Change is inevitable and it can be brutal. What I hope you take away from this book is that although pain exists, so does fun. Fun allows us to cope with life's pain, and sometimes even transcend it, by more fully experiencing life's gifts.

When we mindlessly throw ourselves at fun untethered—although fun is certainly boundless—it never seems to be enough, so we villainize it.

However, when we seek fun out deliberately, not despite our pain, but in harmony with it, we unlock a door to a new world that eludes too many. Not only do we experience more pleasure, but we unlock valuable insight and wisdom as well. And, perhaps best of all, life gifts us with moments of awe and wonder that become accessible when we joyfully connect to our own unique actualization of *The Mystery*.

What are the possibilities if, somehow by magic, we could readily accept that our story will eventually have an end?

Start with the End in Mind

If you want to bask in the wonder of life, realizing your life will eventually have an end is a good place to start—but not in an anxious way, like too many of us do. When we face the reality of our mortality, this can be a powerful trigger that fundamentally changes what motivates us. In purely scientific terms, the research I was able to unearth is primarily anecdotal and retrospective studies,* but there are a handful of studies that can enrich our understanding.

Although it might seem paradoxical at first, many psychologists believe that our relationship with death correlates with life satisfaction. Self-actualization and attitude toward one's mortality seem to be linked. It's one thing to have anxiety about the experience of death. It's natural to have a healthy fear of unpleasant things. What we're talking about here is those who won't accept that life is finite. A scientific study that explored the connection between mortality acceptance and self-actualization was conducted in 1975 by Dr. John W. Gamble.[4] Gamble showed that people who are considered more self-actualized—radically accepting of themselves and others—are also generally more comfortable with the finality of life. In contrast, less self-actualized people experience difficulty when contemplating their mortality.

---

* If you are interested in retrospection, Bronnie Ware's amazing research on regret, which fueled the creation of her bestselling book *The Top Five Regrets of the Dying*, will inspire anyone to start living more deliberately.

Could this relationship work in reverse? Could a simple brush with mortality increase our motivation to self-actualize, as it seems to have for Ric Elias, me, and others? *Yes and no.* A study by Drs. Catherine Nogas, Kathy Schweitzer, and Judy Grenst found no association between death anxiety and the need for achievement.[5] It appears that the fear of death alone is not that motivating. In fact, being afraid of death not only doesn't stimulate us in any productive way, but it can also actually hinder our activities and plans.

But a confrontation with death doesn't necessarily lead to death anxiety. It could lead to death acceptance—and that seems to make the difference. A study conducted by Drs. John Ray and Jackob Najman found that the need for achievement was positively linked to death acceptance.[6] When we accept that life will have an end (instead of fearing it), we become more able to use our awareness of death to our advantage.

In general, death acceptance has been connected to higher meaning in life. For example, when studying people's sense of purpose (with the purpose-in-life test, or PIL) psychologists found that people who scored high on PIL generally had a more positive attitude toward death. John Blazer, a researcher from the University of Miami who was behind one of the studies on mortality and meaning in life, argued that our relationship with death can benefit from mindfully examining our goals and purpose.[7] A person with a sense of meaning (that is not motivated by status and finances) is more likely to be accepting of death.

Life After Death (Acceptance)

Some psychologists believe that death acceptance is life's ultimate goal. According to David Sobel, growth occurs only when we acknowledge death.[8] He writes that the experience of death is separation from loved ones and the things we love. When you can let go of your fear of death, you can let go of the desire to control and manipulate. The fear of failure disappears and the rewards of experiencing life become completely available. Some therapists walk their patients through the experience of their death as a therapeutic tool. "Death Cafes"—informal gatherings designed to normalize talk about death, which can otherwise be taboo—are popping up everywhere so participants can explore the topic together.[9]

We all experience "small" deaths throughout our lives—moving to another town, breaking up with a first love or a long-term partner, changing jobs. These "temporal landmarks" can kick-start aspirational behavior.[10] They can push us through similar psychological motions (albeit less intense). When we let it, experiencing this type of loss can be a portal to new behaviors and insights.

Grief expert Elisabeth Kübler-Ross summarizes this well:

Death is the key to the door of life. It is through accepting the finiteness of our own individual existences that we are able to find the strength and courage to reject those extrinsic roles and expectations and devote each day of our lives—however long they may be—to growing as fully as we are able . . . When you fully understand that each day you awaken could be the last you have, you take the time that day to grow, to become more of who you really are, to reach out to other human beings.[11]

Dr. Randy Pausch, who was a computer science professor at Carnegie Mellon University, is a personal hero of mine when it comes to a healthy approach to both life and death. In his Really Achieving Your Childhood Dreams presentation—a "last lecture" given to a full house of Carnegie Mellon students, fellow faculty, and friends on September 18, 2007— Randy talked about achieving his childhood dreams and helping others do the same.[12] At the time of what would ultimately be his final lecture at Carnegie Mellon, although he looked and sounded healthy, Randy had been given only two to five months left to live following a diagnosis of pancreatic cancer.

Randy had very specific dreams growing up—experiencing zero gravity, playing in the National Football League, authoring an article in the *World Book Encyclopedia*, being Captain Kirk (which he later amended to "meeting Captain Kirk"), winning one of those big stuffed animals in an amusement park, and being an Imagineer with Disney. One could argue that Randy is the godfather of the Fun File. During his last lecture, Randy spoke about how he found ways to achieve (almost all of) these experiences. This is what he said about his life: "I don't know how to not have fun. I'm dying and I'm having fun. And I'm going to keep having fun every day I have left. Because there's no other way to play it." Talking about lessons learned: "Never lose the childlike wonder. It's just too important. It's what drives us. Help others."

Randy's fun-loving, brave, free, seize-the-moment attitude continues to be an inspiration to me and countless others. Even in the face of death, he appeared optimistic and cheerful about life. It's clear that one of the reasons he is well-loved is because his attitude was contagious, and he brought joy to others. But perhaps most importantly, Randy didn't put things off, which left him with little regret. He prioritized life experience, so when he died at the age of forty-seven, he left an important legacy: an ode to the power of pursuing fun. His inspiring last lecture has been watched by millions of people worldwide, and his book *The Last Lecture* that shares the experience of the lecture (as well as Randy's wisdom on life) became a *New York Times* bestseller.[13] In a life cut too short, Randy Pausch changed the world for the better. He made his contribution, while having fun all the way.

The Power of Living an Extraordinary Life

We have been groomed to be pacified by superficial access to the *Nothing*. When we are feeling down, we seemingly enjoy that micro-boost when someone likes our random social media post, so we post another one instead of reaching out to thank the person that made us feel that way.

Extraordinary experiences require us to make deliberate choices. Transformative moments don't often fall out of the sky, but there are definitely ways to increase their frequency. **If you want a twist of fate, start twisting.** Choosing fun every day in small, seemingly superficial ways can, over time, lead you to new patterns of behavior—new and better choices. What starts as a dance with whimsy may lead to you discovering *The Mystery*, with your joy lighting the path. How might your life improve after a month, or a year—or ten years—of making fun a habit?

One Final Request

We've reached the end. Thank you so much for taking the time to read this book. If you've enjoyed it, please share the fun in this book with a friend. My hope is that we can spread the power of fun to as many people as possible. Additionally, if you have any questions or comments, please reach out. I'm here for the dialogue and the further exploration of fun.

Second City, Chicago, Illinois, 4/24/2015

You might have noticed I've started each chapter with a quote from a comedian. In part, this was to honor my brother. We had so much fun together in our shared love for comedy. The quote from Patton Oswalt at the start of this conclusion is a fitting one as we finish up. In it are four words that were the mantra of his wife, Michelle McNamara, whom he met after a performance at a comedy club (an encounter he described as love at first sight). After that first encounter, they became inseparable, married, and had a daughter together. And then, after eleven years of a loving and devoted marriage, Michelle died suddenly and unexpectedly.

Oswalt says he and his wife had had a long-standing philosophical debate. Though an atheist, Oswalt always argued for being open to some "latticework of logic," or a deeper intelligence guiding the universe. Michelle, however, disagreed, saying that "everything happens for a reason" was the world's cruelest lie. On the contrary, everything is shockingly random chaos. "She won the argument in the shittiest way possible," Oswalt quips in one of many laughter-through-tears moments in his heartbreaking Netflix special *Annihilation*. "If there is some intelligence up there with a plan, then his plan sucks."

But his wife offered the antidote, the wisdom that ultimately helped Oswalt climb out of the numbing grief he felt in the months after her death, a time in which all his usual comforting escapes failed him. I believe it is the antidote for all of us when life's pain reaches a nadir. In four simple words, she gave her husband an invitation to step into *The Mystery*:

It's chaos. Be kind.

Says Patton, "If you want to talk to God—or whatever you think God is—go be nice to another person. That is the best way to communicate with the infinite. Be nice to a family member, a loved one, go spread that around . . . You don't know how it will be spread around, but you know that you're literally out there doing good."

Science also supports McNamara's mantra.[14] Along with fun, practicing kindness makes us happier—and the acts of kindness that appear to be the most supportive of our well-being are the ones that connect us to each other in an authentic way and allow us to feel we're freely living in alignment with our identity and values. In that way, fun and kindness make great bedfellows.

And so, as you take the wisdom from this book and develop your own Fun Habit, I leave you with these *six* words: *It's Chaos. Be Kind. Have Fun.*

Acknowledgments

We had a lot of fun creating this book, and it was definitely a team sport. I would like to start by saying thank you to Sara Grace for joining me as a collaborator on this journey and making the entire process as delightful as possible. Lisa DiMona, for being an amazing person and superstar agent, as well as trusting and believing in a book about fun. I'd like to thank Stephanie Hitchcock for her enthusiastic curiosity about the proposal and for her effort helping the book take shape in the best way possible. I am grateful for David Moldawer and his amazing work as an early developmental editor on the project. I owe a debt of gratitude to Urša Bratun for her years of effort helping me research and synthesize the science of fun, which now stands as the foundation of *The Fun Habit*. I'm thankful for Hayley Riggs, for all her years of ideas and blog editing. The Year of Fun exists because of Hayley. Rounding out the immediate *Fun Habit* team are Sabine Andree and Sue Campbell (as well as her team at Pages & Platforms), who were late additions but were essential players in the book's launch.

This book wouldn't have been possible without my family. I am grateful for my parents, Robert and Margaret. I could fill the page with exposition here, but that wouldn't be fun. So, let me just say I will be forever grateful that every time I've not been able to get back up on my own, they have been there to get me moving forward again. Throughout the

ACKNOWLEDGMENTS

process of bringing this book to fruition, they've been my biggest cheerleaders, and that certainly was a lot of fun. I am grateful for my wife, who gave up many moments of fun so I could write this book. I promise to never write another book, just like I have promised to never compete in another Ironman or marathon, earn another degree, or get another tattoo. You've been my unwavering Ironmate the past twenty years despite these false promises. And, of course, the littles: Archer and Sloane. I love you so much. Thank you for the continual lessons in fun. You two are such excellent teachers. Selfishly, one of my favorite parts of creating this book is that it is an artifact that's a piece of me for you two to keep.

I have been blessed to be surrounded by great people most of my life, but there are five groups of friends in particular that have shaped my worldview, and for that I would like to acknowledge them: my groomsmen, the Vodka Train crew, my 1996 Isla Vista roomies, my fantasy football teammates, and my Club One / Active Wellness family. (Please note that from here on out, lists of names have no significant order.) **Groomsmen:** Brian Rucker, Micah Myers (and his wife, Kirsten), Nathan Burroughs (and his wife, Meaghan), Darren Pujalet (and his wife, Genevieve), Luke Aguilar (and his wife, Amy), Rich Gray, Erik Foster, Alberto Feliciano, Brian Manalastas, Alfred "Alfie" DelFavero, Sam Pietsch, and Matthew Szymszyk. **Vodka Train crew:** Nathan Baldwin, Mark Burley, Darren "Daz" Swain, Andrew Page, Todd Mathers, Aine and Philip Murphy, Rebecca Mojsin, and Blaise Agresta. (I would have included some of our tales in this book, but what happens in Outer Mongolia stays in Outer Mongolia.) **Isla Vista roomies:** Claire Bloomberg, Anne Stratman, Amy Bloomberg, Ani (and Monico) Casillas, Lisa Welch Holton, Becky Grove, Erin Dunning, Maya Lise Singer, and Anne Paffrath Ray. **Fantasy football buddies:** Jeremy Carver, Dave Otterson, Jim Monagle, Drew Shimizu, Niccolo De Luca, Glenn Chenn, Scott Carlson, Jon Hallin, Ken Lee, Scott Russell, Andrew Nelson, and Dan Offenbach. **Club One / Active Wellness family:** Bill McBride, Jill Kinney, Carey White, Michele Wong, Kari Bedgood, Meredith DePersia, Ryan McFadden, Elizabeth Studebaker, Jessica Isle, Erica Stenz, Karah Ehrhardt, Jennie Martin, Kenny and Annette Ko, Manda Wong, Alvin

ACKNOWLEDGMENTS

Dizon, Jerry Cardinali, Andy (and Alisah) Spieth, Lauren Suggett, Natalie Jensen, Rosemary Mamisay, Justin Weber, and the rest of the Club One / Active Wellness family. The immense amount of fun I have had with the names contained within this paragraph provide this fortunate soul with a lifetime of reminiscing.

Before *The Fun Habit*, there was the Burrito Project. If you know, you know. Thanks to all my USC classmates who donated to make that endeavor happen. And a special acknowledgment goes out to Patrick Fellows, who took me in as an apprentice for no other reason besides I am bananas (like him), we both love burritos, and we both like endurance sports.

I would like to acknowledge Michael Gervais, Olav Sorenson, Nir Eyal, Ryan Tarzy, Tim Grahl, and Jyotsna Sanzgiri as amazing mentors through various periods of my life. These six have been quite kind with their time and wisdom. I appreciate each of you.

Thank you Ritu Barua, Andy Velez, and Finley Skelton for your help as virtual assistants, and Doan Trang for your illustrative contributions.

I'd like to acknowledge all of the thought leaders that made the time to be interviewed for the Live Life Love Project that have not been acknowledged already: Stuart MacFarlane, Jamie Ramsden, Sean Waxman, David Allen, Jeff Atkinson, Dave Scott, Scott Bell, Chris Talley, Kristi Frank, Jeff Galloway, Todd DiPaola, Tom DeLong, Mark Friedman, Gloria Park Perin, Bryan Pate, J.K. Monagle, Lloyd Nimetz, Gear Fisher, Ed Baker, Brodie Burris, Hammad Zaidi, Thom Gilligan, Margaret Moore, Barbara Lippard, Ellen Burton, Deena Varshavskaya, Liz Applegate, Scot Hacker, Alex Gourley, Erik Allebest, Nadeem Kasaam, Jerome Breche, Brian Russell, Alex Kaplinsky, Ken Snyder, Eric Quick, Sky Christopherson, Tim Ferriss, Matthew Heineman, Sunil Saha, Howard Jacobson, Ned Dwyer, Ari Meisel, Gary Vanerchuk, Mike Leveque, Neville Medhora, Bob Summers, Brad Bowery, Craig DeLarge, Ben Rubin, Ben Greenfield, James Pshock, Chris Bingham, Al Lewis, Drew Schiller, Laura Putnam, Kate Matsudaira, Mitesh Patel, Edgar Schein, Jill Gilbert, John Gengarella, Henry DePhillips, Raj Raghunathan, Chip Conley, Matthew Nock, Cathy Presland, Daniel Freedman, Steve

ACKNOWLEDGMENTS

Groves, Matt Holt, Amanda Krantz, Morten Hansen, Charlie Hoehn, Erik Paquet, Jeffrey Pfeffer, Brad Wills, Anthony Middlebrooks, Laura Vanderkam, Jonah Babins, Noah Kagan, Craig Lund, Cassie Mogilner Holmes, Dike Drummond, Angela Kyle, Timothy Wilson, Gary Ware, Tara Gerahty, Tania Katan, Susanne Cook-Greuter, Karen Pollard, Alexandre Mandryka, Jordan Etkin, Lisa Feldman Barrett, Kaitlin Woolley, Iris Mauss, Todd Kashdan, Tasha Eurich, Jill Vialet, Jedd Chang, Lee Huffman, and Christian Ehrlich.

I'd like to acknowledge my fellow Healthcare Information and Management Systems Society Digital Changemakers, especially our organizer, Michael Gaspar. This world needs more people like Michael. I would also like to acknowledge Kathleen Terry and my fellow Leadership Manhattan Beach alumni. Both of these groups have been instrumental in my growth as a servant leader.

I want to thank Paula Nowick, Kelly Cash, Bryan Wish, Brad Bowery, Eugene Manin, Linda Leffel, Scott Russell, Ken Holt, Lindsey Nicole, Yonina Siegal, Julia Bellabarba, Karen Barletta, and Quin Bee for responding to crowdsourcing prompts that resulted in segments of collective wisdom found in chapter 6 and chapter 9.

Lastly, I would like to acknowledge all the scholars, researchers, authors, and sage people that have shaped my views on fun: Ronald A. Berk, Stanley Cohen, Laurie Taylor, David J. Linden, Willard Gaylin, Elaine Hatfield, John T. Cacioppo, Richard L. Rapson, Erik H. Erikson, Joan M. Erikson, Joseph J. Sandler, Peter Fonagy, Charles Murray, Jeffrey Goldstein, Daniel H. Pink, John B. Miner, Gary Wolf, Henry Sidgwick, John Rawls, Bronnie Ware, Richard M. Ryan, Edward L. Deci, Edward O. Wilson, George Ritzer, Alex Soojung-Kim Pang, Martin E. P. Seligman, Peter Railton, Roy F. Baumeister, Chandra Sripada, Matthew Killingsworth, Susan Cain, Yi-Fu Tuan, Dan Sullivan, Benjamin P. Hardy, Viktor E. Frankl, Harold S. Kushner, William J. Winslade, Benjamin Hale, Karl E. Weick, Catherine Wilson, Daniel L. Schacter, Daniel T. Gilbert, Daniel M. Wegner, Robert Kegan, Shasta Nelson, Dale Carnegie, Sherry Turkle, Stuart Brown, Travis Bradberry, Jean Greaves, Eric Berne, Thomas Harris, David F. Lancy, Kathryn Schulz, Ellen Jane

ACKNOWLEDGMENTS

Langer, Elisabeth Kübler-Ross, Lisa L. Lahey, Brené Brown, Carl Pacifico, Mihaly Csikszentmihalyi, Dylan Walsh, Clare Ansberry, Willibald Ruch, René Proyer, Marco Weber, Sara Wellenzohn, Kristy Holtfreter, Michael D. Reisig, Jillian J. Turanovic, Shin-Hyun Kim, Scott Y. H. Kim, Hong Jin Kim, Hadi Kooshiar, Zohre Najafi, Amin Azhari, Erika Forbes, Peter M. Lewinsohn, Jeremy Pettit, Thomas E. Joiner, Liang Gong, John R. Seeley, Cancan He, Yingying Yin, Hui Wang, Qing Ye, Feng Bai, Yonggui Yuan, Haisan Zhang, Luxian Lv, Hongxing Zhang, Zhijun Zhang, Chunming Xie, Laurie R. Santos, Alexandra G. Rosati, Jennifer A. Hunter, Charles J. Palus, David M. Horth, Minkyung Koo, Jens Timmermann, Lynda Flower, Christian Meisel, Antonio Damasio, Nasir Naqvi, Baba Shiv, Antoine Bechara, Richard M. Wenzlaff, Michael Lacewing, Emma A. Renström, Torun Lindholm, Mark E. Koltko-Rivera, Henry Venter, Eduard Venter, Wulf-Uwe Meyer, Rainer Reisenzein, Achim Schuetzwohl, Marret K. Noordewier, Eric van Dijk, Gregory S. Berns, Samuel M. McClure, Pendleton R. Montague, Vincent K. M. Cheung, Peter M. C. Harrison, Lars Meyer, Marcus T. Pearce, John-Dylan Haynes, Stefan Koelsch, Małgorzata A. Gocłowska, Matthijs Baas, Richard J. Crisp, Carsten K. W. De Dreu, Brian Knutson, Curt M. Adams, Grace W. Fong, Robert Sapolsky, Yu-Chen Chan, Wei-Chin Hsu, Tai-Li Chou, Scott A. Langenecker, Leah R. Kling, Natania A. Crane, Stephanie M. Gorka, Robin Nusslock, Katherine S. F. Damme, Jessica Weafer, Harriet de Wit, K. Luan Phan, Kennon Sheldon, Stefano Di Domenico, Richard Koestner, Barbara A. Marinak, Linda B. Gambrell, Laura G. Burgess, Patricia M. Riddell, Amy Fancourt, Kou Murayama, Rosemarie Anderson, Sam T. Manoogian, J. Steven Reznick, Örjan de Manzano, Simon Cervenka, Aurelija Jucaite, Oscar Hellenäs, Lars Farde, Fredrik Ullén, Konstanze Albrecht, Johannes Abeler, Bernd Weber, Armin Falk, Brendan J. Tunstall, Dean Kirson, Lia J. Zallar, Sam McConnell, Janaina C. M. Vendruscolo, Chelsea P. Ho, Volker Ott, Graham Finlayson, Hendrik Lehnert, Birte Heitmann, Markus Heinrichs, Jan Born, Manfred Hallschmid, Peter Katsingris, John P. Robinson, Steven Martin, Deniz Bayraktaroglu, Gul Gunaydin, Emre Selcuk, Anthony D. Ong, Ayelet Fishbach, Veronika Huta, Alan S. Waterman,

ACKNOWLEDGMENTS

Harald S. Harung, Gill Pomfret, Joe Hoare, Sherry Hilber, Hanna R. Rodenbaugh, Heidi L. Lujan, David W. Rodenbaugh, Stephen E. DiCarlo, Reneé L. Polubinsky, Jennifer M. Plos, D. J. Grosshandler, Niswander Grosshandler, Renate L. Reniers, Amanda Bevan, Louise Keoghan, Andrea Furneaux, Samantha Mayhew, Stephen J. Wood, Stephen Lyng, Sue Scott, Mark D. Austin, Alan Dix, Regan L. Mandryk, Stella M. Atkins, Paul Ekman, Richard J. Davidson, Kiki M. De Jonge, Eric F. Rietzschel, Nico W. Van Yperen, Benjamin Scheibehenne, Rainer Greifeneder, Peter M. Todd, Hazel Rose Markus, Barry Schwartz, Elena Reutskaja, Axel Lindner, Rosemarie Nagel, Richard A. Andersen, Colin F. Camerer, Kirsi-Marja Zitting, Mirjam Y. Münch, Sean W. Cain, Wei Wang, Arick Wong, Joseph M. Ronda, Daniel Aeschbach, Charles A. Czeisler, Jeanne F. Duffy, Max Hirshkowitz, Kaitlyn Whiton, Steven M. Albert, Cathy Alessi, Oliviero Bruni, Lydia DonCarlos, Nancy Hazen, John Herman, Eliot S. Katz, Leila Kheirandish-Gozal, David N. Neubauer, Anne E. O'Donnell, Maurice Ohayon, John Peever, Robert Rawding, Ramesh C. Sachdeva, Belinda Setters, Michael V. Vitiello, James Catesby Ware, Paula J. Hillard, Laura K. Barger, Najib T. Ayas, Brian E. Cade, John W. Cronin, Bernard Rosner, Frank E. Speizer, Bronwyn Fryer, Sandi Mann, Rebekah Cadman, Lydia Saad, John Pencavel, Francesco P. Cappuccio, Lanfranco D'Elia, Pasquale Strazzullo, Michelle A. Miller, John Helliwell, Huong Dinh, Lyndall Strazdins, Jennifer Welsh, Katrina L. Piercy, Richard P. Troiano, Rachel M. Ballard, Susan Carlson, Janet E. Fulton, Deborah A. Galuska, Stephanie M. George, Richard D. Olson, William W. Beach, William J. Wiatrowski, Homa Khaleeli, Elizabeth Frates, Dan Buettner, Sam Skemp, Bryce Hruska, Sarah D. Pressman, Kestutis Bendinskas, Brooks B. Gump, Kim Brooks, Thomas P. Reith, Gareth Cook, David A. Reinhard, Erin C. Westgate, Nicole Ellerbeck, Cheryl Hahn, Casey L. Brown, Adi Shaked, Sarah Alahmadi, Nicholas R. Buttrick, Amber M. Hardin, Colin West, Sanford E. DeVoe, Paul A. O'Keefe, Carol S. Dweck, Gregory M. Walton, Curt Richter, David Premack, Leif D. Nelson, Tom Meyvis, Alyssa Croft, Elizabeth Dunn, Jordi Quoidbach, Dinah Avni-Babad, Ilana Ritov, Chess Stetson, Matthew P. Fiesta, David M. Eagleman, Gilles Grolleau, Sandra Saïd,

ACKNOWLEDGMENTS

Sharon Hadad, Miki Malul, Agnete Gundersen, Michaela Benson, Karen O'Reilly, Nico H. Frijda, Sonja Lyubomirsky, David Schkade, Philip C. Watkins, Kathrine Woodward Thomas, Tamara Stone, Russell L. Kolts, Paul G. Middlebrooks, Marc A. Sommer, Gábor Orosz, Edina Dombi, István Tóth-Király, Beáta B?the, Balázs Jagodics, Phil Zimbardo, John N. Boyd, Fred B. Bryant, Joseph Veroff, Bradley P. Turnwald, Danielle Boles, Alia J. Crum, Colette M. Smart, Scott P. King, Stephen Schueller, Megan E. Speer, Jamil P. Bhanji, Mauricio R. Delgado, Bethany Morris, Greg J. Stephens, Uri Hasson, Oliver S. Curry, Lee Rowland, Caspar J. van Lissa, Sally Zlotowitz, Harvey Whitehouse, John McAlaney, Justin Thomas, Tel Amiel, Stephanie L. Sargent, Pablo Fernandez-Berrocal, Rosario Cabello, Peter Hills, Michael Argyle, Elizabeth Bernstein, William Fleeson, Adriane B. Malanos, Noelle M. Achille, Zhenkun Zhou, Ke Xu, Jichang Zhao, Craig Ross, Emily S. Orr, Mia Sisic, Jaime M. Arseneault, Mary G. Simmering, Robert R. Orr, David Cunningham, Liz Thach, Karen J. Thompson, Shengli Deng, Yong Liu, Hongxiu Li, Feng Hu, Zoya Gervis, Sointu Leikas, Ville-Juhani Ilmarinen, William Pavot, Ed Diener, Frank Fujita, Joshua J. Mark, Steven Fife, Michael J. Tews, John W. Michel, Raymond A. Noe, Judy Willis, Ronald Alsop, David L. Collinson, Frode Stenseng, Jostein Rise, Pål Kraft, Brigitte Wanner, Robert Ladouceur, Amélie V. Auclair, Frank Vitaro, Doris Bergen, Maxime Taquet, Yves-Alexandre de Montjoye, Martin Desseilles, James J. Gross, Desirée Kozlowski, Elizabeth Berry, Barış K. Yörük, Chris Hadfield, Wendy Wood, Nate Staniforth, Heather McIver, Trevor Noah, Michel Hansenne, Moïra Mikolajczak, Abraham H. Maslow, David B. Yaden, Jonathan Haidt, Ralph W. Hood, David R. Vago, Andrew Newberg, Ingrid Koller, Michael R. Levenson, Judith Glück, Mark H. Anshel, Diane Bamber, Ian M. Cockerill, Sheelagh Rodgers, Douglas Carroll, Chantal Seguin-Levesque, Marie-Lyne Laliberté, Luc G. Pelletier, Celine Blanchard, Robert J. Vallerand, Genevieve A. Mageau, Catherine Ratelle, Laude Leonard, Marylene Gagne, Josee Marsolais, Joshua Phelps, Tommy Haugen, Monica Torstveit, Rune Høigaard, Eva Roos, Eero Lahelma, Ossi Rahkonen, Wijnand A. P. van Tilburg, Eric R. Igou, Constantine Sedikides, Jennifer Sommers, Stephen J. Vodanovich, Greg-

ACKNOWLEDGMENTS

ory J. Boyle, Lisa M. Richards, Anthony J. Baglioni, Mary B. Harris, Gustavo Razzetti, Chantal Nederkoorn, Linda Vancleef, Alexandra Wilkenhöner, Laurence Claes, Remco C. Havermans, Kalina Christoff, Alan M. Gordon, Jonathan W. Schooler, Michael I. Posner, Inchara Naidu, Jothi A. Priya, Gayatri Devi, Cory J. Gerritsen, Maggie E. Toplak, Jessica Sciaraffa, John Eastwood, Robert Waldinger, Catherine Caruso, Diana Baumrind, Julee P. Farley, Jungmeen Kim-Spoon, Anna-Beth Doyle, Heather Lawford, Julie N. Kingery, Cynthia A. Erdley, Katherine C. Marshall, Jacob A. Burack, Alexandra D'Arrisso, Vladimir Ponizovsky, Wendy Troop-Gordon, Tarek Mandour, Curtis Tootoosis, Sandy Robinson, Grace Iarocci, Stephanie Fryberg, Deborah Laible, Gustavo Carlo, Marcela Raffaelli, Alex Williams, Kim Reinking, Robert A. Bell, Michael E. Roloff, Karen Van Camp, Susan H. Karol, Jan-Emmanuel De Neve, George Ward, Maria Konnikova, Sergio M. Pellis, Vivien C. Pellis, Brett T. Himmler, and Jaak Panksepp.

If you just made it through the last few pages, please return to chapter 2 and go through the PLAY Model exercise again. My guess is you can find much better options for spending your time than reading a list of names. In all seriousness, I remain grateful for all those named (and inadvertently unnamed) that enabled this book to become reality. *It truly was a lot of fun.*

Sincerely,

Michael Rucker, Ph.D.

Endnotes

Author's Note
1. *We realized the truth:* Keller, Helen. *Let Us Have Faith* (New York: Doubleday, & Doran & Company, Incorporated, 1940).

Introduction
2. *Did I mention that:* Golden, Ryan. "What Does the Outcry over Amazon's Mental Health Kiosks Say About Corporate Wellness Programs?" *HR Dive*, June 16, 2021, https://www.hrdive.com/news/what-does-outcry-over-amazon-amazen-mental-health-kiosks-say-about-corporate-wellness/601942.

Chapter One
1. *We let these important skills:* Ansberry, Clare. "An Overlooked Skill in Aging: How to Have Fun." *The Wall Street Journal.* Dow Jones & Company, June 2, 2018, http://www.wsj.com/articles/an-overlooked-skill-in-aging-how-to-have-fun-1527937260.
2. *The United States has:* Iacurci, Greg. "U.S. Is Worst Among Developed Nations for Worker Benefits." CNBC, February 4, 2021, http://www.cnbc.com/2021/02/04/us-is-worst-among-rich-nations-for-worker-benefits.html.
3. *This was vividly demonstrated by:* Ehrenreich, Barbara. *Nickel and Dimed: On (Not) Getting By in America* (New York: Metropolitan Books, 2010).
4. *Author Rahaf Harfoush notes:* Harfoush, Rahaf. *Hustle and Float: Reclaim Your Creativity and Thrive in a World Obsessed with Work* (New York: Diversion Books, 2019).

ENDNOTES

5 *This so-called algorithmic work:* Pink, Daniel H. *Drive: The Surprising Truth About What Motivates Us* (New York: Penguin, 2011).

6 *Author Ann Larson theorizes:* Larson, Ann. "My Disturbing Stint on a Corporate Wellness App: At Some Point, I Realized the Goal Was to Make My Job Kill Me Slower." *Slate*, April 26, 2021, https://slate.com/human-interest/2021/04/corporate-wellness-grocery-store-work-dangers.html.

7 *Corporations hire popular speakers:* Vaynerchuk, Gary. *Crush It!: Why NOW Is the Time to Cash In on Your Passion*, vol. 10 (New York: HarperCollins, 2015).

8 *Corporations hire popular speakers:* Cardone, Grant. *The 10X Rule: The Only Difference Between Success and Failure* (New York: John Wiley & Sons, 2011).

9 *In his book* Dying for a Paycheck: Pfeffer, Jeffrey. *Dying for a Paycheck: Why the American Way of Business Is Injurious to People and Companies* (New York: HarperCollins Publishers, 2018).

10 *In an interview with Insights:* Walsh, Dylan. "The Workplace Is Killing People and Nobody Cares." Stanford Graduate School of Business, March 15, 2018, http://www.gsb.stanford.edu/insights/workplace-killing-people-nobody-cares.

11 *Findings from the World Health Organization:* Pega, Frank, Bálint Náfrádi, Natalie C. Momen, Yuka Ujita, Kai N. Streicher, Annette M. Prüss-Üstün, Alexis Descatha, et al. "Global, Regional, and National Burdens of Ischemic Heart Disease and Stroke Attributable to Exposure to Long Working Hours for 194 Countries, 2000–2016: A Systematic Analysis from THE WHO/ILO Joint Estimates of the Work-Related Burden of Disease and Injury." *Environment International* 154 (2021): 106595. https://doi.org/10.1016/j.envint.2021.106595.

12 *And despite Taylor's undisguised contempt:* Taylor, Frederick Winslow. *The Principles of Scientific Management* (New York: Harper & Brothers, 1919).

13 *I recall as a doctoral candidate:* Miner, John. *Organizational Behavior 1: Essential Theories of Motivation and Leadership* (New York: Routledge, 2015).

14 *As it is with so many activities:* Bartels, Bjoern. "My Love—Relationship Counter." App Store, December 18, 2010. https://apps.apple.com/us/app/my-love-relationship-counter/id409609608.

15 *It often spikes before:* Schott, B. H., L. Minuzzi, R. M. Krebs, D. Elmenhorst, M. Lang, O. H. Winz, C. I. Seidenbecher, et al. "Mesolimbic Functional Magnetic Resonance Imaging Activations During Reward Anticipation Correlate With Reward-Related Ventral Striatal Dopamine Release." *Journal of Neuroscience* 28, no. 52 (2008): 14311–19, https://doi.org/10.1523/jneurosci.2058-08.2008.

16 *Urged on by dopamine:* "Dopamine Jackpot! Sapolsky on the Science of Pleasure." YouTube, uploaded by FORA.tv, March 2, 2011, https://www.youtube.com/watch?v=axrywDP9Ii0.

17 *For decades science has been:* Brickman, Philip, Dan Coates, and Ronnie Janoff-Bulman. "Lottery Winners and Accident Victims: Is Happiness Relative?" *Jour-

ENDNOTES

nal of Personality and Social Psychology 36, no. 8 (1978): 917–27. https://doi.org/10.1037/0022-3514.36.8.917.

18 *We can indeed improve:* Lindqvist, Erik, Robert Östling, and David Cesarini. "Long-Run Effects of Lottery Wealth on Psychological Well-Being." *The Review of Economic Studies* 87, no. 6 (2020): 2703–26. https://doi.org/10.1093/restud/rdaa006.

19 *Similarly, many preferred four weeks:* Grolleau, Gilles, and Sandra Saïd. "Do You Prefer Having More or More Than Others? Survey Evidence on Positional Concerns in France," *Journal of Economic Issues* 42, no. 4 (2008): 1145–58. https://doi.org/10.1080/00213624.2008.11507206.

20 *Emerging science suggests these practices:* Kable, Joseph W., and Paul W. Glimcher. "The Neurobiology of Decision: Consensus and Controversy." *Neuron* 63, no. 6 (2009): 733–45. https://doi.org/10.1016/j.neuron.2009.09.003.

21 *In fact, some researchers argue:* Twenge, Jean M., Thomas E. Joiner, Megan L. Rogers, and Gabrielle N. Martin. "Increases in Depressive Symptoms, Suicide-Related Outcomes, and Suicide Rates Among U.S. Adolescents After 2010 and Links to Increased New Media Screen Time." *Clinical Psychological Science* 6, no. 1 (2017): 3–17. https://doi.org/10.1177/2167702617723376.

22 *The work of Dr. Jean Marie Twenge:* Twenge, Jean. *IGen: Why Today's Super-Connected Kids Are Growing Up Less Rebellious, More Tolerant, Less Happy—and Completely Unprepared for Adulthood—and What That Means for the Rest of Us* (New York: Atria Books, 2017).

23 *In* The Compass of Pleasure: Linden, David J. *The Compass of Pleasure: How Our Brains Make Fatty Foods, Orgasm, Exercise, Marijuana, Generosity, Vodka, Learning, and Gambling Feel So Good* (New York: Penguin, 2012).

24 *When Dr. Volker Ott:* Ott, Volker, Graham Finlayson, Hendrik Lehnert, Birte Heitmann, Markus Heinrichs, Jan Born, and Manfred Hallschmid. "Oxytocin Reduces Reward-Driven Food Intake in Humans." *Diabetes* 62, no. 10 (2013): 3418–25. https://doi.org/10.2337/db13-0663.

25 *When oxytocin is present:* Barraza, Jorge A., and Paul J. Zak. "Oxytocin Instantiates Empathy and Produces Prosocial Behaviors." *Oxytocin, Vasopressin and Related Peptides in the Regulation of Behavior*, 2013, 331–42. https://doi.org/10.1017/cbo9781139017855.022.

26 *Lightning is spectacular:* Engelking, Carl. "Lightning's Strange Physics Still Stump Scientists." *Discover Magazine*, November 20, 2019. https://www.discovermagazine.com/environment/lightnings-strange-physics-still-stump-scientists.

27 *One theory is that early:* Goldstein, Jeffrey. *Play in Children's Development, Health and Well-Being* (Brussels: Toy Industries of Europe, 2012).

28 *When we bias ourselves toward fun:* Sullivan, Dan, and Benjamin P. Hardy. *The Gap and The Gain: The High Achievers' Guide to Happiness, Confidence, and Success* (Hay House Business, 2021).

29 *Laughter is a force for democracy:* Petras, Kathryn, and Ross Petras. "Nothing Is

Worth More Than This Day.": Finding Joy in Every Moment (New York: Workman Publishing, 2016).

30 *According to Walter Isaacson's biography:* Isaacson, Walter. *Einstein: His Life and Universe* (New York: Simon & Schuster Paperbacks, 2008).

31 *People who show an aptitude:* Feingold, Alan, and Ronald Mazzella. "Psychometric Intelligence and Verbal Humor Ability." *Personality and Individual Differences* 12, no. 5 (1991): 427–35. https://doi.org/10.1016/0191-8869(91)90060-o.

32 *They found that both:* Bryant, Fred B., Colette M. Smart, and Scott P. King. "Using the Past to Enhance the Present: Boosting Happiness through Positive Reminiscence." *Journal of Happiness Studies* 6, no. 3 (2005): 227–60. https://doi.org/10.1007/s10902-005-3889-4.

Chapter Two

1 *Matthew Killingsworth, while completing his:* Killingsworth, Matthew. *Happiness from the Bottom Up*. Diss., Harvard University, 2013.

2 *A 2004 survey of 909 working mothers:* Kahneman, Daniel, Alan B. Krueger, David A. Schkade, Norbert Schwarz, and Arthur A. Stone. "A Survey Method for Characterizing Daily Life Experience: The Day Reconstruction Method." *Science* 306, no. 5702 (2004): 1776–80. https://doi.org/10.1126/science.1103572.

3 *first, research from Dr. Marissa Sharif:* Sharif, Marissa A., Cassie Mogilner, and Hal E. Hershfield. "Having too little or too much time is linked to lower subjective well-being." *Journal of Personality and Social Psychology* (2021).

4 *According to the results:* "American Time Use Survey Summary." *U.S. Bureau of Labor Statistics*. U.S. Bureau of Labor Statistics, July 22, 2021. http://www.bls.gov/news.release/atus.nr0.htm.

5 *And although Pew research indicates:* Livingston, Gretchen, and Kim Parker. "8 Facts About American Dads." *Pew Research Center*, May 30, 2020. http://www.pewresearch.org/fact-tank/2019/06/12/fathers-day-facts.

6 *And although Pew research indicates:* Houle, P., Turcotte, M., & Wendt, M. (2017). Changes in parents' participation in domestic tasks and care for children from 1986 to 2015.

7 *The Pew Research Center reports:* Drake, Bruce. "Another Gender Gap: Men Spend More Time in Leisure Activities." *Pew Research Center*, 7 Feb. 2014, https://www.pewresearch.org/fact-tank/2013/06/10/another-gender-gap-men-spend-more-time-in-leisure-activities.

8 *If you think that four to five hours:* Khaleeli, Homa. "How to Get More Free Time in Your Day." *The Guardian*, 13 Mar. 2018, https://www.theguardian.com/money/shortcuts/2013/jun/07/how-get-more-free-time.

9 *In at least their short-term thinking:* Mogilner Holmes, Cassie. "The Pursuit of Happiness Time, Money, and Social Connection." *Psychological Science* 21, no. 9 (2010): 1348–54. https://doi.org/10.1177/0956797610380696.

ENDNOTES

10 *In one, professors at UCLA:* Hershfield, Hal E., Cassie Mogilner Holmes, and Uri Barnea. "People Who Choose Time over Money Are Happier." *Social Psychological and Personality Science* 7, no. 7 (2016): 697–706. https://doi.org/10.1177/1948550616649239.

11 *Based on the frequent resharing:* Herrbach, Toni. "Age Appropriate Chores for Kids: Printable." *The Happy HousewifeTM : Home Management*, 1 Mar. 2019, https://thehappyhousewife.com/home-management/age-appropriate-chores-for-kids-printable.

12 *One of my favorite examples:* Katan, Tania. *Creative Trespassing: How to Put the Spark and Joy Back into Your Work and Life* (New York: Currency, 2019).

13 *Based on recent findings from Nielsen:* The Nielsen Company. *The Nielsen Total Audience Report, Q1 2018*, p. 34, https://www.nielsen.com/wp-content/uploads/sites/3/2019/04/q1-2018-total-audience-report.pdf. Accessed 21 Jan. 2020.

14 *However, we know from years:* Robinson, John P., and Steven Martin. "What Do Happy People Do?" *Social Indicators Research* 89, no. 3 (2008): 565–71. https://doi.org/10.1007/s11205-008-9296-6.

15 *However, we know from years:* Bayraktaroglu, Deniz, Gul Gunaydin, Emre Selcuk, and Anthony D. Ong. "A Daily Diary Investigation of the Link between Television Watching and Positive Affect." *Journal of Happiness Studies* 20, no. 4 (2018): 1089–1101. https://doi.org/10.1007/s10902-018-9989-8.

16 *At this point, we're all familiar:* Hunt, Melissa G., Rachel Marx, Courtney Lipson, and Jordyn Young. "No More FOMO: Limiting Social Media Decreases Loneliness and Depression." *Journal of Social and Clinical Psychology* 37, no. 10 (2018): 751–68. https://doi.org/10.1521/jscp.2018.37.10.751.

17 *For example, smokers who are:* Cohen, Lee M., Frank L. Collins Jr, and Dana M. Britt. "The effect of chewing gum on tobacco withdrawal." *Addictive Behaviors* 22, no. 6 (1997): 769-773.

18 *And in the world of human desire:* Rietzschel, Eric F., J. Marjette Slijkhuis, and Nico W. Van Yperen. "Task Structure, Need for Structure, and Creativity." *European Journal of Social Psychology* 44, no. 4 (2014): 386–99. https://doi.org/10.1002/ejsp.2024.

19 *Computer users trying to choose:* Scheibehenne, Benjamin, Rainer Greifeneder, and Peter M. Todd. "Can There Ever Be Too Many Options? A Meta-Analytic Review of Choice Overload." *Journal of Consumer Research* 37, no. 3 (2010): 409–25. https://doi.org/10.1086/651235.

20 *The scientists concluded that the brain:* Reutskaja, Elena, Axel Lindner, Rosemarie Nagel, Richard A. Andersen, and Colin F. Camerer. "Choice Overload Reduces Neural Signatures of Choice Set Value in Dorsal Striatum and Anterior Cingulate Cortex." *Nature Human Behaviour* 2, no. 12 (2018): 925–35. https://doi.org/10.1038/s41562-018-0440-2.

21 *The American Psychological Association: Peak experience:* In *APA Dictionary of Psychology.* (2022). Retrieved from https://dictionary.apa.org/peak-experience.

22 *"That type of game that provides":* Mandryka, Alexandre. "Pleasure without

Learning Leads to Addiction." *Game Whispering*, 29 Aug. 2016, https://game whispering.com/pleasure-without-learning-leads-to-addiction.

23 *The man did safely parachute:* Guardian Staff Reporter. "Man Accidentally Ejects Himself from Fighter Jet During Surprise Flight." *The Guardian*, 14 Apr. 2020, https://www.theguardian.com/world/2020/apr/14/man-accidentally-ejects -himself-from-fighter-jet-during-surprise-flight.

24 *When analyzing the interactions:* Grosshandler, D.J, and E Niswander Grosshandler. "Constructing Fun: Self-Determination and Learning at an Afterschool Design Lab." *Computers in Human Behavior* 16, no. 3 (2000): 227–40. https://doi.org/10.1016/s0747-5632(00)00003-0.

25 *In his position paper:* Dix, A. Fun Systematically, 2012, retrieved from http:// alandix.com/academic/papers/ECCE-fun-2004/ecce-alan-fun-panel.pdf.

26 *Stephen Lyng is a pioneer:* Lyng, Stephen. "Edgework: A Social Psychological Analysis of Voluntary Risk-Taking." *American Journal of Sociology* 95, no. 4 (1990): 851–886.

27 *This sets them beyond professional status:* Ritzer, George. *Enchanting a Disenchanted World: Revolutionizing the Means of Consumption* (Newbury Park, California: Pine Forge Press, 2005).

28 *Maslow, too, counted being:* Maslow, Abraham H. *Toward a Psychology of Being* (New York: Simon and Schuster, 2013).

29 *For example, a study of BMX:* Scott, Shane, and D. Mark Austin. "Edgework, Fun, and Identification in a Recreational Subculture: Street BMX Riders." *Qualitative Sociology Review* 12, no. 4 (2016): 84–99.

30 *I was struck by the video:* McRae, Donald. "Sky Brown: 'Sometimes You Fall but I Wanted to Show Me Getting up Again'." The Guardian, August 3, 2020. https://www.theguardian.com/sport/2020/aug/03/sky-brown-gb-skateboarder -fall-getting-up-olympic-games.

31 *In* Toward a Psychology of Being*:* Maslow, Abraham H. *Toward a Psychology of Being* (New York: Simon and Schuster, 2013).

32 *Some might say that's someone:* Anshel, Mark H. "A Psycho-Behavioral Analysis of Addicted Versus Non-Addicted Male and Female Exercisers." *Journal of Sport Behavior* 14, no. 2 (1991): 145.

33 *Excessive fun, in which self-control:* Linden, David J. *The Compass of Pleasure: How Our Brains Make Fatty Foods, Orgasm, Exercise, Marijuana, Generosity, Vodka, Learning, and Gambling Feel So Good* (New York: Penguin, 2012).

34 *To determine whether one:* Vallerand, Robert J. "On Passion for Life Activities: The Dualistic Model of Passion." *Advances in Experimental Social Psychology*, vol. 42, pp. 97–193 (Academic Press, 2010).

35 *Vallerand's experiments show that obsessive passion:* Vallerand, Robert J., Céline Blanchard, Geneviève A. Mageau, Richard Koestner, Catherine Ratelle, Maude Léonard, Marylène Gagné, and Josée Marsolais. "Les Passions De L'âme: On Obsessive and Harmonious Passion." *Journal of Personality and Social Psychology* 85, no. 4 (2003): 756–67. https://doi.org/10.1037/0022-3514.85.4.756.

36 *According to the research:* Hirshkowitz, Max, Kaitlyn Whiton, Steven M.

ENDNOTES

Albert, Cathy Alessi, Oliviero Bruni, Lydia DonCarlos, Nancy Hazen, et al. "National Sleep Foundation's Sleep Time Duration Recommendations: Methodology and Results Summary." *Sleep Health* 1, no. 1 (2015): 40–43. https://doi.org/10.1016/j.sleh.2014.12.010.

37 *In contrast, if we get less:* Barger, Laura K, Najib T Ayas, Brian E Cade, John W Cronin, Bernard Rosner, Frank E Speizer, and Charles A Czeisler. "Impact of Extended-Duration Shifts on Medical Errors, Adverse Events, and Attentional Failures." *PLoS Medicine* 3, no. 12 (2006). https://doi.org/10.1371/journal.pmed.0030487.

38 *Dr. Czeisler also believes:* Fryer, Bronwyn. "Sleep Deficit: The Performance Killer." *Harvard Business Review*, Oct. 2006, https://hbr.org/2006/10/sleep-deficit-the-performance-killer.

39 *If you're one of the:* Zitting, Kirsi-Marja, Mirjam Y. Münch, Sean W. Cain, Wei Wang, Arick Wong, Joseph M. Ronda, Daniel Aeschbach, Charles A. Czeisler, and Jeanne F. Duffy. "Young Adults Are More Vulnerable to Chronic Sleep Deficiency and Recurrent Circadian Disruption than Older Adults." *Scientific Reports* 8, no. 1 (2018). https://doi.org/10.1038/s41598-018-29358-x.

Chapter Three

1 *Although burnout can affect any:* Reith, Thomas P. "Burnout in United States Healthcare Professionals: A Narrative Review." *Cureus*, 2018. doi:10.7759/cureus.3681.

2 *As Wilson explains, people possess:* Cook, Gareth. "How to Improve Your Life with 'Story Editing.'" *Scientific American*, 13 Sept. 2011, https://www.scientificamerican.com/article/how-to-improve-your-life-with-story-editing.

3 *In one experiment conducted by Wilson:* Wilson, Timothy D., David A. Reinhard, Erin C. Westgate, Daniel T. Gilbert, Nicole Ellerbeck, Cheryl Hahn, Casey L. Brown, and Adi Shaked. "Just Think: The Challenges of the Disengaged Mind." *Science* 345, no. 6192 (2014): 75–77. https://doi.org/10.1126/science.1250830.

4 *The research group concluded that:* Alahmadi, Sarah, Nicholas R. Buttrick, Daniel T. Gilbert, Amber M. Hardin, Erin C. Westgate, and Timothy D. Wilson. "You Can Do It If You Really Try: The Effects of Motivation on Thinking for Pleasure." *Motivation and Emotion* 41, no. 5 (2017): 545–61. https://doi.org/10.1007/s11031-017-9625-7.

5 *Participants who received the reminders:* Westgate, Erin C., Timothy D. Wilson, and Daniel T. Gilbert. "With a Little Help for Our Thoughts: Making It Easier to Think for Pleasure." *Emotion* 17, no. 5 (2017): 828–39. https://doi.org/10.1037/emo0000278.

6 *Successful story editing can:* Dweck, Carol S. *Mindset: The New Psychology of Success*. (New York: Random House, 2008).

7 *This small mindset shift:* West, Colin, Cassie Mogilner, and Sanford E. DeVoe. "Happiness from Treating the Weekend like a Vacation." *Social Psy-

chological and Personality Science 12, no. 3 (2020): 346–56. https://doi.org/10.1177/1948550620916080.

8. *At the least, you will:* O'Keefe, Paul A., Carol S. Dweck, and Gregory M. Walton. "Implicit Theories of Interest: Finding Your Passion or Developing It?" *Psychological Science* 29, no. 10 (2018): 1653–64. https://doi.org/10.1177/0956797618780643.

9. *These now-legendary stories:* Avallone, Tommy, director. *The Bill Murray Stories: Life Lessons Learned from a Mythical Man.* Gravitas Ventures, 2018. 1 hr., 11 min.

10. *In the 1920s:* Richter, Curt Paul. "A Behavioristic Study of the Activity of the Rat." *Comparative Psychology Monographs* (1922).

11. *David Premack studied this phenomenon:* Premack, David. "Toward empirical behavior laws: I. Positive reinforcement." *Psychological Review* 66, no. 4 (1959): 219.

12. *For example, if you're trying:* Nelson, Leif D., and Tom Meyvis. "Interrupted Consumption: Disrupting Adaptation to Hedonic Experiences." *Journal of Marketing Research* 45, no. 6 (2008): 654–64. https://doi.org/10.1509/jmkr.45.6.654.

13. *For example, in a study:* Quoidbach, Jordi, and Elizabeth W. Dunn. "Give It Up: A Strategy for Combating Hedonic Adaptation." *Social Psychological and Personality Science* 4, no. 5 (2013): 563–68. https://doi.org/10.1177/1948550612473489.

14. *The people left uncertain stayed:* Wilson, Timothy D., David B. Centerbar, Deborah A. Kermer, and Daniel T. Gilbert. "The Pleasures of Uncertainty: Prolonging Positive Moods in Ways People Do Not Anticipate." *Journal of Personality and Social Psychology* 88, no. 1 (2005): 5–21. https://doi.org/10.1037/0022-3514.88.1.5.

15. *In all six studies:* Avni-Babad, Dinah, and Ilana Ritov. "Routine and the Perception of Time." *Journal of Experimental Psychology: General* 132, no. 4 (2003): 543–50. https://doi.org/10.1037/0096-3445.132.4.543.

16. *The authors concluded that:* Stetson, Chess, Matthew P. Fiesta, and David M. Eagleman. "Does Time Really Slow Down During a Frightening Event?" *PLoS ONE* 2, no. 12 (2007). https://doi.org/10.1371/journal.pone.0001295.

17. *In* The End of History and the Last Man: Fukuyama, Francis. *The End of History and the Last Man.* (Simon and Schuster, 2006).

18. *Having a lot more does:* Hadad, Sharon, and Miki Malul. "Do You Prefer Having Much More or Slightly More Than Others?" *Social Indicators Research* 133, no. 1 (2016): 227–34. https://doi.org/10.1007/s11205-016-1362-x.

19. *They do this by leaving:* Gundersen, Agnete. "Starting Over: Searching for the Good Life—an Ethnographic Study of Western Lifestyle Migration to Ubud, Bali." *New Zealand Sociology* (2017): 157–171.

20. *Dr. Michaela Benson and her colleague:* O' Reilley, Karen, and Michaela Benson. "Lifestyle Migration: Escaping to the Good Life?" In *Lifestyle Migration: Expectations, Aspirations, and Experiences,* pp. 1–13 (Farnham, United Kingdom: Ashgate, 2008).

21. *It's also important not to:* Benson, Michaela. "The Movement Beyond (Lifestyle) Migration: Mobile Practices and the Constitution of a Better Way of Life." *Mobilities* 6, no. 2 (2011): 221–35. https://doi.org/10.1080/17450101.2011.552901.

ENDNOTES

22　*As the psychologist Nico Frijda:* Frijda, Nico H. "The Laws of Emotion." *American Psychologist* 43, no. 5 (1988): 349–58. https://doi.org/10.1037/0003-066x.43.5.349.

23　*For instance, Sonja Lyubomirsky:* Lyubomirsky, Sonja, Kennon M. Sheldon, and David Schkade. "Pursuing Happiness: The Architecture of Sustainable Change." *Review of General Psychology* 9, no. 2 (2005): 111–31. https://doi.org/10.1037/1089-2680.9.2.111.

24　*Even so, most experts agree:* Watkins, Philip C., Kathrane Woodward, Tamara Stone, and Russell L. Kolts. "Gratitude and Happiness: Development of a Measure of Gratitude, and Relationships with Subjective Well-Being." *Social Behavior and Personality: An International Journal* 31, no. 5 (2003): 431–51. https://doi.org/10.2224/sbp.2003.31.5.431.

Chapter Four

1　*On the twentieth anniversary:* Spade, David. 2015. "I'm told that today is the 20th anniversary of Tommyboy." Facebook. March 31, 2015. https://www.facebook.com/DavidSpade/photos/im-told-that-today-is-the-20th-anniversary-of-tommyboy-aside-from-that-making-me/10153717195027678.

2　*Dr. Barbara Fredrickson:* Fredrickson, Barbara L. "What Good Are Positive Emotions?" *Review of General Psychology* 2, no. 3 (1998): 300–319. https://doi.org/10.1037/1089-2680.2.3.300.

3　*Dr. Barbara Fredrickson:* Burton, Chad M., and Laura A. King. "The Health Benefits of Writing about Intensely Positive Experiences." *Journal of Research in Personality* 38, no. 2 (2004): 150–63. doi:10.1016/s0092-6566(03)00058-8.

4　*Researchers from MIT:* Ramirez, Steve, Xu Liu, Christopher J. MacDonald, Anthony Moffa, Joanne Zhou, Roger L. Redondo, and Susumu Tonegawa. "Activating Positive Memory Engrams Suppresses Depression-like Behaviour." *Nature* 522, no. 7556 (2015): 335–39. https://doi.org/10.1038/nature14514.

5　*I have been influenced in particular:* Bryant, Fred B., and Joseph Veroff. *Savoring: A New Model of Positive Experience* (Lawrence Erlbaum Associates, 2007).

6　*This tracks well with the findings:* Ford, Brett Q., Phoebe Lam, Oliver P. John, and Iris B. Mauss. "The Psychological Health Benefits of Accepting Negative Emotions and Thoughts: Laboratory, Diary, and Longitudinal Evidence." *Journal of Personality and Social Psychology* 115, no. 6 (2018): 1075–92. https://doi.org/10.1037/pspp0000157.

7　*Dr. Kevin Rathunde suggests:* Rathunde, Kevin. "Broadening and Narrowing in the Creative Process: A Commentary on Fredrickson's 'Broaden-and-Build' Model." *Prevention & Treatment* 3, no. 1 (2000). https://doi.org/10.1037/1522-3736.3.1.36c.

8　*Some psychologists:* Lieberman, Matthew D., Naomi I. Eisenberger, Molly J. Crockett, Sabrina M. Tom, Jennifer H. Pfeifer, and Baldwin M. Way. "Putting Feelings into Words." *Psychological Science* 18, no. 5 (2007): 421–28. https://doi.org/10.1111/j.1467-9280.2007.01916.x.

ENDNOTES

9 *Experts warn that journaling:* Eurich, Tasha. "Here's Why You Should Journal (Just Not Every Day)." *The Muse*, 19 June 2020, https://www.themuse.com/advice/heres-why-you-should-journal-just-not-every-day.

10 *They found that people appreciate:* Cosley, Dan, Victoria Schwanda Sosik, Johnathon Schultz, S. Tejaswi Peesapati, and Soyoung Lee. "Experiences with Designing Tools for Everyday Reminiscing." *Human–Computer Interaction* 27, no. 1-2 (2012): 175–198.

11 *Thomas and Briggs also made:* Thomas, Lisa, and Pam Briggs. "Reminiscence Through the Lens of Social Media." *Frontiers in Psychology* 7 (2016). https://doi.org/10.3389/fpsyg.2016.00870.

12 *Two, because taking a moment:* Rucker, Michael. "Interview with Jordan Etkin About the Folly of Activity Tracking." *Mike Rucker, Ph.D.*, 23 Dec. 2020, https://michaelrucker.com/thought-leader-interviews/dr-jordan-etkin-activity-tracking-folly.

13 *In general, there are two:* Herold, David M., and Martin M. Greller. "Feedback the Definition of a Construct." *Academy of Management Journal* 20, no. 1 (1977): 142–47. doi:10.5465/255468.

Chapter Five

1 *"has sort of a natural importance":* "Chris Hadfield: How Looking at 4 Billion Years of Earth's History Changes You | Big Think." YouTube, uploaded by Big Think, 24 Mar. 2018, https://www.youtube.com/watch?v=qPvSRPsWhOQ.

2 *What Hadfield describes seems:* Stenseng, Frode, Jostein Rise, and Pål Kraft. "Activity Engagement as Escape from Self: The Role of Self-Suppression and Self-Expansion." *Leisure Sciences* 34, no. 1 (2012): 19–38. https://doi.org/10.1080/01490400.2012.633849.

3 *They allow us to be fully present:* Killingsworth, M. A., and D. T. Gilbert. "A Wandering Mind Is an Unhappy Mind." *Science* 330, no. 6006 (2010): 932. doi:10.1126/science.1192439.

4 *American workers had a record number:* "Study: A Record 768 Million U.S. Vacation Days Went Unused in '18." *U.S. Travel Association*, 11 Nov. 2019, https://www.ustravel.org/press/study-record-768-million-us-vacation-days-went-unused-18-opportunity-cost-billions.

5 *Annual surveys by Expedia:* Expedia.com. "Americans Plan to Take an Additional Week of Vacation This Year, Expedia Reports." *Cision PR Newswire*, 3 Feb. 2021, https://www.prnewswire.com/news-releases/americans-plan-to-take-an-additional-week-of-vacation-this-year-expedia-reports-301221553.html.

6 *The writer Susan Sontag:* Sontag, Susan. *On Photography* (New York. Picador: 2001), pg. 14. (Original publication 1973).

7 *In a book I love called:* Staniforth, Nate. *Here Is Real Magic.* Bloomsbury, 2018.

8 *Jaye Smith, cofounding partner:* Garone, Elizabeth. "The Surprising Benefits of a Mid-Career Break." *BBC Worklife*, 2016, https://www.bbc.com/worklife/article/20160325-the-surprising-benefits-of-a-mid-career-break.

9 *That the case for my friend:* Wills, Brad. 2018. "Why I Left and What I

Learned." LinkedIn. February 5, 2018. https://www.linkedin.com/pulse/why-i-left-what-learned-brad-wills.
10 *Former entrepreneur turned speaker:* Sivers, Derek. "Travel Without Social Praise." Derek Sivers, September 24, 2019. https://sive.rs/tp2.
11 *While the first person tries:* Stenseng, Frode, Jostein Rise, and Pål Kraft. "Activity Engagement as Escape from Self: The Role of Self-Suppression and Self-Expansion." *Leisure Sciences* 34, no. 1 (2012) 19–38. doi:10.1080/01490400.2012.633849.

Chapter Six

1 *Publishing in the journal:* Taquet, Maxime, Jordi Quoidbach, Yves-Alexandre de Montjoye, Martin Desseilles, and James J. Gross. "Hedonism and the Choice of Everyday Activities." *Proceedings of the National Academy of Sciences* 113, no. 35 (2016): 9769–73. https://doi.org/10.1073/pnas.1519998113.
2 *In science we have a saying:* Street, Farnam. "The Map Is Not the Territory." *Farnam Street*, 1 Oct. 2020, https://fs.blog/2015/11/map-and-territory.
3 *Dr. Todd B. Kashdan:* Kashdan, Todd. *Curious? Discover the Missing Ingredient to a Fulfilling Life* (New York: William Morrow & Co, 2009).
4 *In contrast, when we aren't:* Kashdan, Todd. "Science Shows You Can Die of Boredom, Literally." *Psychology Today*, March 2010, https://www.psychologytoday.com/us/blog/curious/201003/science-shows-you-can-die-boredom-literally.
5 *Boredom has been linked:* Kim, Meeri. "Boredom's Link to Mental Illnesses, Brain Injuries and Dysfunctional Behaviors." *The Washington Post*, 17 July 2021, https://www.washingtonpost.com/health/boredom-mental-health-disconnected/2021/07/16/c367cd30-9d6a-11eb-9d05-ae06f4529ece_story.html.
6 *Curiosity is also closely:* Hunter, Jennifer A., et al. "Personality and Boredom Proneness in the Prediction of Creativity and Curiosity." *Thinking Skills and Creativity*, vol. 22, 2016, pp. 48–57. *Crossref*, doi:10.1016/j.tsc.2016.08.002.
7 *A surprise means that we:* Meyer, Wulf-Uwe, Rainer Reisenzein, and Achim Schützwohl. "Toward a Process Analysis of Emotions: The Case of Surprise." *Motivation and Emotion* 21, no. 3 (1997): 251–274.
8 *In their article:* Noordewier, Marret K., and Eric van Dijk. "Surprise: Unfolding of Facial Expressions." *Cognition and Emotion* 33, no. 5 (2019): 915–930.
9 *The team concluded that:* Berns, Gregory S., Samuel M. McClure, Giuseppe Pagnoni, and P. Read Montague. "Predictability Modulates Human Brain Response to Reward." *The Journal of Neuroscience* 21, no. 8 (2001): 2793–98. https://doi.org/10.1523/jneurosci.21-08-02793.2001.
10 *The best ones:* Cheung, Vincent K.M., Peter M.C. Harrison, Lars Meyer, Marcus T. Pearce, John-Dylan Haynes, and Stefan Koelsch. "Uncertainty and Surprise Jointly Predict Musical Pleasure and Amygdala, Hippocampus, and Auditory Cortex Activity." *Current Biology* 29, no. 23 (2019). https://doi.org/10.1016/j.cub.2019.09.067.
11 *In contrast, those high in need:* Gocłowska, Małgorzata A., Matthijs Baas, Richard J. Crisp, and Carsten K. De Dreu. "Whether Social Schema Viola-

tions Help or Hurt Creativity Depends on Need for Structure." *Personality and Social Psychology Bulletin* 40, no. 8 (2014): 959–71. https://doi.org/10.1177/0146167214533132.

12 *It is clear fun promotes:* Tews, Michael J., John W. Michel, and Raymond A. Noe. "Does Fun Promote Learning? The Relationship Between Fun in the Workplace and Informal Learning." *Journal of Vocational Behavior* 98 (2017): 46–55. https://doi.org/10.1016/j.jvb.2016.09.006.

13 *Karl E. Weick, one of America's:* Weick, Karl E. *Sensemaking in Organizations.* Vol. 3. Sage, 1995. Sage.

14 *Austrian psychiatrist and neurologist:* Frankl, Viktor E. *Man's Search for Meaning* (New York: Simon & Schuster, 1985).

15 *Meaning is so important:* Hale, Benjamin. *The Evolution of Bruno Littlemore* (New York: Twelve, 2011).

16 *He believed that to be happy:* Sidgwick, Henry. *The Methods of Ethics* (Indianapolis, Indiana: Hackett, 1874/1982).

17 *The link between well-being:* Kozlowski, Desirée. "What Is Hedonism and How Does It Affect Your Health?" *The Conversation,* 3 Sept. 2017, https://theconversation.com/what-is-hedonism-and-how-does-it-affect-your-health-78040.

18 *It just lets you readjust:* Rucker, Michael. "Interview with Lisa Feldman Barrett About Emotion and Affect." *Mike Rucker, Ph.D.*, 5 Feb. 2021, https://michaelrucker.com/thought-leader-interviews/lisa-feldman-barrett-emotion-affect.

19 *In contrast, when we are distracted:* Quoidbach, Jordi, Elizabeth V. Berry, Michel Hansenne, and Moïra Mikolajczak. "Positive Emotion Regulation and Well-Being: Comparing the Impact of Eight Savoring and Dampening Strategies." *Personality and Individual Differences* 49, no. 5 (2010): 368–73. https://doi.org/10.1016/j.paid.2010.03.048.

20 *Shortly before his death, Abraham Maslow:* Maslow, Abraham H. "The Farther Reaches of Human Nature." *The Journal of Transpersonal Psychology* 1, no. 1 (1969): 1–9.

21 *After studying Maslow's work:* Koltko-Rivera, Mark E. "Rediscovering the Later Version of Maslow's Hierarchy of Needs: Self-Transcendence and Opportunities for Theory, Research, and Unification." *Review of General Psychology* 10, no. 4 (2006): 302–317.

22 *David Bryce Yaden, from the University of Pennsylvania:* Yaden, David Bryce, Jonathan Haidt, Ralph W. Hood, David R. Vago, and Andrew B. Newberg. "The Varieties of Self-Transcendent Experience." *Review of General Psychology* 21, no. 2 (2017): 143–60. https://doi.org/10.1037/gpr0000102.

23 *A band whose purpose was:* Diamond, Michael, and Adam Horovitz. *Beastie Boys Book* (Random House Publishing Group, 2018).

24 *"That's a fallacy":* Decurtis, Anthony "Adam Yauch: 'I Don't Care If Somebody Makes Fun of Me.'" *Rolling Stone,* 28 May 1998, https://www.rollingstone.com/music/music-news/adam-yauch-i-dont-care-if-somebody-makes-fun-of-me-188139.

25 *"Yauch LOVED disguises":* Potts, Erin. "Adam Yauch, Activism & Fake Mustaches."

Medium, 28 Nov. 2017, https://medium.com/@erin_potts/adam-yauch-activism-fake-mustaches-dc101a1524f8.

26 *When they danced:* Flower, Lynda. " 'My Day-to-Day Person Wasn't There; It Was like Another Me': A Qualitative Study of Spiritual Experiences during Peak Performance in Ballet Dance." *Performance Enhancement & Health* 4, no. 1–2 (2016): 67–75. doi:10.1016/j.peh.2015.10.003.

Chapter Seven

1 *A New York Times article:* Williams, Alex. "Why Is It Hard to Make Friends Over 30?" *The New York Times*, 2012, pp. 97–98.
2 *Church membership in the U.S.:* Jones, Jeffrey. "U.S. Church Membership Down Sharply in Past Two Decades." *Gallup*, 13 Aug. 2021, https://news.gallup.com/poll/248837/church-membership-down-sharply-past-two-decades.aspx.
3 *One frequently cited meta-analysis:* Holt-Lunstad, Julianne, Timothy B. Smith, and J. Bradley Layton. "Social Relationships and Mortality Risk: A Meta-Analytic Review." *PLoS Medicine* 7, no. 7 (2010). https://doi.org/10.1371/journal.pmed.1000316.
4 *A critic for U.K. entertainment site:* Fleming, Laura Zoe. "Joke's On Who . . . ?—Impractical Jokers U.K. (TV Review)." *VultureHound Magazine*, 9 Aug. 2016, https://vulturehound.co.uk/2016/08/jokes-on-who-impractical-jokers-uk-tv-review.
5 *Fun Friends are like human growth:* Reis, Harry T., Stephanie D. O'Keefe, and Richard D. Lane. "Fun Is More Fun When Others Are Involved." *The Journal of Positive Psychology* 12, no. 6 (2016): 547–57. https://doi.org/10.1080/17439760.2016.1221123.
6 *You may already be familiar:* Gladwell, Malcolm. *The Tipping Point: How Little Things Can Make a Big Difference* (Little, Brown, 2006).
7 *You may already be familiar:* Christakis, Nicholas A., and James H. Fowler. "Social contagion theory: examining dynamic social networks and human behavior." *Statistics in Medicine* 32, no. 4 (2013): 556–77.
8 *Emotional contagion, a concept pioneered:* Hsee, Christopher K., Elaine Hatfield, John G. Carlson, and Claude Chemtob. "The effect of power on susceptibility to emotional contagion." *Cognition and Emotion* 4, no. 4 (1990): 327–40.
9 *It's credited as likely responsible:* Stamenov, Maksim, and Vittorio Gallese, eds. *Mirror Neurons and the Evolution of Brain and Language*, Vol. 42. (John Benjamins Publishing, 2002).
10 *Researchers studying intrinsic motivation:* Burgess, Laura G., Patricia M. Riddell, Amy Fancourt, and Kou Murayama. "The Influence of Social Contagion within Education: A Motivational Perspective." *Mind, Brain, and Education* 12, no. 4 (2018): 164–74. https://doi.org/10.1111/mbe.12178.
11 *Their game was featured in:* Adams, Russell. "You're It! How I Got the 'Tag' Story." *The Wall Street Journal*, Dow Jones & Company, June 16, 2018, https://

www.wsj.com/articles/inside-a-journalists-pursuit-of-grown-men-playing-tag-1525963582.

12 *Research from Dr. Jeanne Tsai:* Tsai, Jeanne L., Brian Knutson, and Helene H. Fung. "Cultural variation in affect valuation." *Journal of Personality and Social Psychology* 90, no. 2 (2006): 288–307. doi:10.1037/0022-3514.90.2.288.

13 *But as Dr. Iris Mauss:* Rucker, Michael. "Interview with Iris Mauss About the Consequences of the Pursuit of Happiness." *Mike Rucker, Ph.D.*, 9 Apr. 2021, https://michaelrucker.com/thought-leader-interviews/iris-mauss-pursuit-of-happiness.

14 *One tool he found helpful:* MacLeod, Chris. "Does Meetup.com Work for Making Friends?" *Succeed Socially*, https://www.succeedsocially.com/doesmeetupwork.

15 *In one study, adults were:* Hudson, Nathan W., and R. Chris Fraley. "Volitional Personality Trait Change: Can People Choose to Change Their Personality Traits?" *Journal of Personality and Social Psychology* 109, no. 3 (2015): 490–507. doi:10.1037/pspp0000021.

Chapter Eight

1 *Daniel Gilbert famously theorized:* Gilbert, Daniel. *Stumbling on Happiness.* (Vintage Canada, 2009).

2 *Children are the best thing in a parent's life:* Wargo, Eric. "Aiming at Happiness and Shooting Ourselves in the Foot." *APS Observer* 20, no. 7 (2007).

3 *A 2016 study on the "happiness penalty:"* Glass, Jennifer, Robin W. Simon, and Matthew A. Andersson. "Parenthood and happiness: Effects of work-family reconciliation policies in 22 OECD countries." *American Journal of Sociology* 122, no. 3 (2016): 886-929.

4 *Or perhaps kids only make parents:* Blanchflower, David. "Children, Unhappiness and Family Finances: Evidence from One Million Europeans." NBER, 25 Feb. 2019, https://www.nber.org/papers/w25597.

5 *The study termed these people:* Ashton-James, Claire E., Kostadin Kushlev, and Elizabeth W. Dunn. "Parents reap what they sow: Child-centrism and parental well-being." *Social Psychological and Personality Science* 4, no. 6 (2013): 635–42. https://doi.org/10.1177/1948550613479804.

6 *Play is generally defined as:* Yogman, Michael, Andrew Garner, Jeffrey Hutchinson, Kathy Hirsh-Pasek, Roberta Michnick Golinkoff, Rebecca Baum, Thresia Gambon et al. "The power of play: A pediatric role in enhancing development in young children." *Pediatrics* 142, no. 3 (2018).

7 *Meanwhile, those kids who received:* Bonawitz, Elizabeth, Patrick Shafto, Hyowon Gweon, Noah D. Goodman, Elizabeth Spelke, and Laura Schulz. "The Double-Edged Sword of Pedagogy: Instruction Limits Spontaneous Exploration and Discovery." *Cognition* 120, no. 3 (2011): 322–30. https://doi.org/10.1016/j.cognition.2010.10.001.

8 *The insight comes from Professor:* Gray, Peter. "Playing with Children: Should You, and If So, How?" *Psychology Today,* September 6, 2014. https://www.psy

chologytoday.com/us/blog/freedom-learn/201409/playing-children-should-you-and-if-so-how.

9 *The comedian Maz Jobrani has:* " 'Persian Parents Party' | Maz Jobrani—I'm Not a Terrorist but I've Played One on TV." YouTube, uploaded by Maz Jobrani, 6 Dec. 2016, https://www.youtube.com/watch?v=b750fKHXS18.

10 *Jobrani and my coworker:* Lancy, David F. *The Anthropology of Childhood: Cherubs, Chattel, Changelings* (Cambridge University Press, 2008).

11 *And in fact, elsewhere:* Moore, Lela. "From Tokyo to Paris, Parents Tell Americans to Chill." *The New York Times*, 2 Aug. 2018, https://www.nytimes.com/2018/08/02/reader-center/free-range-parenting-outside-united-states.html.

12 *Michael W. Yogman, M.D.:* Yogman, Michael, Andrew Garner, Jeffrey Hutchinson, Kathy Hirsh-Pasek, Roberta Michnick Golinkoff, Rebecca Baum, Thresia Gambon et al. "The power of play: A pediatric role in enhancing development in young children." *Pediatrics* 142, no. 3 (2018).

13 *Further research also indicates:* Cates, Carolyn Brockmeyer, Adriana Weisleder, Benard P. Dreyer, Samantha Berkule Johnson, Kristina Vlahovicova, Jennifer Ledesma, and Alan L. Mendelsohn. "Leveraging Healthcare to Promote Responsive Parenting: Impacts of the Video Interaction Project on Parenting Stress." *Journal of Child and Family Studies* 25, no. 3 (2015): 827–35. https://doi.org/10.1007/s10826-015-0267-7.

14 *They wanted to guide kids:* Shine, Stephanie, and Teresa Y. Acosta. "Parent-Child Social Play in a Children's Museum." *Family Relations* 49, no. 1 (2000) 45–52. doi:10.1111/j.1741-3729.2000.00045.x.

15 *For instance, Dr. Thomas A.:* Harris, Thomas Anthony. *I'm OK—You're OK* (New York: Harper & Row, 1967).

16 *In* The Alter Ego Effect*:* Herman, Todd. *The Alter Ego Effect: The Power of Secret Identities to Transform Your Life* (New York: HarperCollins, 2019).

17 *They celebrate it:* Rucker, Michael. "Interview with Susanne Cook-Greuter About Fun and the Ego." *Mike Rucker, Ph.D.*, 2 Feb. 2021, https://michaelrucker.com/thought-leader-interviews/dr-susanne-cook-greuter-about-fun-and-the-ego.

18 *Dr. Yogman notes that:* Yogman, Michael. "Fathers' Roles in the Care and Development of Their Children: The Role of Pediatricians." *American Academy of Pediatrics*, 1 July 2016, https://pediatrics.aappublications.org/content/138/1/e20161128.

19 *An Israeli study, for example:* Feldman, Ruth, Ilanit Gordon, Inna Schneiderman, Omri Weisman, and Orna Zagoory-Sharon. "Natural Variations in Maternal and Paternal Care Are Associated with Systematic Changes in Oxytocin Following Parent–Infant Contact." *Psychoneuroendocrinology* 35, no. 8 (2010): 1133–41. https://doi.org/10.1016/j.psyneuen.2010.01.013.

20 *Rambunctious, rough-and-tumble play:* Yogman, Michael W. "Games Fathers and Mothers Play with Their Infants." *Infant Mental Health Journal* 2, no. 4 (1981): 241–48.

21 *In* Savoring*, Fred Bryant writes:* Fred B. Bryant and Joseph Veroff, *Savoring: A New Model of Positive Experiences* (New Jersey: Lawrence Erlbaum Associates, 2007), pg 41.

22 *Author Rachel Macy Stafford:* Stafford, Rachel Macy. "Six Words You Should

Say Today." *Hands Free Mama*, 3 Oct. 2020, https://www.handsfreemama.com/2012/04/16/six-words-you-should-say-today.

23 *A recent study at the University of Toledo:* Dauch, Carly, Michelle Imwalle, Brooke Ocasio, and Alexia E. Metz. "The Influence of the Number of Toys in the Environment on Toddlers' Play." *Infant Behavior and Development* 50 (2018): 78–87. https://doi.org/10.1016/j.infbeh.2017.11.005.

24 *Discussing the phenomenon in* Savoring: Fred B. Bryant and Joseph Veroff, *Savoring: A New Model of Positive Experiences* (New Jersey: Lawrence Erlbaum Associates, 2007), pg. 42.

Chapter Nine

1 *In one research project on academic achievement:* Woolley, Kaitlin, and Ayelet Fishbach. "For the Fun of It: Harnessing Immediate Rewards to Increase Persistence in Long-Term Goals." *Journal of Consumer Research* 42, no. 6 (2016) 952–66. doi:10.1093/jcr/ucv098.

2 *Their studies have also revealed:* Woolley, Kaitlin, and Ayelet Fishbach. "Immediate Rewards Predict Adherence to Long-Term Goals." *Personality and Social Psychology Bulletin* 43, no. 2 (2016): 151–62. doi:10.1177/0146167216676480.

3 *In 2020, Drs. Erik Gonzalez-Mulé:* Gonzalez-Mulé, Erik, and Bethany S. Cockburn. "This Job Is (Literally) Killing Me: A Moderated-Mediated Model Linking Work Characteristics to Mortality." *Journal of Applied Psychology* 106, no. 1 (2021): 140–51. doi:10.1037/apl0000501.

4 *As a review of nine studies:* Lammers, Joris, Janka I. Stoker, Floor Rink, and Adam D. Galinsky. "To Have Control over or to Be Free from Others? The Desire for Power Reflects a Need for Autonomy." *Personality and Social Psychology Bulletin* 42, no. 4 (2016): 498–512. https://doi.org/10.1177/0146167216634064.

5 *Self-determination theory:* Deci, E. L., & R. M. Ryan (2012). "Self-determination theory." In P. A. M. Van Lange, A. W. Kruglanski, & E. T. Higgins (Eds.). *Handbook of Theories of Social Psychology* (pp. 416–436). (Sage Publications Ltd.) https://doi.org/10.4135/9781446249215.n21.

6 *This was the conclusion of John Trougakos:* Trougakos, John P., Ivona Hideg, Bonnie Hayden Cheng, and Daniel J. Beal. "Lunch Breaks Unpacked: The Role of Autonomy as a Moderator of Recovery During Lunch." *Academy of Management Journal* 57, no. 2 (2014): 405–21. https://doi.org/10.5465/amj.2011.1072.

7 *In a now widely circulated lecture:* Cleese, John. "Creativity in Management." Lecture given at Grosvenor House Hotel, London, UK, January 23, 1991.

8 *I use this method myself:* Frachon, Kate. "Turn Your Weekly To-Do List into a Raise or Promotion." *Ink+Volt*, 11 May 2017, https://inkandvolt.com/blogs/articles/turn-your-weekly-to-do-list-into-a-raise-or-promotion.

9 *If you're a small business owner:* Jarvis, Paul. *Company of One: Why Staying Small Is the Next Big Thing for Business* (Boston: Houghton Mifflin, 2019).

10 *Authors Adam Gazzaley and Larry Rosen:* Gazzaley, Adam, and Larry D.

Rosen. *The Distracted Mind: Ancient Brains in a High-Tech World* (Cambridge, Massachusetts: MIT Press, 2016).

11 *Once an athlete becomes aware:* Hanin, Yuri L. "Emotions and Athletic Performance: Individual Zones of Optimal Functioning Model." *European Yearbook of Sport Psychology 1* (1997): 29–72.

12 *Research psychologists Robert Yerkes and John Dodson:* Yerkes, Robert M., and John D. Dodson. "The Relation of Strength of Stimulus to Rapidity of Habi-Formation." *Journal of Comparative Neurology and Psychology* 18, no. 5 (1908): 459–82. doi:10.1002/cne.920180503.

13 *That's what Nicholas Epley and Juliana Schroeder:* Epley, Nicholas, and Juliana Schroeder. "Mistakenly Seeking Solitude." *Journal of Experimental Psychology: General* 143, no. 5 (2014): 1980.

14 *After his solo he shared:* "Dave Grohl Lets Fan Play Guitar On Stage. 'Brady'— Foo Fighters PlayStation E3 Party 2003." *YouTube,* uploaded by rage12345678, 30 Oct. 2013, https://www.youtube.com/watch?v=2L83Cmf58Dw.

15 *"In my research, I've found":* Fogg, BJ. "How You Can Use the Power of Celebration to Make New Habits Stick." *Ted,* 6 Jan. 2020, https://ideas.ted.com/how-you-can-use-the-power-of-celebration-to-make-new-habits-stick.

16 *High-performance psychologist Dr. Michael Gervais:* Gervais, Michael. *The Passion Trap* (blog). LinkedIn Pulse, July 10, 2020. https://www.linkedin.com/pulse/passion-trap-michael-gervais.

17 *But it's worth being deliberate:* Sonnentag, Sabine, Carmen Binnewies, and Eva J. Mojza. " 'Did You Have a Nice Evening?' A Day-Level Study on Recovery Experiences, Sleep, and Affect." *Journal of Applied Psychology* 93, no. 3 (2008): 674–84. https://doi.org/10.1037/0021-9010.93.3.674.

Chapter Ten

1 *Pleasure—feeling good—became unsustainable:* Kringelbach, Morten L., and Kent C. Berridge. "Towards a Functional Neuroanatomy of Pleasure and Happiness." *Trends in Cognitive Sciences* 13, no. 11 (2009): 479–87. doi:10.1016/j.tics.2009.08.006.

2 *Over the past decade:* Ehrlich, Christian. "Be Careful What You Wish For but Also Why You Wish for It—Goal-Striving Reasons and Subjective Well-Being." *The Journal of Positive Psychology* 7, no. 6 (2012): 493–503. doi:10.1080/17439760.2012.721382.

3 *There have even been accounts:* Hopkins, Benjamin S., Daniel Li, Mark Svet, Kartik Kesavabhotla, and Nader S. Dahdaleh. "CrossFit and Rhabdomyolysis: A Case Series of 11 Patients Presenting at a Single Academic Institution." *Journal of Science and Medicine in Sport* 22, no. 7 (2019): 758–62. https://doi.org/10.1016/j.jsams.2019.01.019.

4 *In her paper "The Hidden Cost":* Etkin, Jordan. "The Hidden Cost of Personal Quantification." *Journal of Consumer Research* 42, no. 6 (2016): 967–984.

5 *These findings were replicated again:* Kent, Rachael. "Self-Tracking Health

Over Time: From the Use of Instagram to Perform Optimal Health to the Protective Shield of the Digital Detox." *Social Media + Society* 6, no. 3 (2020): 205630512094069. doi:10.1177/2056305120940694.

6   *Dr. Etkin's work taps into:* Rucker, Michael. "Interview with Jordan Etkin About the Folly of Activity Tracking." *Mike Rucker, Ph.D.*, 23 Dec. 2020, https://michaelrucker.com/thought-leader-interviews/dr-jordan-etkin-activity-tracking-folly.

7   *Meanwhile, the children in the:* Lepper, Mark R., David Greene, and Richard E. Nisbett. "Undermining Children's Intrinsic Interest with Extrinsic Reward: A Test of the 'Overjustification' Hypothesis." *Journal of Personality and Social Psychology* 28, no. 1 (1973): 129–37. https://doi.org/10.1037/h0035519.

8   *I saw that play out:* "New Study Brings Value of Activity and Biometric Tracking into Question." PRWeb, 26 Feb. 2013, https://www.prweb.com/releases/fitness/tracking/prweb10470191.htm.

9   *In the very first Ironman race:* Carlson, Timothy. "First Ironman Champion." *Slowtwitch*, https://www.slowtwitch.com/Interview/First_Ironman_Champion__7033.html.

10 *I'm a big fan of:* Thaler, Richard H., and Cass R. Sunstein. *Nudge: Improving Decisions about Health, Wealth, and Happiness* (New York: Penguin, 2009).

11 *Many studies show that what:* Wadhera, Devina, and Elizabeth D. Capaldi-Phillips. "A Review of Visual Cues Associated with Food on Food Acceptance and Consumption." *Eating Behaviors* 15, no. 1 (2014): 132–43. doi:10.1016/j.eatbeh.2013.11.003.

12 *For example, a study showed:* Turnwald, Bradley P., Danielle Z. Boles, and Alia J. Crum. "Association between indulgent descriptions and vegetable consumption: Twisted carrots and dynamite beets." *JAMA Internal Medicine* 177, no. 8 (2017): 1216–18.

13 *Cofounder Daniel Spils shared:* Argument, The. "1 of My 43 Things." Medium, September 9, 2016. https://medium.com/theargument/1-of-my-43-things-271d076c2ba8.

Chapter Eleven

1   **Being** *the change you want:* Ehrlich, Christian. "The Goal-Striving Reasons Framework: Further Evidence for Its Predictive Power for Subjective Well-Being on a Sub-Dimensional Level and on an Individual Goal-Striving Reasons Level as Well as Evidence for Its Theoretical Difference to Self-Concordance." *Current Psychology* 40, no. 5 (2019): 2261–74. doi:10.1007/s12144-019-0158-y.

2   *Albeit satirical, it's funny because:* "Nothing for Hungry Kids." *South Park Digital Studios LLC*, uploaded by South Park, 21 Oct. 2015, https://www.southparkstudios.com/video-clips/lit77f/south-park-nothing-for-hungry-kids.

3   *Most of us feel a draw:* Schwartz, Barry. *The Paradox of Choice: Why More Is Less* (New York: Ecco, 2004).

4   *Fun is obviously an important outcome:* Jessica Blatt Press. "Ideas We Should

ENDNOTES

Steal: Turning Blight into Play Spaces." *The Philadelphia Citizen*, 9 Feb. 2021, https://thephiladelphiacitizen.org/ideas-we-should-steal-turning-blight-into-play-spaces.

5 *In fact, it appears to produce:* Montague, Anne C., and Francisco Jose Eiroa-Orosa. "In It Together: Exploring How Belonging to a Youth Activist Group Enhances Well-Being." *Journal of Community Psychology* 46, no. 1 (2017): 23–43. doi:10.1002/jcop.21914.

6 *Sharing a purpose with others:* Ibid.

7 *Volunteering your time to help:* Umberson, Debra, and Jennifer Karas Montez. "Social Relationships and Health: a Flashpoint for Health Policy." *Journal of Health and Social Behavior* 51, no. 1_suppl (2010): S54-S66. doi:10.1177/0022146510383501.

8 *Volunteering your time to help:* Ibid.

9 *Volunteering your time to help:* Berkman, Lisa S. and S. Leonard Syme. "Social Networks, Host Resistance, And Mortality: A Nine-Year Follow-Up Study of Alameda County Residents" *American Journal of Epidemiology* 109, Issue 2 (1979): 186–204, https://doi.org/10.1093/oxfordjournals.aje.a112674.

10 *Even donating money to charity:* Yörük, Barış K. "Does Giving to Charity Lead to Better Health? Evidence from Tax Subsidies for Charitable Giving." *Journal of Economic Psychology* 45 (2014): 71–83. doi:10.1016/j.joep.2014.08.002.

11 *Children who volunteer and engage:* Johnson, Monica Kirkpatrick, Timothy Beebe, Jeylan T. Mortimer, and Mark Snyder. "Volunteerism in Adolescence: A Process Perspective." *Journal of Research on Adolescence* 8, no. 3 (1998): 309–32. https://doi.org/10.1207/s15327795jra0803_2.

12 *That's largely because of the way:* Breines, Juliana, "Three Strategies for Bringing More Kindness into Your Life." *Greater Good*, Sept. 16, 2015, https://greatergood.berkeley.edu/article/item/three_strategies_for_bringing_more_kindness_into_your_life.

13 *In its busiest night:* ALS Association. "The ALS Association FY 2015 Annual Report." *Issuu*, https://issuu.com/alsassociation/docs/020816-fy-2015-annual-report-websit.

14 *It funded research that led:* "Ice Bucket Challenge Dramatically Accelerated the Fight Against ALS." *ALSA*, http://web.alsa.org/site/PageNavigator/pr_060419.html.

15 *That's right, the group that simply:* Ko, Kellon, Seth Margolis, Julia Revord, and Sonja Lyubomirsky. "Comparing the Effects of Performing and Recalling Acts of Kindness." *The Journal of Positive Psychology* 16, no. 1 (2019): 73–81. https://doi.org/10.1080/17439760.2019.1663252.

16 *One study found that the pressure:* Maslach, Christina, and Mary E. Gomes. "Overcoming Burnout." In R. M. MacNair (Ed.) & Psychologists for Social Responsibility. *Working for Peace: A Handbook of Practical Psychology and Other Tools* (Oakland, California: Impact Publishers/New Harbinger Publications, 2006), pp. 43–49.

17 *He credited his mom:* Aitkenhead, Decca. "The Daily Show's Trevor Noah: 'I Am Extremely Political.' " *The Guardian*, 28 Nov. 2017, https://www.theguardian.com/culture/2016/nov/25/trevor-noah-interview.

ENDNOTES

Conclusion

1 *This has been thoroughly explored:* Solomon, Sheldon, Jeff Greenberg, and Tom Pyszczynski. *The Worm at the Core: On the Role of Death in Life* (New York: Random House, 2015).

2 *"And that urgency, that purpose":* Elias, Ric. "3 Things I Learned While My Plane Crashed." *TED Talks*, uploaded by TED Talks, 22 Apr. 2011, https://www.ted.com/talks/ric_elias_3_things_i_learned_while_my_plane_crashed.

3 *David Bowie, for instance:* Walters, Joanna, and Edward Helmore. "David Bowie's Last Days: An 18-Month Burst of Creativity." *The Guardian*, 26 Mar. 2020, https://www.theguardian.com/music/2016/jan/15/david-bowies-last-days-an-18-month-burst-of-creativity.

4 *A scientific study that explored:* Gamble, John Wylie. "The Relationship of Self-Actualization and Authenticity to the Experience of Mortality." (1975): 3578-3578.

5 *A study by Drs. Catherine Nogas:* Nogas, Catherine, Kathy Schweitzer, and Judy Grumet. "An Investigation of Death Anxiety, Sense of Competence, and Need for Achievement." *OMEGA-Journal of Death and Dying* 5, no. 3 (1974): 245–55.

6 *A study conducted by Drs. John Ray:* Ray, J. J., and J. Najman. "Death Anxiety and Death Acceptance: A Preliminary Approach." *OMEGA—Journal of Death and Dying* 5, no. 4 (1975): 311–15. doi:10.2190/mhel-88yd-uhkf-e98c.

7 *John Blazer, a researcher:* Blazer, John A. "Relationship Between Meaning In Life And Fear Of Death." *Psychology* 10, no. 2 (1973): 33–34.

8 *According to David Sobel:* Sobel, David E. "Death and dying." *AJN The American Journal of Nursing* 74, no. 1 (1974): 98–99.

9 *"Death Cafes"—informal gatherings designed:* "Forthcoming Death Cafes," Death Cafe, https://deathcafe.com/deathcafes.

10 *These "temporal landmarks" can kick-start:* Dai, Hengchen, Katherine L. Milkman, and Jason Riis. "The Fresh Start Effect: Temporal Landmarks Motivate Aspirational Behavior." *Management Science* 60, no. 10 (2014): 2563–82. https://doi.org/10.1287/mnsc.2014.1901.

11 *It is through accepting the finiteness:* Kübler-Ross, Elisabeth. *Death: The Final Stage of Growth* (Englewood Cliffs, New Jersey: Prentice-Hall, 1975).

12 *Randy talked about achieving:* Pausch, Randy. *Really Achieving Your Childhood Dreams* (Network Media Group, Carnegie Mellon University, 2007).

13 *His inspiring last lecture has:* Pausch, Randy. *The Last Lecture* (Hachette Books, 2008).

14 *Science also supports McNamara's mantra:* Hui, Bryant P., Jacky C. Ng, Erica Berzaghi, Lauren A. Cunningham-Amos, and Aleksandr Kogan. "Rewards of Kindness? A Meta-Analysis of the Link between Prosociality and Well-Being." *Psychological Bulletin* 146, no. 12 (2020): 1084–116. https://doi.org/10.1037/bul0000298.

Index

Abby's List: A Dogumentary, 49–50
abundance, 71
Acosta, Teresa Y., 141
activism, *see* collective action
activities
    bundling of, 51, 54, 59–62, 121, 172–73, 193–94, 202–3
    choice of, 106–7
    in social events, 130
adaptation, 10–11
addictions, 12, 39, 42–44, 91, 99, 190
    to social media, 12, 34
Adult state, 141, 142
adventure, 94–96
    see also travel and vacations
affinity groups, 170
affluence, 27–29
Agonizing quadrant, in PLAY model, 23–26, 28–33, 60, 62, 63
Alahmadi, Sarah, 56
algorithmic work, 5, 6
ALS Association, 212–13
Alter Ego Effect, The (Herman), 143
altruism, 213–14
    burnout and, 215
American Dream, 5
American Time Use Survey, 26
amygdala, 80
Anderson, Toni, 32

animals, 15
Anshel, Mark, 43
Ansberry, Clare, 4
Antarctica, 95, 210
anticipation, 9–10, 79, 110
anxiety, 12
AppSumo, 208
Arbery, Ahmaud, 214
Armstrong, Lance, 208
Armstrong, Neil, 101, 102
arousal
    dopamine and, 10
    mistaking fun for, 45, 130
    positive low-arousal emotions, 45, 130
    work and, 164–68
Association for Psychological Science, 132
astronauts, 86–89
athletes, *see* health, fitness, and sports
Atomic Habits (Clear), 193
Austin, Mark, 41
Austin Children's Museum, 141
autonomy, 17, 138, 140, 207
    collective action and, 201–2
    goals and, 184, 201
    work and, 157–64
autoresponders, 92–93
Avallonea, Tommy, 58
Avni-Babad, Dinah, 64

INDEX

awe, 115
Aydelotte, Frank, 19

B

Babins, Jonah, 208
ballet, 118
Bamford, Maria, 180
Barrett, Lisa Feldman, 16, 114–15
Beastie Boys, 116–17, 202
"be here now," 73
beliefs, 55
Benson, Michaela, 66–67
Berne, Eric, 141–42
Berns, Gregory S., 111
Bezos, Jeff, 87
Billboard, 112
Bill Murray Stories, The, 58
Black Lives Matter, 214
Blazer, John, 222
BMX riders, 41
Bonawitz, Elizabeth, 137
boredom, 108, 109, 180–81
Boston Marathon, 210
Bowie, David, 101–2, 220
brain
  boredom and, 109
  choice and, 37–38
  curiosity and, 109
  dopamine and, 9–10, 12–14, 34, 39, 111
  fun and, 3, 15
  happiness and, 9
  hedonic adaptation and, 62
  memory in, 34, 43
  mirror neurons in, 124
  negative emotions and, 80
  oxytocin and, 13–14, 145
  physical expression and, 79
  sleep and, 45
  social media and, 12
  surprise and, 110, 111
  time and, 34, 64
  vices and, 43
brainstorming, 35–37, 68
Branson, Richard, 87
Breines, Juliana, 211–12
Brickman, Philip, 10

Briggs, Pam, 83–84
Brown, Bruce E., 146
Brown, Sky, 42
Bryant, Fred, 78, 145–47
Buddhism, 117
bundling of activities, 51, 54, 59–62, 121, 172–73, 193–94, 202–3
Bureau of Labor Statistics, 26
burnout, 7, 26, 52, 54, 99, 104, 155, 215

C

Caddyshack, 58
Caine's Arcade, 148
calendar, 22–23, 25, 57, 82–83
cancer, 206–7
Cannes Film Festival, 69
Cardone, Grant, 7
Carlin, George, 200
celebrating milestones, 174–75
charitable donations, 205
Charity Miles, 211
Charlestown Boys & Girls Club, 210
Cheung, Vincent, 111–12
childcare, 133
  see also parenting
children
  fun and, 3
  sharing housework with, 32–33
  social impact work and, 209–10
children's museums, 107–8, 141
Child state, 141, 142
Chinchilla, Nuria, 7
chocolate, 63
choices, 224
  options, in SAVOR system, 51, 67–70, 173–74
  overchoice, 37–38, 203
Choose Your Own Adventure books, 217–18
Christakis, Nicholas, 123
church membership, 120–21
Cinema Against AIDS, 69–70
Clear, James, 193
Cleese, John, 16, 160–61
clothes
  ironing, 29
  laundry, 31–32

INDEX

clubs, 126–28
Coates, Dan, 10
Cockburn, Bethany S., 157
cognitive imagery, 21
collective action, 200–216
   activity bundling and, 202–3
   athletic events and, 205–10
   autonomy and, 201–2
   choice fatigue and, 203
   employer opportunities for, 210
   Ice Bucket Challenge, 212–13
   options to get started with, 211
   and personal benefits of giving back, 203–5
   personality and skillset and, 207
   picking a cause, 207
   reminiscing and, 213–14
   self-compassion and renewal and, 214–16
   sharing engagement with, 208
community, 120–21
   see also friends, friendships
commuters, 171
Company of One (Jarvis), 162
comparisons, 11, 37, 65–66
Compass of Pleasure, The (Linden), 13, 43
competence, 157–58, 163, 207
confidence, 160–61
connectedness, 14, 116, 157, 207
Cook-Greuter, Susanne, 116, 144–45
Cornelison, Judy, 175–76
Cornell University, 83
corporate social responsibility (CSR) programs, 210
COVID-19 pandemic, ix, 103, 104, 158, 206–9, 214
Crab Cove, 209
Creative Trespassing, 33
creativity, 112, 118
   Child state and, 142
   at work, 160–61
credit card reward programs, 70
CrossFit, 185
Csikszentmihalyi, Mihaly, 39
curiosity, 108–10, 118
Czeisler, Charles A., 45

D

death, 218–24
   acceptance of, 220–23
   of author's brother, xii, xiv, 47, 105, 218, 219
   memento mori and, 219–20
   self-actualization and, 221–22
   suicide, 12, 51–52, 54
   work and, 7, 157
Death Cafes, 222–23
deaths, small, 223
Deci, Edward L., 157
depression, 12, 34, 77, 99, 205
   clinical, 44
Diamond, Mike (Mike D), 116
Direct Line, 27
Disney World, 89–90
dissatisfaction, xiii, 13
Distracted Mind, The (Gazzaley and Rosen), 165
Dix, Alan, 40
doctors, 51–55
Dodson, John, 167–68
doomsurfing, 31
dopamine, 9–10, 12–14, 34, 39, 111
dot-com era, 155
Dunbar, Robin, 129
Dweck, Carol, 57
Dying for a Paycheck (Pfeffer), 7

E

Eagleman, David, 65
edgework, 41–42, 212
ego-states, 141–42
Ehrenreich, Barbara, 5
Ehrlich, Christian, 184–85, 200–201
Einstein (Isaacson), 19
Einstein, Albert, 15, 18–19
Einstein, Elsa, 19
Elias, Ric, 219–20, 222
email, 29–30, 91
   autoresponder and, 92–93
emotions, 76
   acceptance of, 80
   Child state and, 142
   friends and, 123–24
   intensity of, 41

INDEX

emotions (*cont.*)
  negative, 20, 80–81, 110, 124
  positive, 110
  positive low-arousal, 45, 130
  range of, 20
  work and, 165–66
empathy, 14, 145, 203
  burnout and, 215
Enchanting a Disenchanted World (Ritzer), 41
End of History and the Last Man, The (Fukuyama), 65
endorphins, 43
enjoyment after the moment, *see* reminiscing
ennui, 13
enrichment, 106–7
entertainment, 33–34
  television and movies, 25, 34
Epley, Nicholas, 171
escape, 86–102, 103
  and escaping to, not from, 99–101
  see also travel and vacations
Etkin, Jordan, 84–85, 187, 188, 192
Eurich, Tasha, 82
evolution, 11, 15
Evolution of Bruno Littlemore, The (Hale), 113
exercise, *see* health, fitness, and sports
Expedia, 89
extroverts, 121, 130, 131
Eyal, Nir, 29

F
Facebook, 83, 120, 148
fantasy football, 128, 129
Farley, Chris, 76
feedback, 84–85, 183–84
Fellows, Patrick, 182
Fiesta, Matthew P., 65
Fishbach, Ayelet, 155, 195
Fissell, Jeremy, 76, 163–64
Fissell, Nate, 163–64
fitness, *see* health, fitness, and sports
fixed mindset, 57
flow, 39
Fogg, BJ, 174, 193, 194
Foo Fighters, 174

Ford, Brett, 80
43 Things, 196–97
Fowler, James, 123
Frachon, Kate, 161–62
Frankl, Viktor, 112
Frates, Pete, 212–13
Fredrickson, Barbara, 77, 80
friends, friendships, 119–31
  clubs and, 126–28
  consistency, accountability, and fun in, 127, 130
  of convenience, 25, 125–26
  emotions and, 123–24
  health and, 121
  Jenga study and, 123, 128–29
  learning and, 199
  loneliness and, 129
  making, 125–26
  sustaining, 127
  work breaks and, 170–71
Frijda, Nico, 70–71
Fukuyama, Francis, 65
fun, xiv, 1–21, 104
  as autonomous, 17, 138, 140
  as biased toward action, 15–16
  booster for, 20–21
  enemies of, 42–49
  excessive, 43
  as extraordinary, 17–18
  first use of word, 16–17
  hierarchy of, as pyramid, 105–8
  levels of, 17
  obstacles to, xiv–xv
  as prosocial, 16–17
  simple theory of, 14–18
Fun File, 35–38, 57, 68
  brainstorm in, 35–37
  short list in, 37–38
  structure in, 36–37
fun hacking, 70

G
Gamble, John W., 221
gap year, 95
gateways to peak experience, 38–42
  avoiding enemies of fun, 42–49
  intensity of emotion, 41

INDEX

learning plus self-determination, 39–40
leveling up, 38–39
risk-taking and edgework, 41–42, 212
uncertainty, 40
Gatto, Joe, 122
Gazzaley, Adam, 165
Gervais, Michael, 177
Gervais, Ricky, 154
Ghostbusters, 58, 59
gifts, 146–47
Gilbert, Daniel, 88, 132, 133, 149
Gilligan, Thom, 210
Gladwell, Malcolm, 123, 178
GlowPong, 163–64
goals, 181
   autonomy and, 184, 201
   dopamine and, 10
   happiness and, 181, 184–85, 200–201
   making public, 198
   motivations for, *see* motivation
   naming, 194–95
   SMART, 183, 184, 186, 188, 192
   tiny changes and, 194
GoFundMe, 2
Goldfield, Sharleen and Dan, 97–98
Gonzalez-Mulé, Erik, 157
gratitude, 71, 81
   reminiscing and, 71, 78–79
Gray, Peter, 137
Great American River Cleanup, 209
Greater Good Magazine, 211
Greenberg, Jeff, 218–19
Grenst, Judy, 222
grief, xiv
Grohl, Dave, 174
Grossman, Barry, 161
growth mindset, 57, 205
Guardian, 215
gym, 31, 42–44

H

habits, 29, 35
Hadfield, Chris, 87, 88, 101–2
Hadfield, Evan, 102
Hale, Benjamin, 113
Hanin, Yuri, 165
happiness, xi–xiv, 8–11, 15–18, 20, 104, 117, 130, 147
   adaptation and, 10–11
   brain and, 9
   and comparisons to others, 11, 65–66
   goals and, 181, 184–85, 200–201
   kindness and, 212
   momentary, 24
   parenting and, 132–33
   prescriptions and maps for, 107
   pursuit of, 10
   set point of, 10, 62
   television and, 34
   time and, 28
   tracking, 84–85
   trap of (hedonic treadmill), xii, 8–11, 14, 63, 70, 147, 177
hard fun, 180–99
   activity bundling and, 193–94
   identifying personal motivation in, 190–91
   identifying steps in, 191–92
   key performance indicators and, 189–93
   and naming your goal, 194–95
   quantification and, 186–89
   rewards and, 195–96
   spectators and, 197–99
   see also goals
Hardly Strictly Bluegrass Festival, 138
Harfoush, Rahaf, 5
Harris, Sam, 193
Harris, Thomas A., 142
Harvard University, 106
Hatfield, Elaine, 124
health
   social contagion and, 123
   social relationships and, 121
health, fitness, and sports, 31, 42–44, 146, 165, 185–86
   activism combined with, 205–10
   CrossFit, 185
   fitness trends, 198
   health clubs, 31, 42–44, 188, 214

INDEX

health, fitness, and sports (*cont.*)
  identifying personal motivation in, 190–91
  Ironman, xii, 37, 42, 61, 181–82, 185, 189, 193–98
  key performance indicators and, 189–93
  Peloton, 198
  spectators and, 197–99
  tracking devices and, 186–89
health care workers, 51–55
hedonic adaptation, 62, 147
hedonic experience, 9
hedonic flexibility principle, 107, 113, 115
hedonics, variable, 51, 62, 67, 110, 173, 211
hedonic tone (valence), 15–18, 105
  negative, 17, 34, 110
  neutral, 34
  positive, 17, 107, 110
  work breaks and, 63
hedonic treadmill (happiness trap), xii, 8–11, 14, 63, 70, 147, 177
hedonic value, 106
hedonism, rational, 114
Here Is Real Magic (Staniforth), 96
Herman, Todd, 143
Hershfield, Hal, 26
heuristics, 64
hiking, 130
Hirsch, Jordan, 92–93
holiday jar, 75
hormones
  dopamine, 9–10, 12–14, 34, 39, 111
  oxytocin, 13–14, 145
household tasks, 24, 25, 60
  ironing, 29
  laundry, 31–32
  outsourcing of, 31–32
  sharing with children, 32–33
Huffington, Arianna, 93
Huizinga, Johan, 161
Hustle & Float (Harfoush), 5
hustling, 7, 8, 177, 180
Hwee, Yvette, 210

I

Ice Bucket Challenge, 212–13
Ice Cube, 100
Iglesias, Gabriel, 51
I'm OK—You're OK (Harris), 142
Impractical Jokers, 122
India, 96
Indistractable (Eyal), 29
Individual Zone of Optimal Functioning, 165–66
Industrial Revolution, 5
Information Age, 5–6
ingenuity, 68
Ink+Volt, 162
Inside Out, 76–77, 80
Inside UFO 54-40, 217–18
Insight (Eurich), 82
intentionality, 4, 15, 46–49, 114
International Labour Organization, 7
International Positive Psychology Association, xii
International Space Station, 101–2
interventions, 84
introverts, 16, 121, 129–31
ironing, 29
Ironman, xii, 37, 42, 61, 181–82, 185, 189, 193–98
Isaacson, Walter, 19

J

Janoff-Bulman, Ronnie, 10
Jarvis, Paul, 162
Jenga, 123, 128–29
Jobrani, Maz, 139
John, Oliver, 80
Johnson, Spencer, 73
Jones, Charlotte, 203
journaling, 25, 75, 77–82
  daily, 82
  gratitude, 71
  for wrong reasons, 81–82
Journal of Happiness, 21

K

Kagan, Noah, 208–9
Kashdan, Todd B., 108–9
Katamundi, 210

INDEX

Katan, Tania, 33, 58
Kent, Rachael, 187
key performance indicators (KPIs), 189–93
Kibbutz, 128
Killingsworth, Matthew, 24, 88
Kimmel, Jimmy, 59
kindness, 211–14, 217, 226
King, Jess, 198
King, Martin Luther, Jr., 173
Kingda Ka, xii, 47–48, 220
knowledge work, 6, 159
Ko, Kellon, 213
Koltko-Rivera, Mark E., 116
Kozlowski, Desiree, 114
Kübler-Ross, Elisabeth, 223
Kyle, Angela, 203–5

L

Lam, Phoebe, 80
Lancy, David, 139
La Rochefoucauld, François de, 147
Larson, Ann, 7
Last Lecture, The (Pausch), 220, 224
Lateline, 102
Latham, Gary, 8
laundry, 31–32
learning, 181
    children and, 144–45
    friends and, 199
    self-determination and, 39–40
    work and, 157–58
leisure time, 26–28
leveling up, 38–39
lifestyle migration, 66–67
Linden, David J., 13, 43
Living quadrant, in PLAY model, 23, 24, 26, 28, 38, 39, 40, 42, 46, 62
Locke, Edwin, 8
loneliness, 34, 121, 129
lottery winners, 10
lures, 193–94
Lyng, Stephen, 41
Lyubomirsky, Sonja, 71, 213

M

Maasai Marathon, 210
MacKinnon, Donald, 156, 160

Macleod, Chris, 131
Mandryka, Alexandre, 38–40, 180–81, 183, 184
Man's Search for Meaning (Frankl), 112
"the map is not the territory," 107–8
Marathon Tours & Travel, 210
Marbles Kids Museum, 107–8
Margolis, Seth, 213
Maslow, Abraham, 41, 42, 115–16
Matsudaira, Kate, 161–62
Mauss, Iris, 45, 80, 130
McFadden, Ryan, 175
McNamara, Michelle, 217, 225–26
meaning, 53, 67, 112–16
    fun and, 24
media, 33–34
    news, 31, 33–34
    television and movies, 25, 34
    see also social media
medical school, 53, 54
meditation, 8, 193
meetings, 31
Meetup.com, 131
memento mori, 219–20
memory(ies), 34, 43, 76
    routine experiences and, 64
    thinking about, *see* reminiscing
    time and, 65
mental illness, 44, 109
Meyvis, Tom, 63
Miller, Rob, 146
Mindset (Dweck), 57
mindset, 57–58
    fixed, 57
    growth, 57, 205
Miracle on the Hudson, 219
mirror neurons, 124
Missed game, 144–45
MIT, 77, 106
Mogilner Holmes, Cassie, 26, 27
money, 27–28, 103
    parenting and, 133
    scarcity mindset and, 162
    vacation and, 92
    work and, 162
Monroy, Caine, 148
Montague, Read, 111

INDEX

Monty Python, 160
motivation, 124, 157, 172, 181, 184
   extrinsic, 180, 187–88, 190
   identifying, 190–91
   intrinsic, 124, 137, 188, 190
   quantification and, 186–89
motivational interviewing, 190
Motsinger, Jane, 104–5, 108
moving (relocating), 66–67, 152–53
MTV Music Video Awards, 117
Mulaney, John, 120
Mullick, Nirvan, 148
Murphy, Eddie, 62
Murray, Bill, 58–59, 119
Murray, James, 122
museum, personal, 76
Museum of Walking, 33
museums, children's, 107–8, 141
music, 111–12, 202–3
Myers, Cindy and Mike, 152–53
My Social Book, 83
Mystery, the, 18, 95, 103–18, 201, 216, 221, 225, 226
   curiosity and, 108–10, 118
   other names for, 108
   sense-making and, 112–16
   surprise and, 110–12, 118

N

Najman, Jackob, 222
National Sleep Foundation, 45
needs, pyramid of, 115–16
negative emotions, 20, 80–81, 110, 124
negative occurrences, reinterpreting, 57
Nelson, Leif D., 63
Neverending Story, The, 11–12
news, 31, 33–34
New York Times, 120, 224
Nice-Matin, 69–70
Nickel and Dimed (Ehrenreich), 5
Nielsen, 33
Noah, Trevor, 215–16
Nogas, Catherine, 222
Noordewier, Marret, 110
Nothing, the, 11–14, 25, 28, 33–35, 39, 91, 224

Notorious B.I.G., 10
Novak, Will, 1–4, 13
Nudge (Thaler and Sunstein), 193
nudges, 193–94

O

ocean, 209
Oceanites, 210
options, 224
   overchoice, 37–38, 203
   in SAVOR system, 51, 67–70, 173–74
O'Reilly, Karen, 66–67
Oswalt, Patton, 217, 225–26
Ott, Volker, 14
over-optimizing, 46
Overview Effect, 87
oxytocin, 13–14, 145

P

Pacquet, Erik, 109
pain, xiv, 13, 220–21
parenting, 132–53
   activity bundling and, 60
   benign neglect in, 139–40
   child-centric, 133–35, 138–39
   and children dictating lives of adults, 139
   drudgery in, 24–25, 30–31
   ego-states and, 141–42
   finances and, 133
   free-range, 139–40
   gender roles in, 26–27, 150–51
   happiness and, 132–33
   housework and, 32–33
   long view of, 151–53
   self-direction in, 138–39
   self-expectations in, 140
   selflessness in, 134, 138
   and time for yourself, 149–51
   work and, 98, 133
parenting, and play, 135–36, 139–43
   ideas for, 148–49
   imposing meaning in, 141
   learning and, 144–45
   letting child lead in, 136–39
   physical activities and, 145

INDEX

story editing and, 143–44
toys and, 137, 146–48
transition ritual and, 143
watching children play, 145–46
Parent state, 141–42
passion(s)
harmonious, 43
obsessive, 43–44
work and, 177–79
Pausch, Randy, 220, 223–24
peak experience, *see* gateways to peak experience
Peloton, 198
Pensieve, 83
Personality and Social Psychology Bulletin, 112
personality traits, 131
Pew Research Center, 26–27
Pfeffer, Jeffrey, 7
philanthropy, 210
phones, 12–13, 35
photo albums, 75, 84
photography, 91–92
physical activities, in play with children, 145
physical thrills, 41
physicians, 51–55
planning, 46–49
vacations and, 93–94
play, 106
parenting and, *see* parenting, and play
PlayBuild, 203–5
PLAY model, 22–50, 99
activity bundling and, 60
affluence and, 27–28
Agonizing quadrant in, 23–26, 28–33, 60, 62, 63
Fun File and, *see* Fun File
Living quadrant in, 23, 24, 26, 28, 38, 39, 40, 42, 46, 62
logging activities and, 25
Pleasing quadrant in, 23–24, 26, 28, 34, 60
Yielding quadrant in, 23, 25, 26, 28, 33–35, 60, 125
Pleasing quadrant, in PLAY model, 23–24, 26, 28, 34, 60

pleasure, 13, 14, 106–7, 113–14, 172, 180–81
anticipating, 9–10, 79
consummatory, 9
intentionality and, 114
surprise and, 111
political activism, *see* collective action
Porter, Blake, 9
positional economics, 66, 67
positionality, 66
positive emotions, 110
low-arousal, 45, 130
positivity, toxic, 20
possessions, 146–47
Potts, Erin, 117
poverty, 5
practice, 178
Pratchett, Terry, 86
Premack, David, 60
Premack's Principle, 60
presents, 146–47
Principles of Scientific Management, The (Taylor), 7–8
Proceedings of the National Academy of Science, 106
productivity, 4, 6, 23, 27, 28, 82, 130, 165
Protestant work ethic, 5, 156
Pryor, Richard, 1
Pujalet, Darren, 149–51
Pump It Up, 125
Puritans, 5, 113
purpose-in-life test, 222
Pyszczynski, Tom, 218–19

Q

quality of life, 67
quantification, 186–89
Quantified Self, xii, 186
Quinn, Brian, 122
Quinn, Patrick, 212–13
Quoidbach, Jordi, 115

R

Rathunde, Kevin, 80
rational hedonism, 114
Ray, John, 222

INDEX

Reboot Partners, 98
Redirect (Wilson), 55
regret, 221n
relatedness, 157–59, 163, 168–71, 204, 207
Relativity Theory of Reinforcement, 60
relocating, 66–67, 152–53
REM, 117
reminiscing, 21, 51, 57, 70–71, 73–85, 147
   altruism and, 213–14
   apps for prompting, 74, 82–84
   curating the past to improve the future, 74, 76–82
   feedback and, 84–85
   gratitude and, 71, 78–79
   SAVOR loop and, 84–85
   sharing, 79
   time travel, 74–76
   work and, 174–75
resilience, 52, 77
responsibilities, 24, 114
rest and renewal, 26, 28
Revord, Julia, 213
rewards, 14, 60, 107, 113, 155, 188, 195–96
Reynolds, Ryan, 132
Richter, Curt Paul, 60
Rietzschel, Eric, 36
Rise Festival, 134–36, 138
risk-taking, 41–42
Ritov, Ilana, 64
Ritzer, George, 41
Robbins, Tony, 198
Rolling Stone, 117
Rose, Charlie, 59
Rosen, Larry, 165
roulette analogy, 17
routine, 64
Rucker, Brian, xii, xiv, 47–48, 105, 130, 218–20, 225
Ryan, Richard M., 157

S

sabbaticals, 97–99
Sasse, Arthur, 18–19
Saturday Night Live, 120

Savoring (Bryant and Veroff), 78, 145–46, 147
SAVOR system, 51–72, 74, 77
   activity bundling in, 51, 54, 59–62, 121, 172–73, 193–94, 202–3
   options in, 51, 67–70, 173–74
   reminiscing in, *see* reminiscing
   story editing in, 51, 54–58, 143–44, 172, 190
   variable hedonics in, 51, 62, 67, 110, 173, 211
   work and, 171–75
scheduling, 22–23, 48–49
   vacations and, 93–94
Schroeder, Juliana, 171
Schweitzer, Kathy, 222
Scott, Dave, 195
Scott, Shane, 41
scrapbooking, 75–76, 83
sensory-perceptual sharpening, 79
Sharif, Marissa, 26
self-actualization, 116, 221–22
self-compassion, 214–16
self-confidence, 160–61
self-determination, 39–40, 157
self-development, 100–101
self-esteem, 181, 209
self-evaluation, 99
self-expansion, 87, 109
self-suppression, 101
self-transcendence, 115–16
sense-making, 112–16
serendipity, 171
Shine, Stephanie, 141
Sidgwick, Henry, 113
Siegel, Dan, 80
Sivers, Derek, 99
Slate, 7
sleep, 20, 45
smartphones, 12–13, 35
Smith, Jaye, 98
Sobel, David, 222
social contagion, 123
social events
   activity-driven, 130
   VIP, 68–70
socializing at work, 159, 169–70

INDEX

social media, 12–13, 25, 28, 31, 33–35, 57, 120, 129, 224
   Facebook, 83, 120, 148
   memories and, 83
   vacations and, 91, 99
social movements, *see* collective action
social pollution, 7
social relationships, 120–21, 125, 129
   cultural pressure and, 33
   loneliness and, 34, 121, 129
   social skills and, 130–31
   see also friends, friendships
Social Skills Guidebook, The (Macleod), 131
solitary fun, 16
Solomon, Sheldon, 219
Sontag, Susan, 91
South Park, 3, 202
space travel, 86–89, 101–2
Spade, David, 76
Spils, Daniel, 196–97
sports, *see* health, fitness, and sports
Staddon, Graeme, 205–7
Stafford, Rachel Macy, 146
Stanford University, 106
Staniforth, Nate, 96
Stenseng, Frode, 87, 99, 100
Stetson, Chess, 65
Stipe, Michael, 117
Stop Asian Hate rallies, 169
story editing, 51, 54–58, 143–44, 172, 190
strangers, 171
structure, 36–37
Stumbling on Happiness (Gilbert), 132
success, 5, 53
suicide, 12, 51–52, 54
Sumo 50 Charity RIde, 208–9
Sunstein, Cass, 193
surprise, 20, 39–40, 49, 110–12, 118, 171, 176
Sutherland, Mark, 49–50
Sykes, Wanda, 22

T
tag, game of, 126–27
Tangled, 134

Taylor, Elizabeth, 69–70
Taylor, Frederick Winslow, 7–8
television and movies, 25, 34
terror management theory, 219
Thaler, Richard, 193
Thomas, Lisa, 83–84
ThriveAway, 93
Tibet, 117, 202
time, 22, 29, 46, 64, 103, 123
   activity bundling and, 51, 54, 59–62
   affluence, 27–29
   awareness of, 74
   brain and, 34, 64
   and engaging with work more playfully, 160–61
   happiness and, 28
   how much to spend on fun, 26
   loss of, 34
   memory and, 65
   over-optimizing, 46
   routine experiences and, 64
   tracking how you spend, 25
Timehop, 83
time travel, 74–76
Tiny Habits (Fogg), 193
Tipping Point, The (Gladwell), 123
Tolle, Eckhart, 73
Tomlin, Lily, 103
Tommy Boy, 76
Top Five Regrets of the Dying, The (Ware), 221n
Toward a Psychology of Being (Maslow), 42
toys, 137, 146–48
transactional analysis, 141–42
transition rituals, 143
travel and vacations, 4, 89–94
   adventure, 94–96
   autoresponder and, 92–93
   bringing back gifts from, 146–47
   curiosity and, 109
   holiday jar and, 75
   locals and, 109
   money for, 92
   planning and spontaneity in, 93–94

INDEX

travel and vacations (*cont.*)
   sabbaticals, 97–99
   social media and, 91, 99
   solo, 94
   travel hacking and, 70, 109
Treasure Chest, 75
Trougakos, John, 159, 168
Tsai, Jeanne, 45, 130
Tuazon, Brady, 174
Twenge, Jean Marie, 12–13

U
UCLA, 28
uncertainty, 40, 63
University of Pennsylvania, 28
University of Toledo, 147

V
vacations, *see* travel and vacations
valence, *see* hedonic tone
validation, 12
Vallerand, Robert J., 43, 44
van Dijk, Eric, 110
Vaynerchuk, Gary, 7
Veroff, Joseph, 78, 147
video games, 38–39, 41, 183
VIP experiences, 68–70
Volkswagen, 193
volunteering, 205
Vulcano, Sal, 122
VultureHound, 122

W
Wall Street Journal, 4, 127
Ware, Bronnie, 221n
wealth, 28, 162
Weick, Karl E., 112
well-being, 114
Well-Being Committee, 52–55
Well of Mercy, 103–4
White, Frank, 87
Wills, Brad, 31, 98
Wilson, Timothy, 55, 56, 63
Wish, Bryan, 93–94
Wolf, Gary, 186
wonder, 88
Woolley, Kaitlin, 155, 172, 195

work, 4–8, 24, 27, 28, 53, 154–79, 180
   activity bundling and, 172–73
   affinity groups at, 170
   algorithmic, 5, 6
   analyzing processes in, 32
   arousal and, 164–68
   autonomy in, 157–64
   autoresponder and, 92–93
   being yourself at, 168–71
   boss's expectations and priorities and, 161–62
   boundaries between life and, 7
   breaks from, 58, 63, 159, 168–71
   burnout and, 7, 52, 54, 155
   celebrating milestones at, 174–75
   collective action opportunities through, 210
   competence and, 157–58, 163
   creative space at, 160–61
   days off from, 45
   death and, 7, 157
   detaching from, 179
   emotions and, 165–66
   and energy at end of the day, 155–56, 165, 168
   finish lines in, 6
   friends and, 170–71
   and hours of non-work-related activity, 45
   hustling and, 7, 8, 177, 180
   knowledge, 6, 159
   learning and, 157–58
   long hours of, 28, 46
   marginalized employees at, 169
   meetings in, 31
   options in, 173–74
   overwork, 7, 45, 46
   parenting and, 98, 133
   passion and, 177–79
   perks and, 173–74
   professional excellence and, 178
   Protestant work ethic and, 5, 156
   reawakening Fun Habit at, 178–79
   relatedness and, 157–59, 163, 168–71
   reminiscing and, 174–75
   remote, 6, 156, 158, 171
   sabbatical from, 97–99

INDEX

SAVOR system and, 171–75
scarcity mindset and, 162
self-employed, 6, 156, 162, 163, 171, 173
shortcuts to improve, 175–79
socializing at, 159, 169–70
story editing and, 172
stressful, 157
taking less seriously, 155–56
technology and, 156, 158
vacation time and, 4, 89
variable hedonics and, 173
World Health Organization, 7
Worm at the Core, The (Pyszczynski, Greenberg, and Solomon), 218–19

worrying, 31, 56, 203
Wright, Steven, 73

Y

Yaden, David Bryce, 116
Yauch, Adam, 116–17, 202
Yerkes, Robert, 167–68
"yes, and," 205
Yielding quadrant, in PLAY model, 23, 25, 26, 28, 33–35, 60, 125
Yogman, Michael W., 140, 145

Z

Zenefits, 4
Zugara, 160

INDEX

SAVOR system and, 173–75
sanctity model as and, 102
self-deception &, 156, 162, 171.

T
thought, chape to, 175–79
sociality in, 156, 169–70
sorry-filling and, 172
causally, 197
sticking loss (Rosthchild), 5–6
technology and, 156, 158
victims' aims and, 5, 85
verdicts, hesitancy and, 170
World Trough Certainet toma?
Dying in the Law, The (Rosenthal,
Gronweg, and Schnfeind), 210–19

W

Werking, W. S., 203
Wright, Steven, 79

Y

Yadav, David Foster, 116
Yatra, Arjun, 116–17, 202
Yerkes, Robert, 167–68
Yes and, 207
Yerking up silence(s), RJAY model 25,
25, 28, 28, 38–45, 50, 128
Yorgason, Michael W., 140, 185

Z

Zanella, Vec
Zagmon, Tom

About the Author

Dr. Mike Rucker is an organizational psychologist and charter member of the International Positive Psychology Association who has been academically published in the *International Journal of Workplace Health Management* and *Nutrition Research*. His ideas about fun and health have been featured in the *Wall Street Journal*, *Forbes*, *Vox*, Thrive Global, mindbodygreen, and more. He currently serves as a senior leader at Active Wellness. Learn more at MichaelRucker.com.